CARING

FOR YOUR

PREMATURE

BABY

ALSO BY ALAN H. KLEIN, MD, AND JILL ALISON GANON (WITH CONNIE L. AGNEW, MD):

Twins! Pregnancy, Birth, and the First Year of Life

CARING

FOR YOUR

PREMATURE BABY

A Complete Resource for Parents

ALAN H. KLEIN, M.D., AND JILL ALISON GANON

HarperPerennial
A Division of HarperCollinsPublishers

HarperCollins books may be purchased for educational, business, or sales promotional use. For information please write: Special Markets Department, HarperCollins Publishers, Inc., 10 East 53rd Street, New York, NY 10022.

FIRST EDITION

Designed by Elina D. Nudelman

Library of Congress Cataloging-in-Publication Data

Klein, Alan H., 1946–
 Caring for your premature baby : a complete resource for parents / by Alan H. Klein and Jill Alison Ganon.—1st ed.
  p. cm.
 Includes index.
 ISBN 0–06–273620–5 (pbk.)
 1. Infants (Premature)—Care. 2. Infants (Premature) 3. Parent and child. I. Ganon, Jill Alison, 1952– .
II. Title.
 RJ250.K54 1998   98–18850
 618.92'011—dc21   CIP

 00 01 ❖/RRD 10 9 8 7 6 5 4 3 2

As a pediatrician specializing in the follow-up care of premature and high-risk infants, I have been deeply touched and moved by these babies who often start out with a different beginning and grow up to be laughing, healthy, and happy children. It is to each of them and their parents that I dedicate this book. I hope it helps parents of premature infants to look on the "bright side" and see the true miracles in their children's lives.

—Alan H. Klein, M.D.

I dedicate this book to the memory of my father, Martin Ganon. No children were ever more joyously loved than my sister and me.

—Jill Alison Ganon

Contents

Chapter Five

SUPPORTING YOUR BABY'S RESPIRATORY NEEDS IN THE HOSPITAL

Chapter Six

UNDERSTANDING AND MANAGING BREATHING CONTROL PROBLEMS (APNEA AND BRADYCARDIA)

Acknowledgments

The authors gratefully acknowledge the generous participation of the following families:

Sonia and Alberto Arce, their children Addison and Amelia, and the memory of their son Austin

Daniel Baldwin and Isabella Hoffman and their son Atticus

Behnam and Lisa Heshejin and their sons Michael and Matthew

Michael and Mary Jack and their daughter Truce

Roger and Cheryl Lerner and their daughters Clea and Hannah

Giovani and Madalena Lucci and their children Dex, Hunter, Skyler, Bianca, Madison, Tiffany, and Paris

Dan and Jeanette Mellinkoff and their children Benjamin and Rebecca

Donna and Jack Palmer, their son Alex, and the memory of their daughter Sydney Louise

Donald and Susan Moffat and their children Samantha and Michael, and the memory of their son Brian

Scott and Stephanie Olsen and their daughters Natalie, Amanda, and Melissa

David and Tracy Sereque and their daughters Eva and Eden

Michael and Donnalynn Simonoff and their son Joel

Ronald and Marinka Sjoberg and their daughter Macy

Clark and Donna Staub and their sons Dylan and Rainer

Ken and Patti Stern and their sons Andrew and Taylor

Jack and Anita Valente and their son Jonathan

We wish to thank Dorothy Williams for her professional insights and thoughtful comments as she read several versions of this manuscript during its preparation.

Our thanks to Tricia Medved at HarperCollins for once again being a part of our baby's team.

Thank you to our literary agent Angela Rinaldi for believing in books about babies and families.

Thanks once more to Marge at the Busy Key for creating the transcripts of our conversations with parents.

Introduction

Although 40 weeks is the gestation period for a human infant, any baby delivered after 37 weeks is considered term. A baby delivered prior to 37 weeks is described as premature. Becoming the parent of a premature baby is an emotional roller-coaster ride like no other. Of the approximately four million babies born every year in the United States, more than 400,000 are delivered prematurely, entering the world before either they or their parents are ready for their debut. Whether you are unexpectedly faced with the news that your baby may be born early, or are actually reaching through the porthole of an isolette to touch your tiny newborn, we know that this was not what you were expecting when you decided to have a baby. *Caring for Your Premature Baby* was written for every parent or expectant parent who wonders where to turn for a realistic, encouraging guide to understanding their premature baby's different beginning.

It may also be helpful for us to mention that we found it distracting when describing babies or medical team members to constantly refer to "he/she" or "his/her." The constant use of the dual pronouns interrupted the flow of important information. Our solution was to alternate (by chapter) the gender of babies and medical team members discussed throughout the book.

All the information in *Caring for Your Premature Baby* rests upon a central theme of "family-centered care." What is "family-centered care"? Simply stated, it is an approach to your baby's care that recognizes the expertise of health-care providers, but then takes the vitally important step of asking each of those doctors, nurses, respiratory therapists, social workers, and so many others to acknowledge and earnestly support a family's active participation in their own baby's care. In our model of family-centered care we return over and over to the premise that everyone participating in the care of your baby is a member of your team, and even though the roster of the team will change, the captain of that team is, and will always be, your baby. This book is all about helping you to help your baby by becoming an informed, confident, positive team member. We know that ongoing family-centered care is not easily attained, but we offer it up as a realistic goal, and have made it the indispensable centerpiece of our book.

One of the most significant elements of family-centered care is parent-to-parent support—opportunities for parents who are new to prematurity to meet with parents who are veterans of the experience. The first two chapters of this book are written from the perspective of parents who have faced all the uncertainties of the early days and weeks of prematurity and come out alive and well, and with their miraculous babies in their arms. Hindsight really is 20/20, and we have taken advantage of that fact to offer you a very encouraging outlook as seen by parents who have "been there." For many parents suddenly thrust into the challenging role of caring for their early arrivals, it seems there is no "right time" to reflect on the emotional and psychological aspects of having and subsequently caring for a premature infant. In the first chapters of our book we suggest that parents take the time to examine their own intricate responses to the birth of their premature baby. For example, many families experience the loss of the fantasy of the uncomplicated pregnancy and the chubby term baby. Other parents of premature babies describe feeling oddly detached during the first days following the birth of their child. One mom said, "I was there, but it was as though it wasn't happening to me." But it *is* happening to you and we discuss the importance of acknowledging your feelings.

Caring for Your Premature Baby encourages parents to take care of themselves and each other by demonstrating methods for doing so. This book is a tool to advance the learning curve as you become your baby's greatest booster and most intrepid advocate.

Your questions will begin in the hospital and continue until well after discharge when the supportive environment of the neonatal unit is no longer available—a perfect example of the changing nature of your baby's team. It is almost universal for parents confronted with the possibility or actuality of a premature baby to ask the poignant questions that reflect their concerns:

> *"Will my baby live?"*
> *"Can we hold her?"*
> *"How long will my baby be in the hospital?"*

After hospitalizations ranging from a few days to many months, fragile newborns grow stronger and heartier. As they near discharge from the neonatal unit, new questions arise.

> *"Is he really ready for discharge?"*
> *"What do I need for my baby at home?"*
> *"Am I really able to care for her?"*
> *"Will I need a registered nurse at home to care for my baby?"*

After discharge, premature babies are often brought home to an environment that is unprepared for their arrival and a family with many important questions.

> *"Is she growing normally?"*
> *"Can we take him to the mall?"*
> *"Can we leave her with a sitter?"*
> *"Is it OK to let his big sister pick him up?"*

Caring for Your Premature Baby will help answer these questions and many more as it provides a supportive framework for the nurturing and care of new families with premature babies. You'll find clear, detailed discussions of the numerous medical scenarios, such as respiratory, gastrointestinal, and neurological complications, that you may need to understand. Peppered throughout the book are useful sections called "Dr. Klein Comments . . ." which reflect personal preferences gained through years of experience caring for premature babies. A thorough glossary in the book's appendices provides easy access to the language of prematurity—a complicated jargon that you will come to speak like a native. In researching and writing this book, we spoke with parents of premature babies who generously shared their experiences with us. Some of these experiences are presented in a "Roundtable Talk" we held with a group of parents, and some are tales told by individual parents or couples. We think you will find a lot of hope and inspiration in the stories and pictures of the wonderful babies who have come so far. We have every hope that this book will support and enhance your ability to communicate successfully with the medical members of your baby's team. Finally, in addition to containing a great deal of essential medical information, *Caring for Your Premature Baby* delivers the reassuring message that the vast majority of premature babies who seem so impossibly small and frail at birth are going to become lively, curious, healthy children.

It is our greatest hope that this book will be carried in purses and briefcases, and perused in taxis and at bus stops; and that it also will lie at the top of the pile on your nightstand and next to the phone for ready access. We want you to keep it close at hand for as long as you need it, and hope that when the time comes to retire it, you will have come to regard it as your primer on prematurity. But for now, we believe this book can become a member of your team— helping you to gain confidence and perspective as your baby gains weight and strength. This is the opposite of the coffee-table book that is pristine and elegant, but rarely used. The more dog-eared, coffee-stained, and worn out this book gets, the more confident we will be that we're doing our part for your team.

Chapter One

Your Premature Baby

Not the Miracle You Expected, But a Miracle Nonetheless

A Look Back

It is two weeks—or a month, or five months—since your infant was born prematurely. Today you sit in a rocking chair in the neonatal unit feeding your baby. Your husband is across the room speaking with the charge nurse. You think about all the events that have brought you to this moment. The day you have been waiting for is almost upon you: You've been told that your son, or your daughter, or your twins, will be discharged in the next few days. Is it finally going to happen? You look at each other and share a private moment savoring the incredible victory—your baby is coming home! But wait—the crib your in-laws sent has not even been taken out of the box. And yes, you bought the car seat that was so highly recommended in the consumer magazine, but you've yet to secure it in the back seat of your car. You look around the neonatal unit at all the equipment that has supported your baby's needs, and all the staff who have been so calm and reassuring. As you sit rocking, you realize that your initial ecstasy is undeniably tempered by slight uneasiness. How will you manage without them? Are you really up to the task of caring for this little baby on your own? But as you gaze upon your baby's beautiful face, the one thing you know with absolute certainty is that although many may talk about the miracle of birth, you are holding a real miracle baby right here in your arms.

Not Quite Ready

No one could have prepared you for the extraordinary chain of events that led you to this day. Certainly, it was not what you imagined when you decided to get pregnant. No matter what the circumstances—even if it was unplanned—the feelings of uncertainty you may have experienced during your pregnancy were not about prematurity. And when pregnancy was a much-planned-for, highly anticipated event, the possibility of a premature birth was not what you were thinking when you told your families, "We are going to have a baby!" The experience of becoming parents to a premature baby has had little to do with the fantasy you envisioned as you chuckled at the tiny running shoes in the window of the baby store. It simply didn't enter your mind that your baby would be born prematurely and you would have to leave her at the neonatal unit instead of bringing her home to her beautiful new nursery.

A couple often decides to have a child because they have reached a point in their life together that tells them they are ready to move on to a deeper level of commitment, maturity, and responsibility. They may approach lovemaking with a giddy anticipation that is entirely new. They reflect on childhood and share their memories, good and bad. They talk about their own parents—what they wish to emulate and what they are determined to avoid: "I'll never spank my kid. . . . My mother was right. I *am* glad they made me study piano. . . . We won't force our son to play sports if he doesn't want to. . . . Let's have four kids. . . . No dating 'til she's 16."

The magical time between contemplating parenthood and having children can be filled with all manner of theoretical plans. How will we raise our kids and how many do you want to have, anyway? There is talk and speculation about the child's gender, even early discussions of possible names. But unless you've had personal experience with prematurity, it is the rare couple that automatically contemplates a scenario that begins with a premature birth. Perhaps—if one or both parents work in the medical field, or have a close friend or family member who has given birth to a premature baby—the possibility of having a baby born prematurely is given more thought. But until the possibility becomes reality, even the most informed parents cannot imagine just how the experience will differ from the birth experience that they have been conditioned to anticipate.

For many prospective parents, the first inkling that the pregnancy experience was going to be anything but routine came with the signs of preterm labor. At that point your obstetrician may have done a thorough evaluation that included an assessment of your general health, a physical exam, uterine contraction monitoring, and fetal heart rate monitoring. Additional evaluation might have included an ultrasound to assess fetal well-being and a vaginal culture to check for the presence of bacteria associated with preterm labor. It was at this critical moment in your pregnancy that you heard those two little words "bed rest" for the first time. Once assured that your baby was not in immediate danger, you may have thought this sounded just fine. Time to stop work a few weeks earlier than anticipated and pull the nursery together. As if reading your mind, your obstetrician sat you down and clarified precisely what was meant: There would be no painting the nursery, no cleaning closets, no weekend trip to the beach; just you and the bed and the occasional visitor to bring you some magazines or gossip from the office. Your husband would call to hear you tell him for the hundredth time that you were going nuts, stuck in your bed all day. This was serious. It was all about buying time, and every day of bed rest could mean your baby would deliver one day closer to term.

Lying in bed, you thought back to the early days and weeks of your pregnancy, you remembered your first visits to the obstetrician and the calculating of your due date. You remembered thinking, "9 months, 40 weeks from my last regular menstrual period is the day our baby is due." Do you recall marking those weeks off your calendar? Maybe you planned very carefully, hoping for a conception date that would allow you to have your baby in September, and feel ready to fly to your in-laws to show off your beautiful new baby by Thanksgiving.

But it did not go quite as planned. So there you were in your hospital bed in late June, trying hard to hold off delivery until August. You began to ask questions of your doctor and the nursing staff. They were helpful and encouraging but there were no hard and fast answers to be had. Each day you wondered if your baby would even be out of the hospital by Thanksgiving. You tried to remain optimistic but you were concerned. It was hard to imagine what it would be like. What exactly would it mean to have a premature baby? Would you be able to travel? What would it be like when your extended family met your child for the first time? Would you have the strength, the knowledge, and the emotional and financial resources to care for your baby?

DR. KLEIN COMMENTS ON SPEAKING WITH PARENTS ANTICIPATING A PREMATURE BIRTH

As a pediatrician and neonatologist, my involvement often starts before the baby is born. I go in and talk to the expectant family about what is going on, and answer any questions they might have. It is fair to say that at this point I am always optimistic. It is very important to recognize that even when we are quite certain that the birth will be premature, the outcome is overwhelmingly more positive than it would have been 25 years ago—or even 10 or 15 years ago. We have extraordinary new technology and family-centered care techniques, as well as greater insight into the physiology of premature babies.

If the mother is on bed rest in the hospital, I may take the father up to the neonatal unit to show him where his baby will be cared for. I encourage the mother to envision the baby not being born until 34 to 36 weeks gestation. I have known doctors to tell a mother at 26 weeks to just try for another 2 weeks. Invariably, the mother gives up after 2 weeks, and the baby is born at 28 weeks. I tell moth-

ers to take it one day at a time, with the goal of getting as close to term as possible.

We talk generally about how long the baby is likely to need to stay in the neonatal unit if born prematurely. Prospective parents who are experiencing preterm labor have not yet made the mental and emotional shift from focusing on the pregnant mother to the needs of the infant. They may not yet have interviewed or chosen a pediatrician. I try to spend enough time with them so that they can develop some trust in me before their baby is born. My goal is to establish myself as an informed member of their team who will help them to be the best possible advocates for their baby. Of course, at this point we are not sure that the baby will be premature, so we're hedging our bets a bit. I'm often asked about my experience with premature babies. If families ask me, "What will it be like if my baby is born now?", I try to speak in reasonable generalities. At 33 to 34 weeks gestation the baby will probably be fine. He may have some mild lung problems, and it may be a few weeks before he can suck and swallow on his own. For the parents asking that question at 24 to 26 weeks, the answer is far more complex, and often leads to a discussion about our communication. I encourage parents to talk freely with me about their anxiety. We might discuss the fact that their worries are understandable and not at all inappropriate. I let parents know that they have a choice about how we approach talking about their baby and what is to come:

- I can tell them about the long list of problems that might possibly affect their baby

  o r

- I can tell them about any medical problem that we know has occurred and is having an impact on their baby.

Usually, my preference is to share with parents *what I know is happening for sure,* and spare stressful speculation about *what might happen.* But it is up to the parents. At first, one or both parents may say, "Tell me everything." That usually means that if their child is going to be born at 30 weeks gestation, they want to know about every medical scenario that has been known to occur in infants of that gestational age. While my education as a doctor has familiarized me with the many problems that can happen, my years of experience have led me to believe that we are all

better served if I wait to share information until I *know* we have a particular medical scenario to deal with. I understand that parents who are about to have their baby prematurely have plunged, usually unexpectedly, into unfamiliar territory and need information as well as support. My goal is to supply that information at a rate that I know will be useful to parents' understanding of their baby's condition. So, although I know that the baby born under 30 weeks is going to have a head ultrasound so that we can look for evidence of intracranial hemorrhage, I don't usually talk about that before the baby is born. I use my best judgment in an attempt to spare them unnecessary stress.

I always hope that as our relationship continues through the days or weeks of their baby's hospital stay, parents will come to understand that worrying about *what might happen* may increase their stress unnecessarily. It often works best to let me worry about the "maybes" so that they can save their strength to deal with *whatever is actually occurring.* We work together at developing effective communication. As a physician, I have learned that being a good listener is very important, particularly during stressful times. But at the very beginning, I am simply hoping that my time with the prospective parents has the effect of decreasing their anxiety and reassuring them that I am someone in whom they can place their confidence as they begin the next part of their journey.

Your Baby Arrives

Then your baby was born, at 25 weeks or 32 weeks or just 4 or 5 weeks before your due date. Until that time you had not even heard of the NICU, ROP, CLD, or any of the other abbreviations that are used to describe the array of medical conditions, procedures, and equipment which may have affected or continue to affect your premature baby. But in the days, weeks, or months that have passed you have become all too familiar with the three- and four-letter initials for *retinopathy of prematurity* (ROP) or *chronic lung disease* (CLD) or *continuous positive airway pressure* (CPAP) used by the busy, highly trained personnel of the *neonatal intensive care unit* (NICU).

Having a baby prematurely is never on the wish list of expectant parents. But when it happened, you came to recognize the extraordinary progress that medical science had made on behalf of premature infants. From the researchers toiling in the laboratories and medical schools all over the world, to the people who dedicated their professional lives to the care of high-risk infants and their families, you had extraordinary resources available for your baby's care.

Even as you offered thanks for the miracles of modern science, you struggled to control your worries. You learned to understand that a lack of control does not mean a lack of hope. You quickly mastered rolling up your sleeves and scrubbing up to the elbows with antibacterial soap to do your part in controlling the spread of infection in the unit. Finally, you were astounded to discover that the person who most inspired your medical team toward continued commitment and optimism was not your doctor or the head nurse of the neonatal unit. It was not even you, with your fierce love and determination. It was the person who came into this world at a fragile 600 grams or 1,300 grams and came to be known as the tiger of the neonatal unit. It is your premature baby who has shown you what miracles are all about.

NATHANIEL'S STORY

Olivia and James are the parents of Nathaniel. Nathaniel was born at a little over 26 weeks gestation. He was due October 17 and arrived on July 13. He weighed 2 pounds, 5 ounces (1,070 grams) and was 14 inches long. James says Nathaniel was about the size of their cell phone.

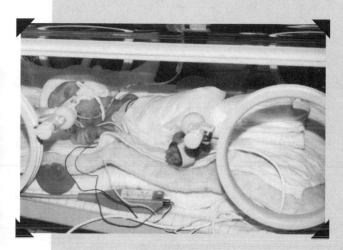

Olivia. The most important thing I learned throughout my pregnancy was to try to let go of something when I couldn't control it. I still don't know all the reasons for my premature delivery. I had some bleeding prior to having my amnio, but I had stopped bleeding before having the procedure. I leaked amniotic fluid immediately afterwards and that was a sign of trouble, but then it stopped, and that was good. There were no problems, leaking fluid, anything, for about four days, and then I discovered a little spot of blood. After that the bleeding stopped. I leaked amniotic fluid from that point on until I delivered my son. I was drinking gallons of water every day. I was on bed rest. I knew that was my job and there was nothing else that I could do. It was hard. James was running around doing everything— preparing my meals, taking care of our two large dogs. I was in bed taking it one day at a time.

James: Olivia started bed rest at about 17 weeks. From 17 to about 23 1/2 weeks she was at home on bed rest and I was taking care of her. Sometimes, when Olivia was still at home on bed rest, she would get upset and say. "I can't stay here anymore." I remember giving her a lot of massages. But our doctor was always reassuring. She told me, "You're doing everything right. Just keep making her breakfast, lunch, and dinner. Help her to stay in that bed as much as possible."

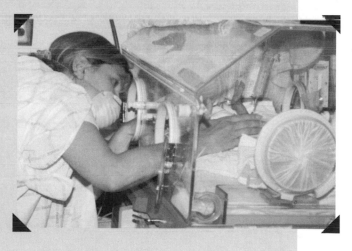

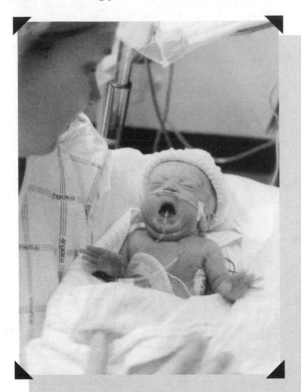

Olivia: We found a doctor with the kind of attitude and approach we felt comfortable with. She actually came out to the house one time. We both felt great confidence in her. I would tell any pregnant woman to trust her instincts about choosing a doctor. When I think about it now it seems so naive, but when our doctor told me to go into the hospital, I thought that I could be there for 12 weeks.

James: She was on bed rest already, but we were advised that she should be on bed rest in the hospital. We knew that the baby was viable and could be monitored along with her. It was a relief in a way, because we lived so far away from our hospital.

Olivia: I felt I had to be positive. . . I told myself that if I cried, that was just going to be less fluid for Nathaniel. As it happens, I got to the hospital on a Tuesday and Nathaniel was born on Saturday. . . not exactly the 12 weeks in the hospital I'd been thinking about.

James: I have a strong belief in the power of spirituality, but it was amazing. I felt thrust into a dual role. The person I was when I was with Olivia, always chipper and upbeat. Our doctor told me straight out, "Look, you need to be really positive around her. Her pregnancy will be affected by her emotional state." But there was also the person I was when I was away from her—confronting all my fears. When I was away from Olivia I'd turn to the doctor and say, "OK. What's *really* going on?" And the doctor would say, "I'm telling her what's really going on."

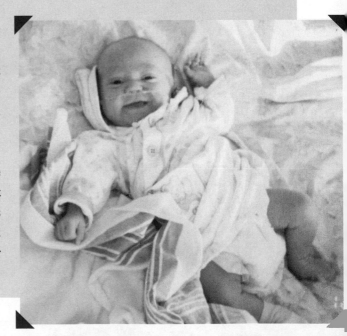

Olivia: As far as spirituality goes, mine soared while I was on bed rest. I really knew that we were being taken care of. I was only allowed to get up for my once-a-week visits to the doctor. Yet each day that went by was good news. I didn't complain that much about wanting to get out of bed. I knew it was my job. It was a hard job sometimes. The hardest thing I have ever done is stay in bed for that length of time. But I knew that each day that went by was such a blessing. I did not want to go into the hospital and be away from James. I just wanted to hold out to 28 weeks.

James: We knew that the difference between 26 and 28 weeks was really important as far as complications for the baby were concerned. Especially for a boy. We understood that every day counted. In the 1960s, just 30 years ago, John and Jacqueline Kennedy had lost a baby boy at 32 weeks gestation. At 32 weeks today you can be in great shape. But today, you're almost guaranteed some ramifications of prematurity below 27 or 28 weeks and we were at 26 and a few days. I was trying to get prepared.

Olivia: When I finally got into the hospital, my feet above my head, I was gushing amniotic fluid. It was a roller coaster. Nathaniel was in breech position. And we were worried about there being so much cord in there with no fluid to slosh around. We were afraid he was going to go into fetal distress by pushing that

cord against the solid wall of my uterus. I remember seeing the glass as half empty at this point... knowing the risk of having this baby at 26 weeks.

I had just hung up the phone with James when I started having contractions. They tried to stop them. First I got the magnesium sulfate, which made me kind of hot. Then they gave me the shot, which made my heart race. The contractions still didn't stop. So now I was having contractions, I was really hot, and my heart was racing. I could feel Nathaniel dropping down. We knew he had to be delivered by C-section 'cause he was breech and so small. We did the C-section. I have to say, I had the best time ever during my pregnancy thanks to that epidural. But I looked at Nathaniel and he looked better than I had anticipated. So I spoke the truth. "He looks good."

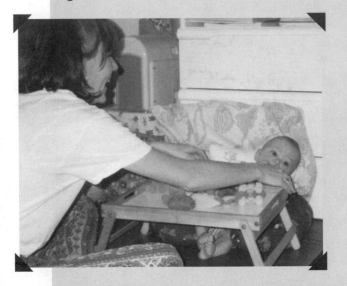

James: I was staying at a friend's house right by the hospital, and I got the call that Olivia was going to have the baby. She started going into labor, they couldn't stop it, and they were taking the baby. I remember driving there, literally talking out loud, "How could she do this to me? I have taken care of this woman. . . I have done everything I possibly could. Why would she do this?" There are 10 grandchildren before Nathaniel in our family. And they're all girls. This is the first boy, and chances are with the ages of everyone in our family with the exception of maybe my one

younger brother, this would probably be the only boy to carry on our family's name. But I stopped thinking about any of that when I got to the delivery room—they had Nathaniel out and I could see just how tiny he was. Olivia introduced me to a guy who was part of the delivery team. "This is Will. He's from Boston." So now this guy in the delivery room is like her best friend. I remember laughing and saying, "She's loopy." It was all so strange. Nathaniel made one loud shriek when he came out. And the confusion really frightened me because the neonatal team came and took the baby. I had to make a choice where to go. I thought, she is with our doctor, whom I trust totally. She'll be okay. So I said, "I'm gonna go with the baby."

Olivia: In many households and ours especially, the father feels like he needs to be the caretaker. He needs to watch over everything. He needs to make sure everything is okay. What happens when that person suddenly doesn't have any control over anything? We almost had a role reversal as far as optimism and pessimism were concerned. I was suddenly the optimist.

James: As much as I can't relate to delivering a child or carrying a child, I felt like I did as much as I could to help and be a part of it. But let's face it, as a man I'll never know what that's like. At the same time, there was so much life still going on outside: dealing with the day-to-day bills and people. I was driving 45 miles back and forth to our house to feed the dogs. I think the father feels less connected. Even though I moved into the hospital room and stayed as much as I could, I felt kind of helpless—things had so little to do with my will. I was angry too. I imagined that if I had been having this baby, he would be okay. Of course I know that is completely untrue, but while it was going on, running up the stairs, running down the stairs, I went through that anger.

Olivia: After the baby was born I thought everything was going to be fine. When I discovered how close my uterus had been to rupturing, I felt doubly blessed. Not only was Nathaniel here, but I was here and my uterus was saved. Now I can have another baby if we decide to try. So I started being much more optimistic than James. I looked at Nathaniel's progress as, "He'll be fine."

James: I think your personality traits can become amplified and magnified in a stressful situation like this. Olivia is very precise. And I tend to wing it. But when the doctor said, "Take one exact teaspoon of this," I had to learn real fast to be more like Olivia for those crucial first four months. She was so on top of it.

Olivia: Handling a premie is so different from handling a term baby. But I have to say, in

some ways I became more like James. I became much more assertive. That was my son and I became a mother tigress. As every premie parent knows, each child really seems to have its own individual course. Any time the baby is getting better, something else can happen. But I always said Nathaniel was going to be all right. It was hard on a day-to-day basis. But I kept trying to be really positive. Nathaniel is nine months now, and he is the happiest baby. Every simple thing seems to give him joy.

James: One of the important factors for me is the relationship between the parents, and how that can be affected by all this. Complications during pregnancy or having a premature baby are almost never a matter of fault. It is so important to realize that. These are simply the cards that have been dealt and this is the hand you've got to play.

Olivia: My experience was that everything I wanted from my pregnancy didn't happen. But it was still all perfect because it was all the way it was supposed to be. My experience with my son is so different and maybe richer, but it just didn't happen the way I'd expected.

James: You have to look at it like you're going to do the best you possibly can and have your faith in each other, and in the whole health-care team that is involved. Whatever your religious denomination, I believe there is a fate factor here, especially while the mother is pregnant. And there's definitely something to be said about being positive.

Chapter Two

Adjusting Your Expectations

Acknowledging, Comprehending, and Accepting Your Baby's Different Beginning

Soon your baby will be coming home! Even the enormity of what lies ahead cannot dampen your ecstatic feelings; but then, you've worked hard to prepare for this moment. You've struggled to become confident about your ability to care for your child. Thinking about leaving your teammates in the NICU makes you a little nervous, but underneath your worry you believe you can do "whatever it takes" to help your baby thrive at home.

But what about caring for yourself and each other? How about the needs of your other children, and how you expect to handle the involvement of the extended family? In the midst of all the phone calls, arranging a time to meet with the home health-care company, dealing with the insurance company, and preparing the nursery, there are a couple of basic issues that may have been lost in the shuffle. As is the case with most of life's most important issues, it is better to give them their due than to brush them aside and simply hope for the best. You'd never dream of taking that approach with your baby's care, so why should you even consider it for yourselves? Many families who delay confronting their complex feelings about coping with a premature baby are forced to examine those feelings during a later marital or family crisis. We will talk more about the intrinsic value of "family-centered care" as it applies to your premature baby later on in this book. But an important part of that care must also focus on you, both as a couple and as parents.

In the days or weeks or months since your baby was born, you called upon inner resources that you may have never suspected were there. Perhaps you sought assistance from parent support groups, private counseling, or other families you met at the neonatal unit. If you had the opportunity to get to know other families with premature babies, you discovered that you shared a kinship that transcended your different ethnic backgrounds, your education, or your bankroll. You have all dealt with a life crisis. Crisis, you learned, can be defined as a significant problem that is not easily resolved. If you thought of it as a story or a movie, it was the turning point marking a time when things would never again be quite the same.

Many health-care professionals in the areas of emotional and mental health have drawn upon the work of Dr. Elisabeth Kubler-Ross and others who examined the ways in which people responded to terminal illness or other life crises. This research offered important insight into the process of recognizing and resolving life crises. First we will list the responses to crisis as outlined by Kubler-Ross in 1969, and then we will offer additional information that is adapted to the specifics of dealing with the birth of a premature baby.

Stages of Resolution of a Life Crisis
1. Denial
2. Anger and Blame
3. Bargaining
4. Sadness and Depression
5. Acceptance

Having named these stages, it is now important to recognize that they are only a framework upon which you may be able to base your own understanding. Not everyone encounters every stage, or goes through the process at the same rate. It is also possible to return more than once to any or several of these stages. You may not feel any of it is applicable to your situation. But by citing some of the factors that may have had or may continue to have an impact on your experience, we hope to encourage you to identify those issues that have particular meaning to you.

We'll also share some words of wisdom from the parents who have had their babies prematurely and survived to tell the tale.

Responding to the Birth of Your Premature Baby

__Denial__ is frequently the first response to the birth of a premature baby. You cannot be fully prepared for your baby's early birth and should not expect it of yourself.

Most parents naturally experience some degree of worry over their unborn children. Early in the pregnancy there are concerns about miscarriage. But by the time a woman is well into her second trimester, those concerns have passed for the most part, and are replaced with another concern. How many of us have heard or said, "I don't care what sex it is, I just want a healthy baby."

Few are heard to say that they just hope their babies are born at term. It is simply not something that the average American woman is taught to think about, nor should she be. We are conditioned to anticipate birth as a time of extraordinary joy. The birth of a child marks your contribution to the next generation of your family. If this is the first child to be born into the family, it is the actual beginning of a new generation. It is momentous and undeniably important. Your parents take out your baby pictures and remark on your chubby thighs, and your precocious early speech. There is quiet speculation about the sex of the child and in-laws comment to each other on how you seem really ready to become parents (and wonder if they are ready to become grandparents). Your friends with children welcome you eagerly to the club, and your single friends feel a tug of wistfulness that you won't be quite as available for spontaneous fun. And through it all, you have your private thoughts, the ones you share with your mate and those that are never expressed to a soul, about how it will feel to nurse your hungry baby and hold her fat little fist in yours. How proud you will be to bring her home to the nursery you've prepared so lovingly.

All these thoughts and all this energy that is gearing up for the birth of your term baby come to a stop when you deliver a baby who must begin life in the neonatal intensive care unit of the hospital. Doctors often say that while parents hear the words being spoken, they seem unwilling or unable to grasp what is being said. Denial of the implications of premature birth frequently marks the beginning of a long process. In addition, there is an absolute necessity for working through the stages of acceptance of the loss of the full-term baby you did not have in order to fully appreciate your baby's "different beginning" (our thanks to William A.H. Sammons, MD, and Jennifer M. Lewis, MD, for their aptly titled book, *Premature Babies—A Different Beginning*). Denial is in fact a very understandable response, particularly when you consider the fact that parents are often unprepared from even the most basic pragmatic angle.

- You may not yet have had your scheduled childbirth classes.
- You are not likely to have determined who your pediatrician will be.
- You don't yet have a "phone tree" for telling friends and family about the birth of the baby, and now you don't know exactly what to say to them.
- How will you allay your other children's concerns about their tiny new baby sister?
- Should the father follow the baby to the neonatal unit or stay with the mother after delivery?
- You've yet to agree on a name for the baby.
- How will the family manage with the baby having to stay in the hospital?
- And how long will she be there?
- The nursery is not yet prepared and you haven't bought any baby clothes.

You may be a partner at a major law firm, a 25-year-old fitness instructor, a firefighter, a physician, or a teacher at an inner-city high school—nothing in your professional experience could have prepared you for the helplessness you endured in those first anguished hours and days. For a person used to feeling "in control," the powerlessness was paralyzing. There are parents who were so overwhelmed by the premature birth of a child, and so fearful that the child may not survive, that they made a decision, sometimes not even consciously, not to get attached to their baby. They resisted naming, touching, holding, or sometimes even looking at their baby. But the power of becoming a parent is not to be denied. Among parents who have endured the tragedy of losing a baby, those who got involved with and attached to their infants—holding, nurturing, naming their baby—fared better with their tragic loss than those parents who resisted attachment.

In most cases there was a member of the staff of the neonatal unit who helped you take the first steps in familiarizing yourself with the environment that was to be your baby's home for however long he needed to remain hospitalized. This was your initiation as a member of the team that would serve your miracle baby so well.

Blame, anger, and guilt are understandable reactions to crisis; you need to allow yourselves the time, and sometimes the expert help, to process these feelings.

Many times parents have the impulse to blame or become resentful about the circumstances surrounding their baby's early arrival. Premie parents often see each other or themselves as being at fault. They may express anger at each other, as well as at all their baby's caregivers, their bosses, their creditors, and everyone else in the world.

- We shouldn't have had sex.
- She should have stayed in bed.
- If he'd have been more helpful, I'd have stayed in bed.

WORDS OF WISDOM

○

"It is usually no one's fault."

○

"Sometimes, if you express your feelings of guilt to your physicians, they may be able to help you to realize you haven't done anything wrong."

- My doctor told me to wait to come in until Monday.
- I'm just too stressed about our finances.
- I'm being punished for having had an abortion as a teenager.

The question of whether the anger or resentment is or is not appropriate does not necessarily need to be resolved. But it is important to note that, once given voice, some of these feelings can dissipate. Letting go of old anger helps parents to get on with the important business of caring for their baby and each other.

Bargaining with a higher power or with yourself is a sort of simplistic attempt to "make it better."

Your hand reaches through the portal of your baby's isolette, and her tiny fingers are curled around your pinkie. "I'll be the best parent there ever was. . . I'll give 10% of my earnings to medical research every year. . . I'll quit my job to stay home with him. . . Just please God, let my baby be OK." This reaching out to powers beyond your control, understanding, or sometimes even belief, is a common reaction to crisis. It is a part of the continuing process of trying to gain control over circumstances that have, at least to some degree, spiraled out of your control. In retrospect, many people describe the emotional essence of bargaining as having its roots in a very childlike response to being unable to be in charge of their own fate. "If mom and dad get me the skateboard, I'll never hit my little sister again." In truth, bargaining is about as effective or realistic in this adult crisis as it was when you were a child: It doesn't really work. But it does serve a purpose in that it can bridge the gap between senseless blame and beginning to accept the reality of your situation.

WORDS OF WISDOM

○

"Sometimes trying to strike a bargain with a higher being can be the start of developing a more genuine faith that will definitely help you in the long run."

○

"It may be helpful to realize that if waiting for your baby to be 'normal' means waiting for her to be like a baby born at term, you may be destined for disappointment. The more accustomed I became to my daughter's prematurity, the more relaxed I became as a mom."

Sadness and depression are normal reactions to the severe health problems that your baby may have. But even as your baby's health improves, both sadness and depression are understandable responses to the loss of the fantasy of the healthy term baby you were expecting. A feeling of guilt often occurs as a result of that seemingly unjustified sadness.

After dealing with the expected roller-coaster highs and lows you experience as your baby's condition seems to alternate between good and bad days, there is the need to come to terms with the feelings of sadness you may experience, even as your baby grows stronger and continues to make progress. "If things are going so well, why do I feel so bad?" It is a harsh reality, but you cannot underestimate the importance of acknowledging that the birth of the premature baby robs you of the fantasy of the healthy term baby. *This is not about failing to love your premature baby. You are sad because of the loss of the fantasy of the chubby, full-term baby that you were going to have.* Think about it. Fantasies about mothering may begin in a very meaningful way at the onset of puberty for young girls. It stands to reason that the thirty-five-year-old woman having her first child has a very well-established impression of what she expects mothering to be about. Many parents, especially mothers, feel terribly guilty because on an unconscious level they continue to mourn the loss of-the fantasy term baby. The pleasure in their baby's increasing vitality is tempered by resentment that the baby is still not "normal"—it was not born at term. Initially parents may resist naming their very small baby, or are afraid to touch or even look at it. Feelings of incompetence, heartache over the trauma your baby must endure, or a sense of being depressed and overwhelmed may give way to guilt. Interestingly, these feelings of guilt may not surface in their entirety until the premature baby is "out of

WORDS OF WISDOM

○

"My wife was reluctant to come with me to speak with a therapist, but I went on my own to talk about my discomfort with how frail and tiny my son seemed to be. I felt like a jerk. . . like the stereotype 'jock' father, but it helped me to actually say the stuff that I had bottled up inside."

○

"Feelings of guilt are sometimes an attempt to make sense out of something that makes no sense. . . It is often a consequence of loss of control, and by confronting your feelings of guilt and helplessness, you may begin to discover what you can do in the present to be a very proactive part of your baby's care."

the woods," so to speak. It is when the baby's immediate survival is no longer in question that the mother or father may begin to acknowledge the deepest sense of loss and eventually feel guilty about it.

Acceptance is not about "giving up." It is about freeing yourself to take up the challenge of maximizing your baby's potential.

Accepting that you are the parent of a premature baby is what allows you to begin to develop "a big plan"—a plan that recognizes your miracle baby for the child she is, and supports the kind of family-centered care that is in your whole family's best interest. Your baby's days or weeks in the neonatal unit have taught you many things; the importance of planning is high up on that list. You've learned when to be in the unit to catch the doctor at the best time. You've developed strategies for pumping your breasts to maximize your baby's success at feeding time. You've organized care for your kids at home and planned aspects of your life you never even thought about before. Energy is at a premium when you are caring for a premature baby. Acceptance of your situation is one of the greatest energy savers you are ever likely to experience.

It can be difficult to let go of some of your worries, even though you can see that your baby's health is improving.

The view of a baby's overall well-being can be very dependent on the parents' perception. There is no question that the families of two infants with similar medical conditions, both born at 30 weeks to different families, may view their experience very differently. If we stop to think about whether the family sees the cup as "half empty or half full," we recognize the need to consider the emotional life of the family as it existed prior to the baby's birth.

The birth of a premature baby can act as a catalyst in revealing the psychological makeup of the family as a whole. A family with ongoing difficulties that have not been resolved, or in many cases not even acknowledged—such as financial problems, a troubled teen, or a rough patch in the marriage—may find a focal point in the birth of a premature baby. Unresolved issues are deflected by worry and stress over the baby, and consequently continue to have a murky, negative impact on the life of the family. Parents are stressed; children are anxious; a general impression of worry or nervousness can pervade the household. There are other factors at play that are preventing them from seeing the miracle that is unfolding right in front of them.

Conversely, for the family that has been more successful at processing the complications of family life, where communication among family members is ongoing, there is a generally more optimistic feeling in the household. This is not to suggest that the family is without its problems. But this family is far more likely to celebrate even modest progress in the new baby's development. Another factor in a family's assessment of their premature baby is prior experience with prematurity. The parents who already have a child born at the extremely premature age of 26 weeks gestation will look at the problems associated with a baby born at 32 or 33 weeks and count their blessings. That is also likely to be the case with a parent or parents who work in the neonatal unit with very premature babies.

WORDS OF WISDOM

○

"I was so incredibly protective of our twins. I never wanted to go out with them once they were both home from the hospital. They were born at 28 weeks and they seemed so tiny. . . . My husband finally convinced me that it would do us all some good to get out into the world, and he was right. They are 16 months and doing great, but I'm still really fierce about not having people with colds come over to the house."

DR. KLEIN COMMENTS ON COUPLES SUPPORTING EACH OTHER

Coping with prematurity, particularly if your baby is experiencing significant problems, is a recipe for marital stress. Every couple copes differently. Some have great shouting matches, hurling accusations and shedding bitter tears. Other couples shut down and retreat from each other until the gulf between them is almost impassable. Sometimes they out and out blame each other. Parents may go from specialist to specialist shopping for "the right answer." This is a typical symptom of being unable to give up on the fantasy of the healthy term baby. So, with a misplaced belief that the medical community is failing to recognize the real truth, parents go from one neurologist to the next, to the next, to find the one doctor who will say "your baby is normal."

I speak sometimes with couples who get into what I can only call superstition: they failed to go to church or temple, or wished someone harm, or had a bad thought about the outcome of the pregnancy. All of this is inevitably terribly damaging to the parents, who may already feel responsible for a baby who was not carried to term. And it can be devastating to the relationship. This is a time for me, as a pediatrician, to clarify what I can. I try to explain what happened, why it happened, and often acknowledge that, in the vernacular of the day, "stuff happens" and we simply have no idea why. I always try to stress (even in those rare cases when there is something that led to the premature delivery) that this is a time to stop punishing each other because of some real or imagined past event, and move forward as allies in the care of their new baby.

Sometimes the parents are not in agreement with each other about their impression of the baby's health and that creates additional tension. One parent continues to reach out for a new prognosis, while the other wants to accept the scenario that has been offered and learn how to maximize that potential. The answer lies in reaching deep inside to find the strength and the patience and the will to go through the process of coming to terms with your baby's "different beginning."

Chapter Three

Welcome to the Team

You're All in It Together

Many parents who come to respect and care for the staff of the neonatal unit start out by resenting and even mistrusting them. Frequently mothers say that they felt like the interlopers—that their baby was somehow not their own, and there was nothing that they could do to participate. How could they hold themselves up to a standard of caregiving that was even close to that of the trained medical staff? This is particularly true if a mother has delivered by C-section and cannot get up to the NICU to see her baby right away. Or sometimes the mother is confined to bed after delivery and her baby has been transferred to a neonatal unit in another hospital. It can be a day or more before she sees her baby, and by then her feelings of helplessness may have grown disproportionately large. But all of us have conquered feelings of inadequacy and uncertainty when the stakes were not nearly so high. Anyone who has entered a classroom with a lesson already in progress, or walked across a high-school gym to ask a classmate to dance, or gone back to school, or called someone for a date, has had experience with facing the fear of inadequacy. Now the stakes are as high as they get, and you will likely find that you are more than up to the challenge.

The Team Approach to Caring for Your Premature Baby

It is often a very traumatic experience to go to the neonatal unit and see your child there for the first time. But this is the time to go on in, and touch and talk to your baby and become a vital part of the team that is going to care for your baby for the next few days or weeks, or in some instances, several months. In the description of the All-Star Team that follows, there are some members missing—you and your baby. All the other members of the team are there with the goal of providing the best possible outcome for your family.

Your All-Star Team

• *Pediatrician* A medical doctor who has specialized in the care of infants, children, and adolescents by spending three additional years after medical school in a pediatric training program. (Board certified in Pediatrics by the American Board of Pediatrics)

• *Neonatologist* A pediatrician who has spent an additional three years in training in a fellowship program specializing in the care of premature and sick full-term infants. (Board certified in Perinatal-Neonatal Medicine by the American Board of Pediatrics)

• *Neonatal Nurse Practitioner (NNP)* An RN who has received additional training as a physician extender to give medical care (as differentiated from nursing care) to neonatal patients under the direction of a neonatologist. (Certified by the state)

• *Primary Care Physician (PCP)* A pediatrician or other suitably trained physician who provides comprehensive, coordinated, family-centered, and continuing care for the children in your family. He is the focus of your children's "medical home." The most effective way to provide for your baby's care after discharge is to promote early involvement of a primary care physician.

- ***Pediatric Medical Specialists*** Pediatricians who have spent an additional two or three years in training in a fellowship program specializing in their chosen area. (Board certified in their chosen field by the American Board of Pediatrics)
    - Cardiologists (heart)
    - Nephrologists (kidney)
    - Hematologists (blood)
    - Neurologists (brain)
    - Endocrinologists (hormones)
    - Gastroenterologists (esophagus, stomach, liver, and intestines)
    - Infectious disease (viral, fungal, and bacteriological infections)

- ***Pediatric Cardio-Thoracic Surgeon*** A medical doctor who specializes in the surgical correction of heart problems in infants and children.

- ***Pediatric Anesthesiologist*** A medical doctor who specializes in giving anesthesia to infants and children.

- ***Pediatric Surgeon*** A medical doctor who specializes in general surgery on infants and children.

- ***Pediatric Ear, Nose, and Throat Surgeon (ENT)*** A medical doctor who specializes in the surgery of the ears, noses, and throats of infants and children.

- ***Pediatric Ophthalmologist*** A medical doctor who specializes in the surgery of the eyes of infants and children.

- ***Neonatal Nurse (either registered [RN] or licensed vocational [LVN])*** A nurse who specializes in the nursing care of premature and ill full-term infants. (Registered and certified by the state)

- ***Head Nurse or Charge Nurse*** A nurse who is given a supervisory role and is primarily in charge of other nursing personnel in a nursing unit.

• *Primary Nurse* An RN who helps direct and coordinate the care of a particular neonatal patient, and when possible, is assigned to that patient. A neonate may have a group of primary nurses. In some hospitals families may be able to select particular nurses whom they wish to have as primary nurses for their infant.

• *Clinical Nurse Specialist* An RN who has advanced training in neonatal care who acts as a resource to introduce new methods of nursing care and assures the quality of ongoing methods of nursing care in a neonatal unit.

• *Respiratory Therapist* A specially trained person who gives inhalation treatments, manages ventilator therapy, measures blood gases, and assists with or performs other procedures involved in the care of breathing problems in infants. (Licensed by the state)

• *Occupational/Physical Therapist (OT/PT)* State-licensed professionals who are experts in the neurological and physical development of infants. They may fill the role of developmental specialist and implement developmentally appropriate care. They will provide and teach you special handling and exercises for your baby that will enhance development and muscle control. They are also experts in infant feeding techniques and may be called upon to help you and your baby transition from gavage to oral feedings.

• *Parent Liaison* A member of the NICU team who has usually had his or her own infant hospitalized in the NICU. The parent liaison is available to help families to learn about the complex goings-on of the NICU, offer guidance in how families might best come to understand and utilize hospital services, and provide or arrange for parent-to-parent support.

• *Social Worker* Professionally trained clinicians who help families deal with the emotional aspects of having a premature or ill full-term infant. They also help in discharge planning by coordinating home care needs, making referrals to outside resources, and assisting with financial concerns.

• *Case Manager* A member of your team provided by the hospital, insurance company, or other health-care organization that deals with issues of medical necessity, length of stay, discharge planning, home medical equipment, home nursing, and community referrals when necessary. The case manager can also explain and help you with issues involving insurance coverage and financial concerns.

DR. KLEIN COMMENTS ON THE TEAM APPROACH TO CARING FOR YOUR BABY

I can't emphasize enough that it is this team approach which ensures the very best possible outcome for your baby. It is certainly prudent to get the lay of the land—to be a little tactful—and understand that there may be several babies with varying degrees of need. But you should not be afraid to ask questions of the nursing staff, the doctors, or any of the ancillary staff. If you have taken the time to observe that your baby responds best to a particular type of touch, don't be timid about sharing that with the nurses. Talk to your baby, offer encouragement, and become involved from the very beginning.

Choosing a Pediatrician

Whatever the circumstances of your baby's birth, it is best if a primary care physician becomes involved in her care as soon as possible, but certainly before discharge. Your baby's primary care physician will serve as the link between you and any pediatric specialists—such as a neurologist, ophthalmologist, or ENT (ear, nose, and throat specialist)—to whom your baby may need to be referred. Your health insurance coverage may require your pediatrician to make all referrals to the specialists who will be necessary to support your baby's medical and developmental needs. Think of the pediatrician as being at the center of your baby's evolving team: making connections with specialists, following up with those visits or consultations, making sure that you have the referrals you need to give your baby the best possible support. Of course, there are as many sets of personal circumstances as there are premature babies being born, so we'll try to lay out several general scenarios for choosing a pediatrician, one of which may apply to your family.

For first-time parents with a premature baby in the neonatal unit, whether for a couple of days or an extended stay, the unit itself may be a great place to begin the search for the right pediatrician. The nurses in the neonatal unit (many of whom may have children of their own) are a great resource for developing a "short list" of pediatricians to consider. You might also want to speak with your neonatologist about recommending a pediatrician. If you have had an extended hospital stay and had the opportunity to develop a relationship with a particular neonatologist, she may have valuable insight into which primary care physician might best serve the medical and family-centered needs of you and your baby.

You might also talk to your obstetrician and ask for a recommendation. If you have already chosen a pediatrician, you may want to mention this to the nurses in the NICU and see if they are familiar with her practice. Depending on your baby's clinical course and the complications that arise, it might be appropriate to reconsider your initial choice and look for a doctor who has more experience dealing with the complications of prematurity.

Speak with your friends about their pediatricians. Of course, while you may agree with your friends on everything from politics to who makes the best pizza in town, this does not mean you will share the same criteria for choosing a child's doctor. Keep in mind that an endorsement from a friend, while helpful, is not likely to take the place of an interview with a prospective physician. If this is not your first baby, your current pediatrician is likely to care for your new baby. This may be the perfect arrangement, but if you think your premie will receive better care with a doctor who sees a greater percentage of high-risk infants, don't hesitate to go with your best judgment.

The Pediatric Interview

As a new parent, you want to choose the pediatrician who is right for your family. But how can you tell? What are the questions you should ask? And once you ask them, how do you know if you're hearing the right answers? The fact that you are in new territory should tell you one thing: You want to develop a relationship with a pediatrician who has experience dealing with the medical issues that will be relevant to your baby.

It is also important to recognize that you will need to communicate well with this person—that means talking and listening—and he or she will need to do the same for you. Effective communication leaves room for misunderstandings to be clarified, and for divergent philosophies to be heard. You may not need to be "on the same page" about every element of your baby's care, but you do need to be in the same book. It is important to find out about a doctor's general approach to issues such as medication, and the need for feeding or sleeping schedules. It will be an ongoing source of frustration to you and your pediatrician if you continually see a need for a particular health protocol or medication when she does not feel it is necessary. Or if you feel most at ease with a very holistic approach, a pediatrician with no interest in such methods will not work for your family. If you are someone who requires exacting details about all elements of your pediatrician's approach to health care, you will not be happy with a doctor who is impatient in discussing her approach.

Questions to Ask at the Pediatric Interview

A pediatric interview can be conducted in several ways. Some parents schedule an interview, start out by asking the pediatrician to describe her practice, and follow up with questions that have either been generated from the doctor's comments or prepared earlier. Other parents prepare a detailed list and begin the interview by asking their own questions. The goal here is to get practical information about this doctor's approach to pediatrics, and to assess your "gut reaction" to the person to whom you may entrust the medical care of your very precious child.

The following list covers some of the questions you might want to ask. You may not be interested in all of them, but they will give you an idea of the range of subjects that you should be able to discuss comfortably with a prospective pediatrician. It's a good idea to discuss these questions with your mate beforehand so that you have some idea about what answers you both are looking for before the interview takes place.

- Will you be involved with our baby's care while she is still in the hospital?
- How soon after discharge will you see our baby?
- Do you have a number of patients in your practice born at our child's gestational age?
- What is your schedule for follow-up after discharge of premature babies?
- What happens at a checkup?
- How much time do you spend with a patient at a checkup?
- Who will answer my questions if I call the office?
- What are your office hours?
- What happens if we call after office hours?
- Is this your own practice or are there other pediatricians we might see in this office?
- If it is a group practice, can we request to see you exclusively?
- What is your philosophy regarding immunization?
- What are your thoughts about breast-feeding?
- Can you speak with us about your philosophy regarding medication and the use of "alternative" approaches to health care?
- Where did you take your training?
- Do you have children of your own?
- What do you think about circumcision?
- What hospitals are you associated with?
- Are you board certified?

We cannot overemphasize the importance of having your primary care physician (or pediatrician) become familiar with your baby as early as possible. The earlier your pediatrician gets involved (whether by phone or by visiting the hospital) the more comfortable you'll feel about continuity of care once your baby is discharged. Families whose babies have spent many weeks or even months in the hospital often develop a quite appropriate dependence upon the medical judgment of members of their team. Parents often come to know exactly who to turn to when questions come up. One of the most important factors in preparing for discharge is a family's readiness to leave the round-the-clock support of the unit, while maintaining confidence in their ability to carry on at home with their baby. Once you have been discharged from the hospital, the members of the team will change, but you and your pediatrician will continue to pursue the goal of the best possible health for your baby.

Chapter Four

Parenting Your Baby in the Neonatal Intensive Care Unit

Working Toward a Goal of Family-Centered Care

The team approach that we've described is an important element of a progressive system of providing health services that has come to be known as *family-centered care*. The statement below, as well as the essential components of family-centered perinatal care that follow, is excerpted from the Perinatal Care Policy Statement published in the *Quarterly Bulletin of the National Perinatal Association.*[1] *Perinatology* is a specialized area of health care concerned with infants throughout antepartum (prior to birth), neonatal, and postnatal care. This publication targets health-care professionals, but the insights offered here will be of value to any parent with a premature baby in a hospital nursery.

> *Family centered perinatal services are defined as those which recognize and cultivate the strengths of families and respects their concerns, attitudes, values and ethics. This model of care recognizes that the efforts of health care providers support the work of families and communities who contribute the primary resources, support and dedication to their children. In a family centered model, families and health care providers form full partnerships for the purpose of developing, implementing and evaluating perinatal health services.*

Essential Components of Family-Centered Perinatal Care

- The development of mutual respect and trust between families and health-care providers;
- The honest sharing of information between families and health-care providers and the recognition that family-identified concerns deserve as much attention as health-care-provider–identified needs;
- Collaboration between families and health-care providers to support informed decision making which recognizes that while health-care providers possess professional expertise, families possess a unique ability to recognize and anticipate proper courses of action which best fit their individual family priorities;
- The recognition of the diversity that exists among both families and health-care providers, including differences in racial, ethnic, religious, economic, educational, and geographic backgrounds;
- The appreciation of the value of family-to-family support with the development of opportunities within the perinatal system for families to access this support; and
- An understanding that it is families who provide the consistency of care beyond the perinatal period and that the perinatal system has the obligation to support the family in developing the confidence and competence necessary to carry out their responsibilities.

Although the idea of family-centered care is beginning to take hold in many hospital nurseries throughout the nation, actual practice is quite variable and sometimes difficult to achieve. Consumers of health care are growing more and more informed about their needs and their rights, but they are occasionally still faced with a long-established precedent of deferring to the expert advice of the health-care establishment. The model of family-centered care for the premature infant does not dispute the expertise of health-care providers, but it asks those providers and the families themselves to recognize the intrinsic value of family participation in their baby's care.

If you are fortunate, steps are being taken at your hospital toward satisfying the goal of family-centered care. With these goals in mind, you can speak with the health-care providers at your unit. Let them know you are aware of and interested in the concept of family-centered care. If there is a well-established program, they may seek you out! But don't be afraid to ask questions; contribute to conversation by offering what you know about the principles of family-centered care, and be confident in the value of your participation in your baby's well-being in the hospital nursery.

Learning the Ropes

We've all heard the time-honored phrase about how "the squeaky wheel gets the grease." In the neonatal intensive care unit, there is likely to be a whole lot of squeaking going on. Every parent is there to advocate for their baby. As you have probably experienced, the staff, who are there to help you to help your baby, are often confronted with a dizzying number of requests. One of the most important things you can do for yourselves, your baby, and the overworked staff is take a little time to get the lay of the land. When do the shift changes occur? How likely is it that the nurse or doctor you question today about the results of a test will be there for follow-up tomorrow? Recognize that, particularly in the early days of your baby's stay, you may be more distraught than you realize and your communication skills may fail you.

Parents entering the NICU for the first time are often fearful and are understandably quite self-involved. It is to parents' advantage to use a little patience and diplomacy as they begin to interact with the staff. This gets a little easier when you start to have faith in the team that has gathered to care for your premature baby. Several days or several weeks later, many parents discover that they have also become a devoted cheering section for the little fighter in the isolette right next to their baby. Then it gets a bit easier to hold off with your questions if you see that the team's energy has been appropriately diverted to a more pressing problem in the next isolette. Of course, it may be that yours is the critical care issue, and at that time you will appreciate the immediate attention given to your baby. As you learn your way around the NICU, you'll discover that even within this unit designed to provide intensive care, the levels of care needed will vary from hour to hour and from infant to infant. In the case of a premature baby with complications, there may be many unfamiliar machines and monitors, such as an apnea and bradycardia monitor (see chapter 6 for a detailed discussion of the breathing control problems known as apnea and bradycardia); a tube down an infant's throat to facilitate use of a respirator, which may be next to the isolette; a catheter placed through an infant's umbilicus (belly button) and into the umbilical artery to allow for blood drawing, fluid infusion, and connection to a blood pressure monitor; several IVs for various medications; a sensor wrapped around an infant's foot or hand to measure *oxygen saturation* (the amount of oxygen being absorbed by the blood). Try rating your needs on a scale of one to five, one being the most serious. Use that scale to self-regulate the immediacy of requests you make for the time of the busy, caring staff.

It is unreasonable to expect that all staff and all parents will get along without misunderstandings. It is helpful to determine the chain of command so that you can seek to address any problems you may have with any of the personnel who are working with you. You should have a choice about taking your concern or complaint either to the person who is directly involved or speaking with that person's direct superior. Remember, the goal should always be to improve a troubling situation, not necessarily to be acknowledged as being right. Try to create opportunities to speak with your doctors on a reasonable, regular basis. Write your questions down, and write or make a tape recording (with permission) of your doctors' responses. This is particularly important if one parent cannot be present to discuss an important element of your baby's condition or care. If possible, step outside the nursery with

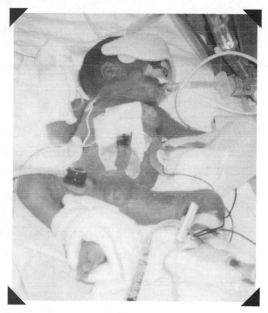

An endotracheal tube, IV's, and an umbilical catheter support the medical needs of this premature infant.

your doctors and ask to use a private office or meeting room if you anticipate the need for a long conversation. Sometimes you will want to ask one or two questions "on the fly" with the understanding that an in-depth conversation will have to wait for another time. If your doctor is researching a particular issue for you, he may need time to gather information. Ask your doctors how they would best like to communicate with you. Offer your fax, work, or pager numbers if that will facilitate communication.

Nursing care in the neonatal intensive care unit is labor intensive and can be highly stressful. In the vast majority of cases, nurses who specialize in the care of preterm and other at-risk infants are there because they love babies and are dedicated to their well-being. However, it is not hard to imagine that their obvious competence, coupled with your inexperience, can create a complex emotional and psychological mine field. Yes, you are thankful for their expert care, but this is your baby and irrational though it might be, you want them to stop interfering. The focus in some nurseries on family-centered care goes a long way toward alleviating those tensions. Even if your unit is not set up to teach and support family-centered care, you can take some steps on your own to build an alliance with your baby's nurses. As the days go by and you get to know the nursery personnel, you will probably have the opportunity to choose a primary care nurse. Let that person know that you are aware of the benefits of family centered care and that you want instruction that will help you to participate as fully as possible in the care of your baby. Wait for the right time and ask exactly what you can do to help. If you have friends who want to help, ask if they can deliver a basket of fruits and nuts or some homemade cookies to the NICU staff on your behalf. Let the staff know that you appreciate their efforts. When you see someone doing an exceptional job, say thank you and write a brief note to that effect to be delivered to the personnel director of the hospital and for inclusion in a personnel file. By all means, be a squeaky wheel, but squeak a little diplomatically.

There is no question that having a premature baby is a very difficult life event. Each day your baby spends in the neonatal unit has the potential to fill you with hope or weigh you down with worry. Many parents have found that taking the following steps during their baby's hospitalization made them even more effective members of the team:

*Become knowledgeable about the use of medical
equipment, such as monitors.*

When you realize that a specific issue or event is causing you to become uneasy, identify the event and figure out who is the most appropriate person on your baby's team to address your concerns and explain what is going on. You may be able to determine why a nurse is making a notation on your baby's chart, or that the monitor alarm that is so frightening to you is alerting the team to a benign event that need not cause you to worry. This may be an opportune time to take notes about the details that are explained to you about the monitor: what the numbers mean; why the beeping occurs; how the monitor is set. In an odd way, you have been dropped into a class that you never anticipated taking, and you need all the study aids you can get!

*Recognize your underlying emotional state, as well as that of
your family, as you confront the stress of your baby's prematurity.*

We've talked about the complexities of the emotions you are facing when you become parents of a premature baby. Now, as you try to take in all the information about your infant's care, you may feel ill-equipped to handle the flood of accompanying emotions. This is not likely to be the time to take on those fundamental emotional problems that were with you coming in to this situation. Nevertheless, if you attempt to develop some coping strategies for dealing with the issues at hand, you may begin to feel a little more in control of your emotions. Try to take a moment to recognize that by seeing to your own emotional well-being, you are providing good care to your baby.

A mother's loving touch.

INSIGHT FROM A PARENT LIAISON

Dorothy Williams, parent liaison for the neonatal unit at a large urban hospital, is herself the mother of twins born prematurely. She offers sound, compassionate advice to any parent with a premature newborn who is hospitalized:

For any parent who voices the concern that their baby belongs to the nurses, or to the neonatal unit, I tell them that nothing could be further from the truth. This is your baby, and your parenting began while the baby was in utero and continues whether it is at home or in the neonatal unit. Babies, whether they are term or premature, thrive in the presence of several elements, of which three are perhaps the most important to talk about when you have your baby in the neonatal unit.

1. The Consistency of Parenting

When you have a new baby born at term who goes home right away, you can insulate yourselves with your baby. You are there as primary caregivers, and maybe there is some extended family. But there are a limited number of people who care for this infant. When the baby shows she needs something by moving or crying or a change in facial expression, the parent is the one who is there, and begins to build up a relationship. With a baby in the neonatal unit, the parent is still the one constant in that baby's life. Nurses, who are unquestionably your baby's closest ally on a moment-to-moment basis, change shifts, have

days off, get assigned to other rooms. There are changes among doctors, respiratory therapists, and a host of other staff in the unit. So as the parent, you are the constant in your child's life and it is very important to acknowledge the importance of that role and to understand that while it may not be the start you were expecting, you have nevertheless begun to fulfill your destiny as the true constant in your baby's young life.

2. Being Your Baby's Advocate

You may have a gnawing concern that you did not succeed in keeping your baby from being born too early. But give yourself some credit and recognize that it is the rare case where a parent has willfully caused their baby to be born too soon. And in most cases, you have done everything possible to prolong your pregnancy and give your baby every protection while she was still in utero. Now it is time to move on to the next step, which is getting involved in learning how to advocate for your baby in this most unhome-like of environments. It may seem odd at first to think of yourself as needing to advocate for your baby, surrounded as she is by all this technical expertise. But you are vital members of your baby's team of caregivers. In fact, as the baby's parents, you are the only members who cannot be replaced. Life in the neonatal unit is not only about the care provided by your baby's medical experts, with all the complex technology and decision making that implies. One of the important elements of family-centered care is your participation as an observer of your baby in her environment. You can keep a watchful eye on environmental variables such as the timing and type of stimulation your baby receives; the positions in which the baby is maintained; and the kind of touch to which she responds positively. By becoming first an alert observer, and then a diplomatic communicator, you will have the opportunity to have a strong, effective, and healthy influence on your baby's stay in the neonatal unit.

3. Learning About Responsiveness

Your baby cannot speak for herself and so you are, quite literally, her voice. But to be an effective voice for your baby, you must learn to understand what the baby wants to communicate. Babies have a lot to tell us if we know how to comprehend their language. A baby's language is one of heart rate and breathing; of skin color changes, movement, and positioning; of sneezes, hiccups, coughs, and grunts. Becoming fluent in this secret language of babies makes you an effective interpreter. You learn that instead of arriving at the nursery and hoping your baby will be awake, there is a pattern to her sleeping and wakefulness. You will really come to know your baby's likes and dislikes and be able to share these insights with the staff. By taking your cues from your baby, you learn how to provide the kind of interaction that will be in her best interest. And you also foster the beginnings of the relationship that you yearn to have with your baby.

Breast Milk for Your Baby in the Neonatal Unit

Providing breast milk for your baby is one of the most important things a mother can do as a member of her baby's team. Not only does it supply the very best nutrition, but it has the added benefit of creating an undeniably positive emotional effect on a mother. A father can also participate right away, helping at feeding time, and encouraging his wife as she works at the sometimes frustrating job of establishing and maintaining her milk supply. The father who becomes knowledgeable about breast-feeding, and the hygienic storing of breast milk, is speaking volumes about how much he supports his wife in this emotional time.

It is important for the mother of a premature baby to know that her baby needs and can use her breast milk even if she is unable to nurse at her breast at first. Most infants born at less than 34 weeks are not able to suck, swallow, and breathe in a coordinated fashion necessary to nurse. One of the first tangible efforts a mother can make on behalf of her child is to start pumping her breasts after the birth of her baby. At first, if your baby was born at less than 34 weeks gestation, she will be receiving nourishment and fluids intravenously. Within a number of days, she will begin taking nourishment from a tube that goes through her nose or mouth and into the stomach. This is known as gavage or tube feeding. As soon as you begin to pump your breasts, you can begin to help nourish your baby. Colostrum, which is the thin milky fluid that comes from the mother's nipple before the milk "comes in," can be introduced to your baby by gavage soon after birth. For the best results, a mother should be advised to use a double setup electric breast pump 10 to 12 times a day for a total of 100 minutes of pumping daily. Pumping should begin as soon as possible after delivery in order to take advantage of changing hormone levels that will enhance lactation. Many mothers of premature babies have described the feeling of connectedness they felt as a result of supplying milk for feeding, even though it was not yet at the breast. If a baby is staying on in the NICU after her mother has been discharged, the father may bring stored, refrigerated breast milk to the hospital and have the nurturing experience of feeding his baby.

It is important to determine approximately how much milk your baby is taking in at a feeding so that you can try to stay ahead of the demand. The goal is to establish an expressed milk supply that will be about 50% ahead of your baby's demand by the time you are two weeks postbirth. This extra milk is "money in the bank" in the event of a temporary dip in a mother's milk supply. Fresh breast milk is best, so you can work with the neonatal unit nursing staff to develop a schedule for pumping your breasts right before feeding time. You will need guidance as you attempt to establish your milk supply. The nurses in your unit will help you to choose the right electric breast pump and help you learn how to use it. It is very important to begin this process firm in the belief that *you will be breast-feeding your baby*. Uterine cramping while pumping (the result of the release of the hormone oxytocin) is not unusual in the early days of establishing your milk supply. Don't worry about when your baby will actually begin to nurse at your breast, or how long you're going to breast-feed. Just immediately assume this wonderful, proactive role in your baby's care. Interestingly, when the time comes that your baby can actually nurse at your breast, you may discover that she finds it easier to coordinate her sucking, breathing, and swallowing at the breast than at the bottle.

You are likely to be encouraged to begin to try nursing your infant at your breast by about 33 weeks. You may breast-feed and then offer a supplement if your doctor recommends it. Taking the opportunity to nurse your baby while still in the neonatal unit can help you to have a strong foundation for continuing to breast-feed once you get home. You may need to continue pumping if your baby is not yet sucking vigorously enough to maintain your milk supply.

Kangaroo Care: Skin-to-Skin with Your Baby

The concept of "skin-to-skin" or "kangaroo care" was originally developed in South America, where the nurseries in local hospitals did not have enough isolettes to warm their premature infants; they came up with skin-to-skin contact to help the babies to stay warm. Of course, people all over the world have carried their babies this way for centuries, but the opportunity to see such a simple but momentous form of care take hold in the modern NICUs of the United States is particularly gratifying. Parents, nurses, and physicians report a variety of wonderful findings in their experience with kangaroo care: babies have less frequent episodes of apnea and less bradycardia (see chapter 6 for a detailed discussion of apnea and bradycardia); they gain weight more rapidly, sleep less fitfully, and have an easier time regulating their body temperature. Fathers can be equally successful with this wonderfully nurturing opportunity with their baby.

Susan Luddington is the nurse–midwife credited with bringing kangaroo or "skin-to-skin" care to the United States after visiting infant care units in Bogota, Colombia. She was quoted in the *Los Angeles Times*.[2]

> *Kangaroo care was not being used in the United States because it's unconventional and anti-technology. We have relied on technology for the survival of these babies. My charge was to test the natural approach to see if it was safe and has a benefit. And we have documented both.*

Kangaroo care initially brings a mother together with her premature baby, as she holds the upright infant, dressed only in a diaper, between her bare breasts during feeding. During kangaroo care, a premature infant will begin to root toward her mother's breast even before the infant is able to breast-feed. There are reports of babies who participated in daily "skin-to-skin" sessions of 1 hour and began to breast-feed from 32½ to 34 weeks. If you consider how challenging it can be for a premature baby to establish successful breast-feeding, you can realize what a significant development skin-to-skin care is for families with premature babies. Mothers who had difficulty nursing their older babies once they were home continued with kangaroo care and reported good results.

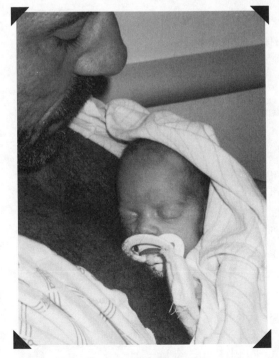

Father enjoys skin-to-skin contact with his little girl.

DR. KLEIN COMMENTS ON KANGAROO CARE AND BREAST-FEEDING

I am very happy to say that I have seen firsthand some wonderful results from the practice of kangaroo care in the hospital neonatal unit. In our nursery, we start kangaroo care when babies reach about 1,000 grams. We start the baby off once a day for approximately one hour. If it seems to be going well, and the parents are eager to continue, we'll increase it. Sometimes we have mother and baby have their time together in a room down the hall. I am aware of some facilities that start with even smaller babies. In some hospitals they begin even when the babies are still on respirators. And keep in mind that this is a wonderful option for fathers too! With the exception of actually breast-feeding his baby, a father is equally equipped to provide the warmth, closeness, and nurturing that characterize this wonderful technique. Infants receiving kangaroo care do seem to have less apneic episodes, less bradycardia, and an improved ability to maintain body temperatures. I have seen young babies begin to root toward their mother's breast even before they are ready to breast-feed. Recently, one of the families I was encouraging to use kangaroo care had their baby begin to breast-feed at 32½ weeks. It was wonderful for the whole family. When I have a mother who has taken her baby home and is having difficulty nursing, I recommend kangaroo care. It is a simple and often very satisfying opportunity for parents and their babies.

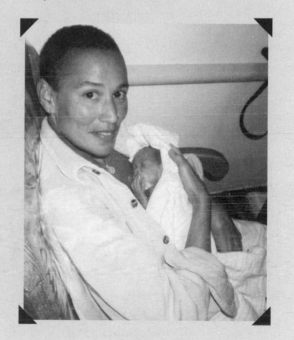

Neonatal Individualized Developmental Care and Assessment Program (NIDCAP)

In the 1980s, Heidelise Als, PhD (Associate Professor of Psychology [Psychiatry] at Harvard Medical School, and Director of Neurobehavioral Infant and Child Studies, Children's Hospital, Boston), directed research that was designed to study whether the compromised respiratory status and overall health of preterm and other at-risk infants could be improved by providing care that was guided by direct observation of each infant's behavior in the neonatal intensive care unit.

The Neonatal Individualized Developmental Care and Assessment Program (NIDCAP) developed as a result of that research. Today many neonatal units throughout the United States are using the NIDCAP model to create programs that provide individualized care to high-risk and preterm infants. Two elements are key to the success of the program:

- The infants' families are supported, instructed, and encouraged to participate in a manner that takes full advantage of their competencies. There is an emphasis on family-centered care.
- Health-care professionals responsible for the long- and short-term care of these infants are trained in developmental observation and assessment.

The NIDCAP approach to premature baby care seeks to maximize the developmental potential of the infant, and concludes that observation of the infant itself is key to attaining the best developmental outcome. There are often attempts to provide privacy for parents and their infants. Parents are taught to become aware of their baby's patterns of responsiveness, tolerance, and preferred patterns of stimulation, such as talking, singing, music boxes, taped music, recorded heartbeats, tastes, smells, and various tactile sensations. The success of NIDCAP in neonatal units throughout the United States appears to support the theory that individualizing the preterm infant's environment, as well as the style and pattern of daily care, can lead to maximizing developmental outcome and decreasing a preterm infant's length of stay in the neonatal unit.

Specific modifications based on observation and assessment of each baby's own environment might include:

- reduction of lighting; minimizing visual clutter and auditory stimulation
- swaddling in buntings and securing infants with rolled blankets or hammocks
- placements that include side-lying, flexed, and prone positions; discouraging extension; having limbs gently contained when turning or alternate positioning is needed
- unnecessary handling kept to a minimum
- providing opportunities for grasping and sucking
- the individual infant's tolerance for handling and procedures is noted and timed to avoid overtiring

Making the Best of a Tough Situation—Your Baby Knows You're There

There is much that can be done to mitigate the fact that you are not at home with your baby. The most basic advocacy that you provide is your presence in the neonatal unit. Your touch, your scent, your voice, the simple fact of your consistent presence in the nursery is meaningful to your baby's well-being. Studies indicate that babies who are touched are less prone to have episodes of apnea. Even a baby as young as 26 weeks may grasp her parent's finger. Although every facility has its own set of rules regarding who can visit the babies and when they can be there, most will try to be as accommodating as possible. It is not unusual for units to allow parents to visit the nursery almost all the time. There may be hours for sibling visitation that give your other children an important opportunity to become invested in rooting for their tiny new sibling. The staff in the neonatal unit welcomes the family involvement that they know is in their patients' best interest. It is this obliging attitude that is at the core of the family-centered care that is so important to you and your baby.

It is no secret that the routine care in the neonatal unit has an impact on its tiny residents. Babies often must cope with lights being on all the time; they must tolerate heel sticks to draw blood; there is a constant changing of personnel; there are many loud sounds. Many nurseries have adopted an individualized approach to caring for infants. Parents can play a vital role in this new approach to individualized care of premature babies.

The sound of your voice is already familiar to your baby. Both of you probably spoke to her before she was born, and certainly you spoke with each other. It is an important part of the baby's environment in utero to hear voices and sounds from the outside. It stands to reason that you should continue to provide that stimulation to your baby once she is born. If you listened to music while driving in the car or loafing around the house on Sundays, your baby was listening too. It is perfectly appropriate for you to bring a tape player to the nursery and continue providing those same stimuli to your baby. Some families record the voices of their children at home making welcoming messages for the new baby. This serves the additional purpose of offering the kids at home a way to "be there" for their new sibling.

Health Insurance: Be a Savvy Consumer

The first thing you should do is read your policy from cover to cover. Few people anticipate complications with their baby's birth, so in the case of a premature baby, you may not have done this by the time the baby is born. If you did, you are ahead of the game. Many people find it helpful to jot down questions that come up while reading the policy. Afterward, you or another member of your team (a physician, social worker, or case manager) can speak with a representative from your insurance company and discuss your concerns. Always be sure to ask for the name of the person with whom you speak, and find out if they have a telephone number that will enable you to contact them directly the next time you have a question. It is not inappropriate to request to speak with a supervisor if you feel your questions are not being answered clearly. Some of the concerns you may have as the parent of a premature baby are:

- What (if any) are the annual and/or lifetime financial caps on the policy?
- If there are long-term special needs, can you get an additional policy that will kick in if limits are reached on the first policy? This is a question best asked of your insurance agent.

- Is your family eligible for federal, state, or local government subsidies or programs?
- What are the lifetime limits on durable medical equipment (DME), such as apnea monitors or other devices needed to care for your baby at home?
- Will your policy pay for outpatient occupational therapy, respiratory therapy, physical therapy, and/or home nursing visits?

Many people are looking for ways to tighten the purse strings in order to prepare for adding a new member to the family. But if both parents are insured before you become pregnant, consider holding on to and putting your baby on both policies. The money you will save by dropping one policy will look inconsequential compared to the increased financial coverage you may get from having your baby covered by a second policy.

TRUCE'S TALE

Truce entered the world at the threshold of gestational viability for a baby. She was 24 weeks postmenstrual age (PMA—a method of calculating the gestational age of an infant as determined by counting from the date of the mother's last period) and weighed 1 pound, 11 ounces. At the time Truce's mother Mary shared her story, Truce was 8½ months old and was tipping the scales at a beautiful 16 pounds, 8 ounces. Truce's story will ring true to all parents who have endured the emotional roller-coaster ride of caring for their very premature baby.

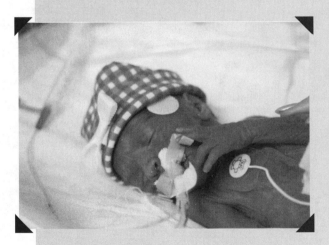

I had no reason to anticipate having a premature baby. I had a very healthy pregnancy. My mom had me when she was 40. My sister was 40 when she gave birth to my niece. I was 39 when I was pregnant and I'm probably the healthiest and most fit of all the people in my family. I certainly was not worried about having a baby at my age. The night she was born I heard her make a tiny cry when she was delivered. . . they put her up to my cheek for a moment. . . I didn't even get a chance to look at her before they put her in a transport incubator and whisked her away. I told my husband to go with her, and he has since told me that he was afraid to go. He had been in New York just hours before. His office reached him on the flight back to California to tell him to come directly to the hospital. He got to the hospital at 9:00 P.M., and I gave birth at 10:25. My faith was strong. . . very strong. I knew that if the Lord was giving us our baby at a point where she *could* survive, that she was meant to be. In my heart, when I was able to carry her to 24 weeks, I just said, "Thank you, God." I remember my husband saying, "Do you understand what the percentage (survival rate) is for a baby this young?" And I said, "Yes, 50%. Isn't that great?" He could not believe I was saying that. He's a statistics person and did not like those odds. For me it was, "Thank you God. You've given us 50%, and I know you'll do the rest."

I was not able to go in and see her right away because of concerns about infection. Five and a half hours after she was born they let me go in to her. Oh, how my heart ached. . . Truce was so young, her eyes were still fused for the first two days. She couldn't even look at us. She had IVs in every limb and in her belly button. Her arms were the size of my smallest finger, and her legs were very small and scrawny and spread out. Her skin was so thin and translucent. . . like a newborn bird or a little mammal. She didn't really look like a baby. But at the same time, she had arms and legs and her hands were so beautiful. All I could do was look at her and see a budding child. I knew her right away. The idea of using Truce as a name came to me as a child when I first learned its meaning. The idea that a truce was about making peace seemed terrific to me. My husband also liked it and we named her Truce the moment we knew she was coming into this world. She was on a warmer for the first 2½ weeks because there were too many IVs to manage her in an isolette. She was also on a high-frequency respirator, and I quickly learned that the staff needed to have easy access to her. I started pumping my breasts as soon as I could, and pumped for the 3 months she was hospitalized. At the beginning, she was receiving nutrition through an IV. After the first week, they tried her on 0.5 ml of diluted breast milk and discovered she could tolerate it, so she began to receive diluted breast milk via tube. I know that did a lot for her, so I kept up with the pumping.

I believe that even before she could open her eyes, she knew we were there. Her nervous system was so immature that she startled a lot. . . She was so jumpy. A baby born at 24 weeks is not prepared to deal with the outside world. We learned that touching her too much could make her uncomfortable. We would put our hands under her tiny hand and she would conform her hand to ours. Somehow, it was enough to let her know we were there. We would sing softly to her and pray with her and read her stories. Every day she would respond to us. . . kind of opening her eyes or turning her head when we opened the door of the isolette. I certainly knew that I was her mother and Michael knew he was her father and we didn't care how much she responded in those early days. We were going to just keep giving as much as it took. That was all that mattered. We had no expectation of what she would give in return. We had to do everything possible to help her and be there for her. Seeing your baby at such a premature age is like being at a window and looking in on what would be occurring in

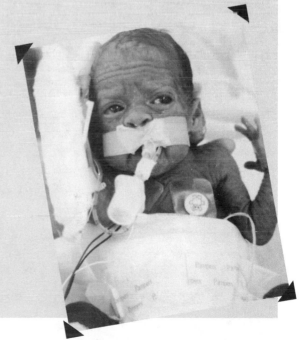

utero. Seeing the lanugo hair on that tiny body. . . and her eyes still being fused. . . We got to observe where the fat on her body was distributed and how it changed over time. Her nose and hands and feet seemed so large until she grew into them. She was like a little wrinkled old man. I remember thinking, "This is what she would have looked like if she was still growing inside me." She looked absolutely nothing like she looks now.

When I think of Truce's time in the hospital, it is as though she followed several courses. . . facing down one obstacle and then confronting another. In her first week she had an intraventricular hemorrhage (IVH) [see chapter 7 for a detailed discussion of this problem], and we had to hope and pray that it would resolve and that she would not need to have a shunt put in. And it did resolve. Actually, it resolved slowly, getting a little better each week. She had an episode that was thought to be a seizure, and a subsequent EEG at 27 weeks was abnormal. She was placed on phenobarbital to keep her from having any more seizures. She was taken off the phenobarbital at 5½ months, and her last EEG was completely normal. We are very aware of keeping in touch with what is going on for Truce developmentally, and even in the hospital we invited the occupational therapists to get involved with our daughter's care. But that first month, it was like climbing uphill all day, every day. When Truce was about 7 or 8 weeks old, having come through her brain hemorrhage and a serious infection and all the other complications of being born so early, we were told that she appeared to have another serious infection or possibly necrotizing enterocolitis (NEC). It was about a 5-day stretch where we went from not knowing which antibiotic was best to treat her, to the possibility that she might need surgery, and finally the understanding that they were able to treat her and get her back on track.

Underlying all of this, as is typical of very early babies, Truce had an underdeveloped (immature) respiratory system. Like I said, she started on a high frequency respirator, but switched to a regular respirator after the first three days. She needed a lot of oxygen and seemed to desaturate very frequently. I remember sitting in that hospital every day for 12 to 13 hours, watching the meters on her monitor go up and down and up and down. I started asking questions right away and knew that her oxygen levels were very important. It was 5½ weeks before she came off the respirator and began nasal continuous positive airway pressure (NCPAP) for about 2 weeks; then she was able to use a nasal oxygen cannula.

I think it is important for parents to know about kangaroo care. With a premature baby, you are learning every step of the way. We started doing kangaroo care at 30 weeks and I believe it helped us a lot. I had read a book about it, and the hospital had just approved a decision to begin to implement the program. But no protocol was really established at that point. I spoke to the neonatologists and they

approved it as long as I could coordinate with the nursing staff. By that time, I had more or less been camping out at the unit and was pretty much a fixture there. I had a list of the nurses we most enjoyed working with, and they were very supportive of our getting started with kangaroo care. Truce was still hooked up to IVs and we had to be very careful about her oxygen levels. But the nurses knew that I would be the first one to suggest putting her back down if she began to suffer in any way. We started slowly—once a day for 5 minutes at a time. We continued at home and I think it was helpful in establishing breast-feeding. Truce made it clear she was ready to stop at about 5 months. She kind of sets the pace for many things.

One of the things I want to say to parents is that you need to be an advocate for your child. We got to the point where we were such veterans at the hospital that we would pull parents aside and tell them not to hesitate to ask questions. Don't just assume that everything is right. The doctors and nurses caring for these babies have so much pressure on them. Parents need to be a part of the dialogue and a part of the decision-making process. You are taking in so much that you may not realize how much you are learning and how capable you are of coping with the situation, however stressful. I saw my husband and myself as partners in Truce's team of wellness. I never thought that we were just parents and the doctors and nurses were taking care of her. We were a part of her care and we asked questions because we needed to know why they did what they did. Spending so much time there, I learned about how to care for my daughter. We came right out and said, "We want so much to help care for Truce, and help you. What can we do? Please let me change her. . . . Can I bathe her?" And the staff was very responsive and supportive. By the time we came home, I was not as intimidated as I might otherwise have been.

I look at Truce now and every day I'm thankful for our progress. But I can tell you that I never doubted that she'd make it. Faith is a tremendous thing. I don't know how anyone gets through this kind of experience without it. You do lose your ability to believe and you just have to know there is something bigger in control. I'd have to say that it has been the hardest year ever for our marriage, but we had and still have a very wonderful relationship. We never went out or managed to take time for each other; everything we did was solely with the thought of bringing our baby home. Once she came home, we were still pretty much confined to the house for a couple of months. But now, almost 9 months later, we are starting to get back to our relationship and our life. Two of my girlfriends are trying to coax me into having a baby shower now. I kind of want to wait until Truce's first birthday and throw a huge party. I just keep telling my husband, "We have a healthy baby. Don't forget that." Our daughter is one of the most jovial, curious children you will ever meet. She's a real explorer and loves being out in the world. She has a wonderful, hearty laugh and is well entertained by our talking with her and looking at books or pictures. When you go from having a baby who is not well and has so many needs, and you slowly come to realize that you are making your way towards your child's good health, you kind of have to pinch yourself. We just went and got those little professional portrait pictures done. I came home and looked at the proofs and thought, "Wow. My daughter with no tubes, no tape across her face. This is pretty neat."

Chapter Five

Supporting Your Baby's Respiratory Needs in the Hospital

Lung Development

As the lungs of a fetus develop, two bronchial tubes that began in the fetal trachea divide into bundles of smaller tubes (bronchioles). Bubblelike air sacs (alveoli) form at the end of the bronchioles. The alveoli develop continuously throughout gestation, along with a rich accompaniment of very small blood vessels (capillaries). The proximity of these exquisitely small capillaries to the alveoli enable the exchange of oxygen and carbon dioxide between the bloodstream and the lungs.

Before birth, there is actually very little blood that flows through a baby's lungs. Instead, the blood is shunted from the right side of the heart into the left side of the body through the *ductus arteriosus*. The ductus arteriosus is a blood vessel in the fetus that connects the pulmonary artery to the *aorta*, which is the large artery coming from the heart that supplies the body with oxygen-rich blood. At birth, the blood has to make the transition from flowing through the ductus arteriosus (bypassing the lungs) to flowing through the lungs to pick up oxygen for the rest of the body. In a healthy baby, the ductus arteriosus closes within the first 24 hours after birth. (Later on we'll talk more about *patent ductus arteriosus*, a condition where the ductus fails to close, which can be a problem for your premature baby.)

As the lungs develop in utero, they begin to produce a substance called *surfactant,* which will be vital to the baby's ability to breathe without assistance after birth. While in utero the fetal lungs are filled with fluid. Although the lungs begin to produce surfactant and grow proportionately larger as the baby grows, they are not yet a functioning element of fetal physiology. It is not until after delivery that a baby relies upon his lungs to breathe. Before birth the transfer of oxygen from mother to baby occurs through the miraculous switching station we know as the placenta.

Once the baby begins to breathe on his own, the surfactant (which has a somewhat soapy feeling) coats the alveoli to prevent them from collapsing in on themselves. Surfactant changes the surface tension on the surface of the alveoli, keeping them partially expanded, and making it easier for the baby to take subsequent breaths. Compare a baby's first breath to the powerful effort you must exert to inflate a new balloon. If you let some of the air out (keeping the balloon partially inflated) and blow the balloon up subsequent times, the effort needed is not nearly so great as it was the first time. A baby's first breath requires great effort, but then surfactant makes subsequent breathing easier because the alveoli remain partially inflated. The closer a baby comes to term, the more time he has had to produce the necessary levels of surfactant. However, this is somewhat complicated by the fact that some of the surfactant that is present at birth can be destroyed as a result of:

- the baby's failure to breathe well on his own at birth
- increased fluid in the lungs because of blood flowing back through the ductus arteriosus or retained fluid in the lungs

Ultimately, it is the amount of *usable* surfactant that will have an impact on the baby's ability to breathe easily after birth. As the fetus matures in utero, surfactant production increases. Premature male infants appear less likely than female babies to have enough surfactant to sustain normal respiration after birth. But by the gestational age of 34 to 36 weeks, almost all babies will be able to breathe without assistance. It is also very interesting to note that while some maternal conditions such as diabetes can cause a delay in surfactant production, others are thought to enhance surfactant production in the developing fetus. If the mother has an infection before the baby's birth, or the fetus is stressed for some other reason (such as ruptured membranes), this may cause enhanced maturation of the lungs. Chronic hypertension in the mother, which may have the effect of promoting pulmonary maturity, may also result in early delivery. Adrenal steroids (not to be confused with the steroids associated with bodybuilding) given to the mother prior to birth also promote surfactant production.

Once the Baby Is Born

At birth, as a baby takes his first breath, it is the beginning of the lifelong job of providing his own oxygen. An infant's first independent action is to take a big breath in order to fill the lungs with air and begin to breathe and maintain respiration. Within the first minutes of each baby's life, he or she will be evaluated and given an *Apgar score*. The Apgar evaluation is a method of assessing a baby's well-being at birth using five criteria:

- heart rate
- respiratory rate
- skin color
- muscle tone
- reflex irritability

The baby can receive up to two points for each category. The Apgar score is assigned at 1 minute, 5 minutes, and occasionally there is a third evaluation at 10 minutes.

Sometimes, if an infant isn't breathing well enough at birth and has a low Apgar score, he may need a little bit of help. This can be accomplished by placing a mask (that is attached to a bag) over the baby's face. As the bag is pumped, a mixture of air and oxygen is forced down into the lungs, which may be enough of an assist to get the baby breathing on his own. Further measures such as *intubation* (the insertion of a narrow tube into the baby's nose or mouth in preparation for delivering additional respiratory assistance) may be needed in the delivery room to assist a baby with breathing problems.

When There Are Breathing Problems

When symptoms of breathing problems occur, the doctor is likely to check the baby's oxygen saturation with a pulse oximeter (a device attached to a sensor wrapped around a foot or hand to measure oxygen saturation) and draw blood to check the blood gas. Blood gas is a measurement of how much oxygen (O_2), carbon dioxide (CO_2), and acid (pH) is in the blood. The doctor uses this information as a tool in interpreting the severity of the baby's lung condition and deciding what therapy is needed. Symptoms of breathing difficulties in an infant may include:

- turning blue in room air and a need for oxygen
- grunting
- flaring nostrils
- sucking in (retracting) of the skin between the ribs when the baby takes a breath, because the lungs (which can't take in adequate air) aren't expanding fast enough to fill the air cavity.

If your premature baby continues to have breathing problems after delivery, your baby's doctor will probably want to do a chest X ray and consider the following possible causes:

- *Transient Tachypnea of the Newborn (TTN)* This problem is caused by a delay in absorption of lung fluid after birth. It has a characteristic X ray, usually requires only minimal extra respiratory support, and resolves rapidly within 3 days (usually less than 24 hours) after birth.

- *Respiratory Distress Syndrome (RDS)* This is the most common single cause of respiratory problems in the premature infant and is described in detail below.

• **Pneumothorax** This is the accumulation of air outside the lungs within the chest cavity. It occurs because of a rupture of the alveoli and is often associated with other lung problems, such as RDS. If it is serious it may be referred to as a collapsed lung, and this can cause respiratory compromise. These severe cases will need to be treated by placing a tube (chest tube) into the chest cavity to remove the air.

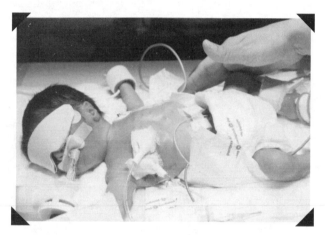

Chest tube in place to treat a pneumothorax.

• **Congenital Heart Disease** Various forms of congenital heart disease can appear as respiratory distress at birth. Your baby's doctor may want to get an echocardiogram (ultrasound of the heart) in order to diagnose this problem.

• **Structural Problems with the Lung** The initial chest X ray done after birth can often alert your baby's doctor to structural problems, such as a diaphragmatic hernia or diaphragmatic paralysis.

• **Pneumonia** This lung infection often occurs after prolonged ruptured membranes or placental infection. It is usually easily treated with antibiotics and resolves in 5 to 10 days. It is sometimes difficult to distinguish infection from RDS and premature infants are often treated with antibiotics at birth "just in case."

Controlling Infection

Like almost all other systems in the premature infant, the immune system's ability to fight off infection is compromised because of its lack of development. As the birth weight and gestational age of an infant decreases, the risk of infection increases. Severity of a baby's illness and the length of stay in the neonatal unit also add to infection risk. Fortunately, treatment for infections with antibiotics is readily available and generally is without complications. When doctors in the neonatal unit are suspicious of infection, they are likely to obtain blood, urine, and sometimes spinal fluid (from a spinal tap) for culture; call for various laboratory studies, such as a complete blood and platelet count; and start treatment with antibiotics while awaiting the results of these tests.

The signs of infection (sepsis) are often nonspecific, and it is important to start treatment as early as possible. Although each "septic work-up" is likely to cause anxiety for parents, it may be comforting to realize that most of them are negative, with only a few revealing significant infection. If any of the cultures are positive for bacteria or fungus, your baby's doctors will probably prescribe a course of antibiotics lasting from 7 to 14 days for a bacterial infection, and possibly up to 4 weeks for a fungal infection. If a spinal tap was not part of the initial work-up and the blood culture is positive, a spinal tap may be called for. If the spinal tap is also positive for infection, then *meningitis* (infection of the lining of the brain) is present and extended treatment may be needed. Luckily, most infections are readily treatable by today's sophisticated antibiotics and resolve without any long-lasting complications.

Ongoing Respiratory Care

For babies who appear to need ongoing respiratory care, the doctor is likely to insert a catheter into either the umbilical artery or a peripheral artery in order to facilitate drawing blood for blood gas measurements. Depending on the severity of the problem, the next step might be the use of nasal CPAP (continuous positive airway pressure). Nasal CPAP provides a flow of oxygen and air delivered by small prongs inserted into the infant's nose that keep the lungs well aerated and prevents them from collapsing. The baby whose lung disease is more severe may need to be *intubated* and placed on a *respirator* (also called a ventilator), which will mechanically pump moist, oxygenated air into the lungs for as long as it is needed. If the baby has low blood pressure or a low red cell blood count, he may require either some extra blood or fluid given through one of the catheters in order to bring up the blood pressure. The younger the baby's gestational age, the more likely it is that he will require a respirator for some period of time.

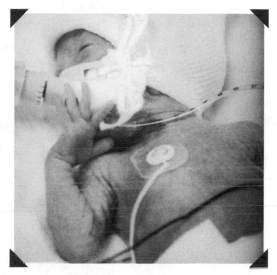

Nasal CPAP (continuous positive airway pressure)

Sometimes a baby can do some breathing on his own and only needs the respirator to do some of the work. If an infant requires high settings on the ventilator, high pressures in particular, it would not be uncommon to sedate and paralyze him for some period of time. An infant who develops pockets of air in the lungs outside the airways—*pulmonary interstitial emphysema* (PIE)—or who requires very high settings may be put on a special kind of ventilator that uses lower pressures and much higher respiratory rates. Some very small premature infants may initially require this type of ventilation. There are two kinds of high-frequency ventilators that can be called upon for this special circumstance:

- The *jet ventilator,* which is a high-frequency ventilator that enables a baby to be ventilated at a rate of anywhere from 200 to 600 breaths per minute.
- An *oscillating ventilator,* which is very high frequency (720 oscillations per minute).

Respiratory Distress Syndrome (RDS)

Respiratory distress syndrome occurs when a baby's lungs have not matured sufficiently and there is not enough surfactant to promote adequate breathing. The earlier the gestational age, the greater the likelihood of developing respiratory distress syndrome. Recent replacement therapy with various commercial surfactant preparations has led to a much improved outcome of this previously deadly problem. This is given through the ventilation tube and there are variable dosage regimens. In some cases a baby may be small enough and gestationally young enough to require intubation to assist his respiratory effort, but that same baby may not be sufficiently troubled as to need extra surfactant. It is very important for parents to understand that there are various parameters that a doctor will consider in deciding whether or not to give the baby surfactant:

- Some physicians will prescribe it for all babies under a certain weight.
- Other physicians may give it only to babies with specific symptoms that they associate with RDS.
- Some doctors only prescribe surfactant if the baby's X-ray looks like it's diagnostic for RDS.
- A physician may feel that particular blood gas measurements must be present before using surfactant.

Surfactant can be associated with pulmonary hemorrhage (bleeding into the lungs). It is like every medication that is available in modern medicine in that there are positive and negative aspects associated with its use. A physician balances these factors in deciding whether or not to go ahead with surfactant treatment. The protocol on how long it's given is also variable. Some neonatal units will give it every 12 hours, while another hospital may utilize it until the baby's blood gases and oxygen requirements suggest it is no longer needed. Typically, RDS that is untreated with surfactant gets worse for the first 24 hours and then improves over the next few days. When a baby receives surfactant, that time course changes and many of them get better quite rapidly. It is not unusual in an uncomplicated case for a baby to be off a respirator in 1 to 2 days. Smaller babies are more likely to need more prolonged ventilator support. As the commercial surfactant works to keep the lungs from collapsing, the baby begins to produce and use its own surfactant with greater efficiency.

The description of the development of your baby's lungs mentioned the *ductus arteriosus*, which is a blood vessel connecting the pulmonary artery to the *aorta* while a baby is still in utero. Prior to birth, the ductus arteriosus channels much of the blood flow to the rest of the developing fetus while bypassing the lungs (for the most part). This temporary connection between the aorta and the pulmonary artery functions very efficiently, supplying the body with oxygen-rich blood from the placenta. As the healthy newborn baby begins to use its lungs, the ductus arteriosus should close within 24 hours; this allows blood to flow through the lungs, where it picks up the oxygen that is so vital to all human life. When the ductus arteriosus fails to close, it is called *patent ductus arteriosus* (PDA). Your doctor will probably want to do an echocardiogram (ultrasound evaluation of the heart) if she thinks a PDA is interfering with your baby's lung condition. If found to be open, it usually can be closed with a medication called Indocin. In some cases, especially in very small babies, surgical closure is necessary.

Recently some doctors have been giving adrenal steroids to very small infants during the first week of life in an effort to decrease their time on the respirator, as well as reduce the incidence of bronchopulmonary dysplasia (see below).

Bronchopulmonary Dysplasia (BPD)

Bronchopulmonary dysplasia (BPD) is a syndrome seen in premature infants whose treatment for respiratory problems has required an extended period of mechanical ventilation. Classically, BPD is characterized by the triad of the following findings in infants over 28 days old:

- oxygen dependence
- abnormal X-ray findings
- chronic respiratory symptoms

Today, as more and more infants with birth weights under 1,000 grams survive, there are many babies who are still on oxygen at 28 days old. However, not all of these babies will go on to be diagnosed with ongoing chronic respiratory problems. It has been proposed that the continued use of oxygen at 36 weeks postmenstrual age (PMA) is a more sensitive and exacting predictor of ongoing respiratory problems in these small premature infants.

With the arrival of surfactant treatment in the late 1980s, there was hope that the incidence of BPD would be markedly decreased. Surfactant treatment did succeed in decreasing the severity of classic severe BPD: initial acute respiratory distress syndrome was prevented or improved and the length of time spent on ventilators was greatly diminished. But although surfactant treatment decreased the severity of BPD, it failed to eliminate it completely. Many of the infants who are now able to survive their initial acute lung disease because of commercially available surfactant go on to develop *late-onset chronic lung disease of extreme prematurity*. Fortunately, the severity of illness in these babies appears to be less severe as a result of the use of surfactant. In addition to those babies diagnosed initially with RDS, there are some who will also develop chronic lung disease *even though they never had initial acute lung disease, or their disease was minimal*. These babies, usually with birth weights under 1,000 grams, may develop progressive and severe respiratory problems that we describe as *chronic respiratory insufficiency of prematurity*. For parents, it may be helpful to understand that your doctor is likely to refer to any of these conditions as *chronic lung disease* (CLD), and the medical course of action is the same for all.

If we look at the general population of babies under 1,000 grams birth weight who survive, approximately 20 to 25% of them will develop CLD. Why do these babies develop lung disease? We know that prolonged ventilation is a factor, but even babies who are not ventilated for extended periods and do not have a lot of lung injury are subject to chronic respiratory problems. We also know that the more premature a baby is, the greater the likelihood of CLD. Infection in the newborn, or even exposure to the room air itself, may be contributory factors.

Caring for Your Baby in the Hospital with CLD

Recovery from CLD may take weeks, or it may go on for months or even years in the most severe cases. Once again, this is a time when your baby's team will need to work effectively together to ensure the very best possible outcome. In the beginning (while still hospitalized) your recovering baby with CLD may be under the care (or have the consultation) of the neonatologists in your neonatal unit. It is best if the members of your baby's team who are vital to this particular aspect of care (neonatologists, the primary care physician, the primary nurse, case managers, social workers, and other relevant personnel such as respiratory therapists and occupational therapists) meet informally or formally on a regular basis to discuss strategies for care. If there is a primary care physician on your team, the neonatologist will want to keep her appraised of your baby's condition, as she will ultimately be handling your child's ongoing health care after discharge. In keeping with the tenets of family-centered care, when possible, parents should meet (or at least speak) with the primary care physician and neonatologists on a regular basis to discuss their baby's progress and problems, and their concerns. *This can be a very stressful experience for parents. It is important to remember that you are dealing with a chronic illness, and that slow growth over a prolonged period of time (often months to years) will lead to recovery.* Your presence in the neonatal unit, supporting your baby's nourishment, and patiently taking cues about how he likes to be touched or spoken or sung to is the very best kind of advocacy you can provide.

The positive news here is that babies recovering from chronic lung disease continue to grow new healthy lung tissue and most reach a point where they have only minimal breathing problems. At that point the baby may be able to breathe on his own without any additional oxygen.

Oxygen Therapy

Of the several treatment options used to care for your baby with CLD, oxygen therapy is the mainstay. If a baby needs extra oxygen because of CLD and isn't getting it, constriction of the pulmonary blood vessels will occur, making it harder for the heart to pump blood through the lungs. Over an extended time this can lead to *failure of the right side of the heart* (cor pulmonale). Fortunately the pulmonary blood vessels are surprisingly sensitive to oxygen, and respond to minute changes in oxygen saturation. As oxygen saturation increases with oxygen therapy, blood vessel constriction decreases, and strain on the right side of the heart is relieved. In general, the blood vessel constriction continues to decrease into the normal range as oxygen saturation increases to a range between 90 and 96%. In the most severely affected infants with CLD, blood vessel constriction may never fall into the normal range even at saturations equal to 100%. In addition to preventing strain on the heart, oxygen is also needed to ensure optimal weight gain and growth in premature infants with CLD. The exact level that optimizes growth is not known. Many doctors caring for these babies like to keep oxygen saturation above 92%, while other physicians prefer a higher level (over 95%).

However, since excessive oxygen is widely thought to be associated with a condition called *retinopathy of prematurity* (ROP), your neonatologist and primary care physician will probably initially try to keep the saturation between 90 and 95%. They will rely on the judgment of a pediatric ophthalmologist to say when your baby's eyes are *fully vascularized* (have their full compliment of tiny blood vessels to the periphery of the retina) and no longer at risk for ROP so that oxygen levels can be liberalized. *This usually occurs at or after 37 weeks PMA.* At that point the allowable range for oxygen saturation can be liberalized. *It is important to understand that this higher saturation should not be interpreted as a worsening of your baby's condition.* In fact, it represents a positive step, because we believe that babies grow best with the use of the highest, safe oxygen saturation levels. It is interesting to note that there is active research going on looking at the relationship between oxygen saturation levels and ROP. Preliminary data suggests that infants with ROP may actually do better with slightly higher oxygen saturation levels. (See chapter 9 for a detailed discussion of ROP.)

A recent study[1] confirms that the decision to use oxygen, as well as how much oxygen to use, is best determined by evaluating an infant's oxygen saturation (while using various levels of oxygen or room air) throughout 8- to 12-hour recordings during sleep and awake time, and while feeding.

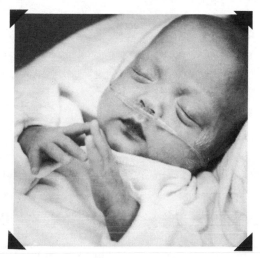

A baby with CLD on oxygen therapy provided by a nasal cannula.

DR. KLEIN COMMENTS ON OXYGEN SATURATION IN INFANTS WITH CLD

In an older infant with CLD who has fully vascularized retinas and is no longer at risk for the development of retinopathy of prematurity (ROP), my approach to prevent strain on the heart, as well as allow for optimal growth, requires consistent maintenance of oxygen saturations at 95% or greater. Some infants with milder CLD may become hypoxic (under-oxygenated) during feeding or sleep, even without an oxygen requirement when they are awake or at rest. More specifically, I tell parents that my goal for an infant with fully vascularized retinas is to keep oxygen saturation above 95%, for 95% of the time, with less than 1% of the time below 90%.

While your baby is hospitalized, a mixture of oxygen and air is provided most easily through a nasal cannula at a continuous flow rate of 1/2 to 1 liter per minute. The amount of oxygen being delivered is controlled by changing the *amount of oxygen* mixed with air with a blender. In this way, the *fraction of inspired oxygen mixed with air* (F_1O_2) can then easily be increased during feeding or when desaturation (a decrease in blood oxygen level) occurs. As you get closer to discharge, your doctor will most likely order that your baby's method of oxygen delivery be changed to a *low-flow* system (also delivered through a nasal cannula). This means that oxygen delivery will be controlled by changing the flow rate of oxygen. Low-flow oxygen delivered directly to the nasal cannula (without a blender in between) gives remarkably high F_1O_2. If more than $^1/_2$ to $^3/_4$ liter per minute of oxygen is needed, then your doctor will probably decide that your baby is not yet stable enough to be discharged home.

Diuretics

It is not unusual for the baby with CLD to have *pulmonary edema* (excessive fluid in the lung tissue). This may be treated with a diuretic such as furosemide (Lasix) or chlorothiazide (Diuril), which helps the kidneys to rid the body of excess fluid through increased urinary output. Lasix, and to a lesser extent Diuril, have also been shown to have a direct beneficial effect on the lungs by reducing airway resistance and improving lung function. The dosage regimen for either Lasix or Diuril is quite variable, ranging from one to three doses per day, or in the case of Lasix, two doses per day, given every other day, may also be used.

Electrolyte abnormalities can occur as a result of treatment with either Lasix or Diuril. The following complications may be associated with the use of Lasix:

- hearing loss
- hypercalciuria (too much calcium in the urine)

Extreme hypercalciuria can cause calcium to crystallize in the urine, with the result that nephrocalcinosis (calcium deposits in kidney tissue) and renal stones may occur.

If hypercalciuria persists while on Lasix, one strategy is to start a low dose of Diuril, which increases calcium reabsorption by the kidney and counteracts this effect. Nephrocalcinosis usually disappears once diuretic therapy is stopped.

When diuretic treatment is pursued, your doctor will monitor your baby's electrolyte levels. If significant electrolyte depletion occurs, supplementation with potassium chloride or sodium chloride is a likely response. Another therapeutic possibility is the use of a potassium-sparing diuretic, such as spironolactone, in conjunction with Lasix or Diuril. The baby who responds favorably to the use of a diuretic will show a decrease in oxygen requirement and/or a decrease in pCO_2: this is good evidence that this drug will be useful long term. Not all infants, however, respond well to diuretics, and a therapeutic trial is needed to justify long-term use.

DR. KLEIN COMMENTS ON THE USE OF DIURETICS

Although I know that many neonatologists do not like to use Lasix because of side effects, I have found in my practice that the every-other-day dosage regimen for Lasix (2 milligrams per kilogram of body weight per dose by mouth, given twice a day, every other day)[2] maintains the positive effect that this drug has on lung function, while avoiding the negative effects on electrolyte and calcium metabolism. In my experience, Lasix is the preferred diuretic.

Bronchodilators

Your doctor may decide on a course of treatment that includes the use of *bronchodilators,* a medication commonly used for asthma. The decision to use them in preterm infants with CLD is based mainly on the following considerations:

- Bronchial smooth muscle in preterm infants responds to bronchodilator therapy.
- Preterm infants with BPD have an increased incidence of a family history of asthma.

However, not all preterm infants with CLD respond to this type of therapy with improvement in their pulmonary function or other ongoing symptoms. A therapeutic trial of medication, and/or pulmonary function studies before and after therapy, can be helpful in deciding which infants are appropriate for long-term treatment. In a stable infant with CLD, these treatments are most easily given by "blowby" with a *nebulizer,* a device that breaks the medication up into small particles resulting in a fine mist which is directed toward the baby's nose. In the hospital, blended O_2 is used for nebulization, while at home a handheld nebulizer is used.

A favorable response to an initial trial of treatment is indicated by a decrease in respiratory rate and/or wheezing, and a decrease in O_2 requirement. If the treatment response is in question, then pulmonary function tests (PFTs) before and after treatments can be helpful. These tests can also be helpful in differentiating those severely affected infants who have broncho-tracheomalacia (commonly referred to as "floppy airways") and large airway obstruction, rather than reactive small airway disease, and in whom bronchodilator therapy may be unnecessary and even counterproductive.

Although *methylxanthines* such as aminophylline have been used in the past to treat many of these infants, they are now infrequently used. *Anticholinergic therapy* with either atropine or ipratropium bromide may also be useful, but there is little published experience with this type of drug in preterm infants with CLD.

Corticosteroids

Although corticosteroids for treating infants with established CLD is controversial and often sparks vigorous debate, their use is extremely common and thought to be helpful. Many CLD infants who are stable and recovering have been treated with steroids, or are maintained on tapering doses. Doses are often restarted or increased when there is a need.

The theory behind steroid treatment is several-fold:

- Their anti-inflammatory properties help to prevent or improve the inflammatory processes that occur in the lung in infants with CLD (similar to their use for other forms of reactive airway diseases).
- They also may directly and/or indirectly affect various aspects of lung repair. Steroids also have been shown to increase the number of beta-receptors, which is thought to enhance the response to beta-adrenergic bronchodilators.

Recently there have been some studies suggesting that infants who develop CLD have decreased adrenal function at birth.

Babies who have been on long-term steroid therapy (more than 10 days) are at risk for adrenal suppression, and should be tested for hypothalamic–pituitary–adrenal axis function, and need to be managed appropriately.

DR. KLEIN COMMENTS ON THE USE OF CROMOLYN IN TREATING CLD

Theoretically, cromolyn's ability to prevent the release of inflammatory and bronchoconstrictor mediators should be helpful in CLD. However, recent studies have not proven this to be the case in infants with CLD. This may be due to the variable role that airway hyperreactivity plays in CLD. Cromolyn is not a course of action that I would typically use in treating a premature baby with CLD.

Nutritional Support for Infants Recovering from CLD

Babies with moderate to severe BPD have been shown to have up to 50% greater energy requirements. The requirements are probably not that high for babies with less severe CLD, for most infants who receive adequate oxygen therapy, and those who are not ventilator-dependent. However, many infants with CLD do require more calories then normal to sustain adequate growth (20–30 grams per day). Some infants may need as much as 130 to 180 calories per kilogram of body weight per day in order to sustain a growth rate of 20 to 30 grams per day. This may be quite difficult to provide, because it is often necessary to restrict total fluid when treating CLD. The volume of fluid that may be tolerated can be increased by using and/or increasing diuretic therapy.

One strategy that can be successful in providing increased calories for these infants is to start with 24 or 27 calories per ounce of premature infant formula, and then add Polycose powder to increase nonfat calories, and MCT oil (7.6 calories per cubic centimeter) or safflower oil (8 calories per cubic centimeter, for older infants) to add fat calories. In a similar fashion, *human milk fortifier* (HMF) may be added to breast milk to give 24 calories per ounce, and then *medium chain triglycerides* (MCT) oil added.

As is the case with healthy premature infants, coordinated sucking, swallowing, and breathing develops in most infants with CLD between 34 and 36 weeks. As mentioned earlier, the ability to breast-feed develops a little earlier (33–34 weeks). Although oral feeding can be very satisfying both to a recovering baby and the parents, desaturation often occurs during feeding and in the time that immediately follows. In order to facilitate and encourage oral feeding, your doctor may recommend increasing oxygen during and immediately after feeds. Although it is interesting that many infants will have fewer episodes of desaturation when nursing at the breast, breast-feeding alone (without supplementation) may not always provide adequate calories for the baby's growth.

A resistance to oral feedings (oral defensiveness) often develops in infants who have been intubated for a long time. This can make oral feeding very difficult to start, even when the infant is developmentally and medically ready. It is important for parents to know that there is help to be found for this problem. Occupational therapy (OT) evaluation and subsequent therapy can be helpful in decreasing oral defensiveness.

In some infants, prolonged gavage feeding may be needed. If long-term gavage feeding is expected, then gastrostomy and tube placement may be necessary. Your doctor may discuss the use of prolonged nasogastric tube (NGT) feeding as a possible alternative to gastrostomy, but it has several drawbacks in infants with CLD. Nasogastric tube feeds utilize a weighted silastic tube that obstructs one-half of the nasal airway, and is likely to contribute further to oral defensiveness.

Gastroesophageal reflux (GER—the abnormal passage of stomach contents back up into the esophagus), which often occurs in infants with CLD, may present a particularly difficult problem. It is possible for a baby to have reflux that may not be clinically significant; however, clinical symptoms that your doctor may consider significant are:

- poor feeding with marked oxygen desaturation during and after feeds
- apnea during or immediately after feeds
- spitting up and/or *emesis* (vomiting)
- crying or increased irritability during feeds

A pH probe study is the best way to look for GER and to try to assess the relationship between reflux and particular symptoms. Gastric emptying studies may also be helpful. Gastroesophageal reflux can be decreased by medications, such as cisapride, which increase gastric emptying.

The decision to insert a gastrostomy tube (a tube that is surgically inserted directly into the stomach in order to provide a direct infusion of nutrition to a baby who has problems with oral feeding) is often made reluctantly by physicians, and greeted unhappily by parents. It is no doubt helpful for parents to take a longer view and recognize that gastrostomy may best serve their baby's overall needs. It allows a more normal sleep pattern after discharge for both parents and the infant, solves nutritional problems associated with poor intake, and therefore enhances growth and speeds recovery. If gastrostomy and gastric feeds are needed, then fundoplication (a surgical procedure designed to decrease the amount of stomach contents that go back up into the esophagus) in order to reduce reflux is almost always needed. After a gastrostomy tube is placed, tube feeds may be given continuously overnight, and oral feeds can be tried during the day. This is another case in which an occupational therapist trained in infant feeding problems and techniques can be very helpful.

Chapter Six

Understanding and Managing Breathing Control Problems (Apnea and Bradycardia)

Take a Moment to Recognize How Far You've Come

For the parents who are about to take their baby home, the first bewildering days in the NICU may be the last thing they want to remember. But it can be helpful, as you anticipate confronting the new challenge of caring for your baby at home, to recall your days as a greenhorn in the NICU and recognize how far you've come. Every parent whose premature infant has been hooked up to an apnea and bradycardia monitor remembers when they saw it for the first time. Most parents encountering the highly technical environment of the neonatal intensive care unit recall being intimidated by the sight of their little baby hooked up to a monitor. Certainly, there was some degree of relief that their baby was in capable hands. Initially, however, it was a daunting experience. So take a moment to recognize how capably you rose to those challenges before meeting the new challenges of bringing your baby home.

What Is Apnea?

As you began to learn your way around the complicated and highly technical environment of the neonatal intensive care unit, you may have heard your first discussion of *apnea*. You discovered that apnea is defined as a "cessation of respiration"—a period of time during which your baby is not breathing. Both premature babies and infants born at term have irregular respiratory patterns, often breathing fast for several moments and then having short periods of time when they even stop breathing. As infants get older the duration of time of irregular breathing patterns is replaced by more regular respiration. Premature infants born at less than 34 weeks gestation often experience prolonged periods of apnea. An apneic episode in either a premature or term baby that lasts for 20 seconds or longer, or a shorter period of apnea that is associated with a significant decrease in heart rate or oxygen saturation, is considered "significant" and will be of concern to those caring for your baby. Apneic episodes that are briefer than 15 seconds are common and of less concern.

What Is Bradycardia?

Bradycardia is the term used to describe a sustained (a period of at least 5 seconds) heart rate that is lower than normal for your baby. The normal heart rate should decrease as a baby matures. As with many of the variables that are used to evaluate a baby's health or development, there is a range of normalcy, and the heart rate described as normal by your doctor may vary somewhat from these figures. The following table lists age-specified lower limits of normal heart rates:

Postmenstrual Age	Lower Limits (Heartbeats per Minute)
up to 44 weeks	80
44 to 52 weeks	70
over 52 weeks	60

—Michigan Association of Apnea Professionals, 1994

The Baby with Apnea and Bradycardia

It is important to recognize that babies who are having one or more apneic episodes daily or significant episodes that require vigorous

stimulation need to have further assessment to look into what is causing their apnea. Apnea can be symptomatic of many of the problems
that are associated with prematurity. The following possible causes of
apnea should be considered:

• *Infection* Premature infants are born prior to full development of
their immune system and thus are very susceptible to bacterial, viral, and
fungal infections. Apnea may be the first sign that a premature infant is developing an infection, and evaluation to rule out an infection is one of the
first things that is done when an infant has significant apnea.

• *Impaired Oxygenation* Because low oxygen levels (hypoxia) is a
known cause of apnea in preterm infants, oxygen levels should be carefully
monitored. If an infant with apnea has an oxygen saturation less than 95%
(as determined by pulse oximetry, normal ≥95%), with or without rapid res-
pirations, a trial of oxygen by nasal cannula may stop the apneic episodes.

• *Various Metabolic Disorders Such as Low Blood Sugar or Low Calcium Levels* Your baby's blood sugar and calcium levels will be checked to
make sure that these easily treatable causes of apnea are resolved.

• *Thermal Instability* It is well known that infants who are either warmed
too rapidly when they are cold or placed in an incubator that is too warm
may have apnea. This is easily fixed by adjusting incubator temperatures.

• *Gastroesophageal Reflux (GER)* This term refers to the abnormal passage of stomach contents back up into the esophagus that occurs frequently in
both premature and full-term infants. Further discussion will occur in chapter 8.

• *Intracranial Hemorrhage* As discussed in chapter 7, most infants will
have had an ultrasound of the brain to make this diagnosis. If an infant
doesn't respond to apnea medication, a repeat ultrasound of the brain may
be warranted.

• *Seizure* Apnea and bradycardia are a very unusual manifestation of
seizures. An EEG (electroencephalogram; a measurement of brain wave ac-

tivity) to rule this out may be needed if apnea and bradycardia persist in spite of treatment.

• *Necrotizing Enterocolitis (NEC)* Apnea may be the first manifestation of this problem. (See chapter 8 for a detailed discussion of NEC.)

• *Mother's Cocaine Use During Pregnancy* Apnea and bradycardia are known to occur more frequently in infants exposed to cocaine in utero. Many neonatal units screen all infants after birth for in-utero drug exposure.

• *Anemia (low red blood cell count)* As premature infants grow and frequently have blood withdrawn for various tests, the amount of red blood cells in the body decreases, resulting in a low hematocrit, commonly referred to as anemia. This low red blood cell count may be a cause of apnea. This is easily treated with a blood transfusion.

Blood Transfusions

When a premature baby is ill, additional red blood cells may be necessary to carry vital oxygen from the lungs to the rest of the body. This may be accomplished through a blood transfusion. Most blood transfusions occur in sick babies during the first two weeks of life. If the red blood cell count is low (as determined by measuring the *hematocrit* [Hct] or *hemoglobin* [Hb]), the occurrence of various symptoms may indicate that the rest of the body is in need of additional oxygen. These symptoms may include:

- tachypnea (a rapid respiratory rate)
- tachycardia (a high heart rate)
- apnea
- poor feeding and inadequate weight gain

Like all other treatment strategies used in the neonatal unit, there are possible complications associated with blood transfusions, and their positive effects must be weighed against these negative complications. Blood transfusions may transmit various viral infections. Although all blood given to premature infants should be and is screened for major viral illnesses such as *hepatitis B, cytomegalovirus* (CMV), and *human immunodeficiency virus* (HIV), there is still a very small possibility that a child could get one of these or some other viral disease from a blood transfusion. On very rare occasions an infant may even get a bacterial infection (sepsis) as a result of a blood transfusion. With these complications in mind, most neonatal units have adopted various strategies to try to limit the need for transfusions and the exposure to blood from several different donors. Neonatal intensive care units have found that by having specific criteria for transfusions (such as an Hct below a specific number), they are able to limit the need for blood transfusions. By separating the blood from one donor into many small packets that can be used at different times, and extending the storage time that blood can be kept before it is used, the exposure to many different donors can be limited. Some studies have suggested that treatment with *recombinant human erythropoietin* (a commercially available product that stimulates the production of red blood cells) may decrease the number of transfusions in premature infants. Nevertheless, its routine use remains controversial, because most blood transfusions are given too early in an infant's course for the erythropoietin to take effect.

Many hospitals have a "directed donor" program where the parents can request that blood for their baby be donated by a known person, such as the father or a friend of the family. If you have been asked if you wanted to designate a directed donor, feel free to do so. However, if this becomes a problem for you, rest assured that the strategies we've mentioned above are currently in use to decrease donor exposure and maintain the safety of all blood transfusions, even if a directed donor is not available.

Idiopathic Apnea of Prematurity

It is very important to look to clinical and laboratory evaluations for additional insight into a baby's apnea before assuming that you are dealing with what is called *idiopathic apnea of prematurity* (apnea in a premature infant that is neither induced or related to another disease). Babies with this type of apnea will grow out of it as they mature. If this diagnosis is made, it can be treated with respiratory stimulant medications, caffeine, or aminophylline. This irony has not escaped the notice of numerous mothers who have commented that they gave up coffee during their pregnancy only to have their newborns become instant "coffee achievers." Typically, if your baby is apnea- and bradycardia-free for 5 to 7 days in the hospital, medication is discontinued and the baby is observed carefully. Treatment may be reinstated if significant episodes reoccur. Many parents are able to bring their premature babies home with apnea monitors as well as either caffeine that is given once a day or aminophylline that is given three or four times a day.

Distinguishing Apnea from Periodic Breathing

When a baby has three or more apneic episodes lasting between 3 and 10 seconds within periods of normal breathing of 20 seconds or less, it is called *periodic breathing*. It appears to be a benign respiratory problem that is most likely the result of immaturity of the baby's respiratory control center. Assuming the baby's color and heart rate remain normal, this is not usually a problem for a premature baby. Even full-term babies have periodic breathing and short apneic episodes, and in most cases these episodes will decrease and respiration will become much more regular as a baby gets older. Some clinicians will send babies who have an abnormal amount of periodic breathing home on apnea monitors.

The Apnea and Bradycardia Monitor in the Hospital

The staff in the NICU is faced with the challenging task of explaining the use of various monitors to the understandably concerned parents of a premature baby. The monitor you saw your baby attached to in the NICU was there to detect and display variations in your baby's breathing and heart rates. You learned that the small, sensitive monitor leads attached by adhesive to your baby's chest were connected by a slender wire to a lead box that was in turn connected to a monitor.

Many hospitals use *trend recording monitors* that record all the needed data continuously for a period of time up to 24 hours. By evaluating the data of the last 6, 10, or 24 hours, members of your baby's team can determine whether a breathing or heart rate event was what they would consider significant.

You gazed back and forth from your infant, to the monitor screen next to him or her. You watched as your baby's breathing and heart rates appeared before you as squiggly lines darting horizontally across the screen, or you listened to the beeps emanating from the monitor as they translated your baby's vital signs. You wondered about the significance of the numbers that appeared intermittently on the monitor screen. At various times, alarms might have gone off to alert your baby's caretakers to a problem. Was the heart rate too slow or too fast? Had the baby stopped breathing? Or maybe there was no problem at all, only what is called "a loose lead alarm," when one of the leads adhered to the baby's skin somehow became detached.

One of the most important concepts for parents to grasp is that the alarm limits on the monitor in the hospital are purposely set to alert a member of the team to make a preemptive strike on your baby's behalf. The alarms are set to go off before either the baby's drop in heart rate reaches a level that is considered "significant," or an apnea episode is long enough to be considered serious. This allows the nursing personnel or any medical person in the area to check out your baby before a problem develops. Typically, the lower heart rate alarm is set at 100 beats per minute and the apnea alarm is set to go off if apnea lasts for longer than 15 seconds. When an alarm goes off, a medical person will look in on your infant. The heart rate may be back up to normal or the baby may already have begun to breathe again. If need be, your baby will be stimulated by being lightly touched or jostled; this can be enough to increase the heart rate or encourage the baby to start breathing again. In a severe case, the baby may require a more aggressive treatment, such as the use of a face mask and bag to ventilate (breathe for) her. Sometimes manual external pressure applied to the heart through the chest is necessary. These more serious events are not the norm, and parents who understand the use of the monitor in the nursery are often spared unnecessary anxiety.

Using a Monitor at Home

There is little consensus in the medical community about which babies should go home on an apnea monitor. Some, but not all, physicians will prescribe home monitoring for a premature baby who continues to be on a respiratory stimulant at the time of discharge. An infant who has had a documented episode of apnea within 5 to 7 days prior to discharge is likely to be sent home on a monitor. Guided by the principles of family-centered care, parents remain informed about their baby's medical assessment as the time for discharge draws near.

The *event recording monitor* is the monitor of choice for home use. The event recording monitor is not a continuous recording monitor. Instead, it records the apnea or bradycardia event itself, alarm settings, alarm summaries, and heart rate and respiration wave forms that were being recorded when the event occurred. This data can then be "downloaded" from the monitor by the home health-care company and analyzed.

Either the company providing the monitor (DME provider) or a separate home health-care agency should provide personnel to train parents or other caretakers in the use of the equipment. Parental understanding of the need for home monitoring, as well as your readiness to handle monitoring at home, should be discussed before your baby is discharged.

- Do you understand your baby's diagnosis? What symptoms are to be expected? How long is monitoring likely to be necessary?
- Do you comprehend the purposes and responsibilities of home monitoring?

Parent education is equally vital to the success of home monitoring:

- Parents and additional caregivers must receive adequate instruction in where to place the monitor; how to attach the sensors to the baby's skin and provide appropriate skin care; operation of the monitor itself—setting sensitivity, and responding to, interpreting, and logging alarms.

- Infant CPR instruction must be provided for parents as well as other friends or family members who may spend time alone with the baby.
- Important details of a successful home care plan should be developed. Phone numbers for the fire department, pediatrician, hospital, home health-care company, DME provider, and of course 911 should be in prominent view next to every telephone in the house.
- It is important to follow medical instructions on when to use the monitor. You must use the monitor when your baby is sleeping, in the car, or unattended in a room at home. Do not withdraw or modify home monitoring unless you've discussed it with your doctor.

The financial implications of home monitoring can be considerable. If, as you near discharge, it appears that home apnea monitoring is likely, you may want to speak with the discharge planners at the hospital. They should be able to help you to determine which home health-care expenses will be covered by your health insurance carrier. It is also important to find out if you are eligible for any additional government financial assistance in caring for your baby.

DR. KLEIN COMMENTS ON HOME APNEA MONITORS

There is little agreement in the medical community as to which babies should be sent home on monitors with respiratory stimulants and which babies should be kept in the hospital for a specified period of time without episodes and off respiratory medication. Some neonatal units require infants to be apnea-free and off medication for 5 to 10 days before they will send them home without a monitor.

I think premature infants should be home with their parents and out of the hospital environment as early as possible. This is best for the psychology of the family unit and also decreases exposure to hospital-acquired infections. Therefore, I often send infants home with monitors on caffeine, which I prefer, because in my experience it is more effective than aminophylline and has the added advantage of needing to be given only once a day.

I routinely recommend event recording monitors when monitoring is indicated. This instrument, which records specific abnormal events, has been shown to decrease the length of time the monitor needs to be used after discharge. If no significant alarms occur at home, I discontinue the caffeine after 4 weeks and continue the monitor without medication. If another 4 weeks go by and the infant has reached at least 44 weeks PMA without a significant alarm, I discontinue the monitor. With this approach, using the event recording monitor so that I don't have to rely on caretaker's observations, almost all my premature infants who had apnea are off monitors at home by 44 to 46 weeks PMA.

Caring for Your Baby at Home on a Monitor

Earlier the numerous feelings that characterize the homecoming of your premature baby were discussed: the joy that is tempered by uncertainty about your own abilities as primary caregiver. Parental feelings about taking a baby home on a cardiorespiratory monitor are frequently characterized by a similarly complex response. Some parents take comfort in the presence of the modern technology, perhaps feeling that it provides a sort of buffer for their own inexperience. Other parents see the monitor as a symbol of their child's vulnerability and resist its presence in their home.

Central to successful home monitoring is the belief that the decision to monitor at home is the best possible action to take under the circumstances. After that, a family's ability to distinguish between what is within their control and what is beyond their influence is also very helpful. Finally, there is each parent's belief system that may provide an effective coping mechanism. Some view the experience as a challenge; others imbue it with a deeper meaning and rely upon faith in God or philosophical principles to guide them.

There are also many practical concerns expressed by parents. They may question the reliability of the monitor, or their own expertise in operating it. These concerns can be further compounded by the high cost of skilled home health care, parents' fatigue, and the lack of outside support from friends or family who are unable (or whom parents see as unsuitable) to shoulder the responsibility of caring for a baby on a home monitor. One of the most important elements of preparing for discharge is to have a regular backup person who can come to your home to provide child care when needed, so that you can jump into the shower or even take a half-hour walk. While some parents have friends and family waiting in the wings to help, others will have to think a little longer and work a little harder to develop a support system. Instead of feeling panic at the prospect of leaving your mother-in-law at home with your baby, contact your home health-care provider and ask that she receive a refresher course in CPR. Many providers also provide instruction in foreign languages that might be helpful for your extended family. Always take the standard precaution of keeping the 911 number in prominent view next to every telephone in the house. Having spent days, weeks, or sometimes months as members of the team caring for your baby in the NICU, suddenly you are promoted to a management position and must take some initiative in reconfiguring the team.

Management Strategies

In an article entitled "Parents Coping with Infants Requiring Home Cardiorespiratory Monitoring,"[1] the following strategies were identified for coping with the stress of having your baby at home on a monitor:

- Some parents used a problem-focused strategy of vigilance to manage the constant threat of danger:
  "I kept a constant check on the baby."
  "I slept in the baby's room or she slept with us. I never left her alone."
- Parents used a novel and logical problem-solving approach and created their own actions:
  "I used a bulletin board with a schedule attached so I could remember when to give medications and do assessment checks on my baby."
  "I introduced my infant to the local fire department so that when I called 911 they would know why they were coming to my house."

- Some people decided not to allow any other people to assist in caring for their baby:

    "I felt like I was the mother and had to take care of the baby while the nurses watched—I felt like I was the only one who knew exactly what to do for my baby."

- There were parents who sought information from books or advice from other people:

    "When I went to the library, I only found two books on the subject of premature babies and one on monitoring. There isn't much written on the subject."

It is clear that there is no single coping strategy that applies to all families, nor is it realistic to assume that caring for your baby on a monitor will get easier with each passing day. What can improve is your confidence in your own instincts and abilities. Ultimately, the test is in "taking the pulse" of the whole family after 3 days, then a week, then a month, until with the passage of time you come to gain confidence in your ability to be your baby's primary home caregiver.

Chapter Seven

Supporting Your Baby's Neurological Needs

Brain Development

In recent years, researchers into the wonders of the human mind have been excited to discover that the structure of the human nervous system is not genetically hardwired at birth, as had been previously assumed. Instead, *the neural wiring of a newborn infant's brain continues to develop after birth in response to its new surroundings and experiences.* The developing nervous system of the unborn baby is also affected by its intrauterine environment. The growing baby floats in a sea of amniotic fluid, contained within the uterus that, neuro-behaviorally speaking, becomes familiar territory.

The developing nervous system is influenced by hormonal and other complex chemical changes that are a natural part of the progress of pregnancy. The unborn baby's developing neurological impulses are also influenced by the world outside—he is along for the ride as his mother goes about the business of living. The unborn baby hears music and voices, feels the motion of walking and car rides, and receives nutrition via the placenta at different times throughout the day. But the new understanding that the baby's brain, whether premature or term, can be influenced by the environment *after birth* should be of particular interest to parents of premies.

In the case of a very premature birth, the fetus, which has had only six months to develop in utero, is now exposed to the neonatal unit and is confronted with an entirely new sensation. . . *a whole raft of entirely new sensations.* There is the sudden variation in temperature, the sensation of being handled for the first time, a change from the warm liquid of the womb to the shock of air upon skin; there is the need to breathe with his lungs, or try to; a leg stretching out is neither supported by amniotic fluid, nor is it met by the familiar constraint of the uterine wall. The radical shift into this unfamiliar extrauterine terrain is thought to influence the development of the brain, and have a profound influence on neuro-behavioral development in preterm infants. Is it accurate to say these babies are "stressed"? Surely, by our standards, lying in the warm, secure, fluid-filled environment of the uterus is less stressful than being placed in a room with noise, bright lights, and all these people rushing around. But the implications of thrusting a baby with an immature nervous system into a radically altered environment go far beyond what we perceive as *stress.*

Anyone with a premature baby born at a sufficiently young age as to have an immature nervous system will benefit by reading chapter 4 of this book, in which the Neonatal Individualized Developmental Care and Assessment Program (NIDCAP), developed by Heidelise Als, PhD, is discussed. Dr. Als tells us:

> *With the advances in medical technology, even very immature nervous systems exist and develop outside the womb.*[1]

This is wonderful news for the parents of premature infants, because it reinforces the importance of recognizing your baby as the leader of his team. Simply stated, by watching and responding to your baby as he continues to grow outside the uterus, you can support his continuing neurological growth. Dr. Als has based much of NIDCAP on her belief in the premise that underlying neurological status and brain function are expressed in observable behavior. What kind of touch seems to soothe? How does he respond to opportunities for low light? For even the baby born very prematurely at 24 weeks, most, if not all, the brain cells have been created and are where they need to be. But the connections between those cells, the body's very own "information highway," have not had the time to come to completion in utero. Dr. Als concludes:

> *The information presented (from detailed observation of the fetus displaced from the uterus into the NICU) indicates that an individualized, behavioral-development approach to care improves outcome not only medically but also behaviorally and neurophysiologically. Such an approach emphasizes at an early stage the infant's own strengths and apparent developmental goals. . .* [1]

As a parent of a premature baby, you have the opportunity not only to observe your child build his neurological highway, but by following its cues, you may play an important role in following up on its successful construction. You, along with the medical and nursing members of the team, have an opportunity to let your baby lead you toward his own successful developmental outcome.

What Can You Do to Help Your Baby in the NICU?

The short answer is—plenty! Supporting the healthy development of your premature baby's nervous system begins in the hospital when he is born. Most neonatal units are very supportive of having parents involved in their baby's care from the very beginning. The dedicated nursing staff will help you to familiarize yourself with several important ways in which parents of premature babies can support their development:

• *Positioning* One of the first things parents of a premature baby may notice is that their baby assumes an *extended* rather than a *flexed* position after birth. As a baby grow in utero, its limbs and body are supported by amniotic fluid, the head and neck is bent forward, and legs and arms are drawn up and held close to the body, assuming the classic "fetal" or flexed position. After delivery, the effect of gravity on a premature baby causes it to assume an extended position. The muscles needed to maintain the flexed position have not yet had the time to develop the strength needed to over-come the effects of gravity. As a result, the baby naturally assumes an ex-tended rather than flexed position. One or more of your baby's team (perhaps a physical or occupational therapist or a member of the nursing staff) will help to determine which positions best suit your baby's need to achieve a flexed position.

• *What Your Baby Sees and Hears* By the time your baby is 29 to 30 weeks PMA, he can look at your face and also discern bold black-and-white patterns. Like you, your baby may develop a preference for certain visual stimuli and may also want variety. Hanging a simple mobile at a dis-tance of 10 inches from your baby's face, or placing a picture of boldly drawn black-and-white geometric shapes on the wall of the isolette, pro-vides excellent stimulation. Of course, you must be tuned in to your baby's signals as to whether he is engaged by this stimulation, or perhaps would like it only intermittently. Babies usually show great interest in faces, so the very best visual stimulation may be your loving face at a range of about 10 inches from his eyes. The 24-week-old fetus responds to sound (tones) while in utero. As you observe your baby, you will notice him begin to turn his head toward the source of your familiar voice. *Talking softly to your baby is important to both of you.* As always, remain alert to signs of overstimula-tion of the very young baby. If speaking seems to make your baby tense up, you may want to stop talking for a little while, and try again later. Simple music played at low volume on a cassette recorder placed in the isolette may provide pleasant stimulation for your baby. You can also record the voices of siblings and grandparents and play them for your new baby when the moment is right.

• *Holding, Touching, and Rocking Your Baby* We know that very im-mature fetuses can respond to touch (even while still in utero) by a reflexive startling motion. This apparent "rejection" can be terribly hard on the parent of a young premature baby. Understand that this reflexive drawing away from touch is the neurological response of an immature nervous system. Take this opportunity to discover what sort of touch is comforting to your baby. If stroking seems to elicit a startle response, try letting your baby hold your pinkie or place his tiny hand upon yours. Eventually you may find that your baby takes comfort in your increasingly familiar hand firmly on its chest, or the sensation of his hand held within yours. How does the baby respond to being held? This is the time to speak with the nursing staff about *kangaroo care* (see chapter 4). The opportunity to rock as you hold your baby upright in your arms may provide just the right balance of comfort and stimulation. As always, let your baby "tell you" what is comforting. The incredible emotional satisfaction of knowing that you are a comfort to your baby will soon follow.

Family-centered care should be at the core of your team's approach to observing, assessing, and caring for your child. The success of Dr. Als' individualized approach to newborn care is supported by pretty impressive data. It decreases hospital stays, improves weight gain, and decreases costs for care. Whether or not your neonatal unit has formally adapted NIDCAP, you can work with your team to participate in your baby's successful development.

When There Are Neurological Problems

Periventricular-Intraventricular Hemorrhage (PV-IVH)

Periventricular-intraventricular hemorrhage (internal bleeding in the brain that is also referred to as IVH) is a condition that is usually unique to the premature baby. In 90% of cases, it occurs within 3 days of birth. Diagnosis is made by ultrasound of the brain. If severe, it may be associated with the subsequent development of *hydrocephalus,* an abnormal buildup of fluid in the brain's *ventricles,* which are the open spaces in the brain tissue that carry fluid and probably serve to decrease the weight of the brain. It is certainly accurate to say that the incidence of periventricular-intraventricular hemorrhage increases in (gestationally) younger, sicker babies. Even 10 years ago the occurrence of intraventricular hemorrhage in babies under 1,500 grams was as high as 40%. Fortunately for parents of premies born today, it is now thought to occur in the 15 to 20% range. There are no studies that highlight specific causes for this considerably improved picture, but it is safe to speculate that general improvement in diagnostic, medical, and nursing techniques in the neonatal unit can share the credit.

Periventricular-intraventricular hemorrhage occurs primarily in an area of the brain called the *germinal matrix* (a layer of cells that surround the ventricles). As a baby develops in utero, the cells of the germinal matrix migrate to other parts of the brain. In fact, if you were to examine the germinal matrix of a 16-week-old fetus, you would discover that it is much larger than it is in the 24-week premie. It continues to decrease in size and is smaller still in the 32- to 33-week-old baby. This is one reason why PV-IVH tends to be more of a problem as gestational age at birth decreases.

The cause (or causes) of the bleeding is not 100% clear, but it seems to be related to fluctuations in blood flow and the inability of that area of the brain to regulate blood flow. Radical changes to the baby's blood pressure, oxygen deprivation, or some other insult to the brain can result in the rupture (breaking) of the delicate blood vessels of the germinal matrix. Periventricular-intraventricular hemorrhage can be separated into four grades, with grade 1 being the least serious and grade 4 the most likely to result in ongoing neurological problems.

Grade 1 PV-IVH: A Germinal Matrix Hemorrhage The hemorrhage is either contained in the germinal matrix layer next to the ventricle and does not extend into it, or does so only slightly, resulting in less than 10% of the ventricle area becoming filled with blood.

Grade 2 PV-IVH The germinal matrix hemorrhage extends into the ventricle, and fills 10 to 50% of the ventricle with blood.

Approximately 75% of premature infants with PV-IVH have either a grade 1 or 2 bleed.

Grade 3 PV-IVH Greater than 50% of the ventricular area fills with blood, often resulting in expanded ventricles.

Grade 4 PV-IVH Hemorrhage into part of the brain tissue outside the germinal matrix, in addition to a grade 3 intraventricular hemorrhage. Hemorrhage into the brain tissue outside the germinal matrix may also occur (albeit less frequently) in grades 1 and 2.

DR. KLEIN COMMENTS ON PV-IVH GRADING SYSTEMS

Grading systems are important primarily as a way to predict subsequent neurological outcome. Although different neonatal units may use different grading systems, two things are clear: First, the risk of developing post-PV-IVH hydrocephalus is directly related to the volume of blood that enters the ventricle. Thus, the occurrence of neurological deficits associated with hydrocephalus is increased in grade 3 and 4 PV-IVHs as compared to grades 1 and 2. Second, neurological complications associated with bleeding into the brain tissue itself (outside the germinal matrix) are dependent on the size of the hemorrhage in the brain and how much brain tissue is actually destroyed. *Hemorrhagic infarction* is the term used to describe this phenomenon.

Hydrocephalus

If your baby has a PV-IVH, your doctor will closely monitor the development of his head circumference. If there is an unusual increase in the rate of head growth, there is the reasonable concern that hydrocephalus may be developing. This will most likely be documented on repeat head ultrasounds. The term *hydrocephalus* refers to an abnormal collection of fluid on the brain that can cause pressure on the brain tissue, the result of which may be brain damage. The urgency is to diagnose and treat the hydrocephalus before brain damage occurs. In the case of a grade 3 or 4 bleed, there can be fluid accumulation in some of the pathways or interference with the parts of the ventricle that absorb the fluid. In those cases, a baby may be diagnosed with hydrocephalus. Under such circumstances, the baby's neurosurgeon will place a tube into the ventricle which exits the skull through the top of the baby's head and ends in a reservoir that is placed under the skin. Fluid can then be removed from the reservoir as necessary to relieve any increased pressure on the brain. Over a period of time the excess fluid resolves and the reservoir can be removed. Sometimes the excess fluid production persists and a more permanent solution must be used in order to avoid brain damage. In that case, a *ventriculo-peritoneal shunt* (a thin tube with a one-way valve) is placed into the ventricle and passed (under your baby's skin) all the way to the abdominal cavity, where the fluid that has accumulated in the brain is able to drain into the abdominal cavity and be reabsorbed by the body. The shunt should not be placed unless it is clear that the hydrocephalus is not going to resolve.

Periventricular Leukomalacia (PVL)

This condition is caused by an interruption of the blood flow to the brain tissue and subsequent injury to the brain cells because of the resulting lack of oxygen. It can be associated with any grade of IVH. The imaging diagnosis is made either by ultrasound or a CT scan. These areas appear as holes in the brain tissue and may simply decrease in size until they disappear, or they may grow larger and present a problem. There is no treatment, and no clinical diagnosis is possible unless the baby has neurological symptoms.

Major and Minor Neurological Deficits

Cerebral palsy (CP) is the term most often used when we refer to *major neurological deficits* in premature infants. It is defined as impaired muscular power and coordination from brain damage that presents itself as abnormalities in muscle tone (tension) and movement. It is what doctors refer to as a *static neurological condition,* which means that the brain damage does not change as a child gets older. *It is important for parents to understand that the severity of CP can range from complete inability to move various muscles, to only mild weakness that may be very difficult to detect without sophisticated testing.* In premature infants, it more often involves the lower rather than the upper extremities and may or may not be associated with cognitive deficits. Cerebral palsy affects 5 to 15% of babies weighing less than 1,500 grams at birth who survive.

The term *minor neurological deficits* is used to describe less severe developmental disabilities that include abnormalities in fine motor control, learning disabilities, and behavioral problems that may interfere with school performance in older children.

Prognosis

Small PV-IVHs have little if any effect on long-term neurological outcome. The incidence of neurological problems increases as the grade of the PV-IVH increases. Approximately 65% of premature infants with grade 3 PV-IVH are free of major neurological handicaps. In infants with grade 4 PV-IVH, outcome is dependent on the size of the bleed (hemorraghic infarction) in the brain tissue. Infants with massive brain involvement who survive have little if any chance of being completely normal. If you and your baby are in this difficult situation, consultation with a pediatric neurologist may help you understand the severity of your baby's condition and help you to consider other possible options, such as discontinuing life support. (This very tough decision is discussed in more detail in chapter 14.)

Infants with only a small localized area of brain tissue damage from hemorrhage clearly have a much more favorable outcome. Although cerebral palsy is common in these infants, a considerable number of these infants have normal intellectual function.

With regard to periventricular leukomalacia, the complete correlation between PVL and subsequent neurological problems has yet to be determined and is an area of ongoing research. In general, the effect of PVL on subsequent development depends on the size and location of the area of involvement. Periventricular leukomalacia is a cause of cerebral palsy affecting primarily the lower extremities, but also, with more extensive involvement, affecting the upper extremities and intellectual function as well.

Infants with post-hemorrhagic hydrocephalus (PHH) who survive will have a 50% chance of having normal or only slightly abnormal neurological development.

Supporting the Neurological Needs of Your Growing Child

In the first months of your baby's life it is hard to say what, if any, the developmental implications will be. As we've discussed many times, the most important thing for parents to understand is that they need to be advocates for their children from the very beginning. After discharge from the hospital, an early intervention or *infant stimulation program* can be enormously helpful for significantly premature babies (those born at less than 30 weeks gestation). These programs, overseen by physical therapists, occupational therapists, or other specialists, are tailored to supporting your baby's particular developmental needs. These health-care professionals are trained to teach you gentle exercises, positioning, and other helpful ways to interact with your baby.

You will become more expert than you ever imagined possible as you seek out the specialists, outpatient therapies, play groups, or infant stimulation programs that best suit your baby's needs. As your baby grows older, your hospital or pediatrician may arrange for a follow-up visit to a multidisciplinary clinic for further assessment by a team that may include a developmental pediatrician, child psychologist, speech pathologist, occupational therapist, physical therapist, or any other developmental specialist who can better evaluate your child's particular set of developmental issues. Participating in this process will help you to be informed about decisions such as whether your baby would benefit from occupational or physical therapy. It is probably a good idea for all babies born under 30 weeks gestation to have this type of follow-up assessment. Babies older than 30 weeks with any significant problem, either medical or neurological, will also benefit from the opportunity to be seen by a pediatrician who specializes in development. If you have any concerns, talk with your pediatrician. She may recommend a visit to a developmental specialist (a pediatrician who is familiar with all types of developmental problems) as your child grows older.

We know that some premature babies can have subtle neurological problems when they get older. There can be attention and distractibility issues for older infants and school-age children. In the case of the school-age child, your pediatrician may recommend an appointment with a child psychiatrist for an assessment and possible follow-up use of medication.

Your Baby's Developmental Milestones

This is another time to remember that *it is correct to correct for your baby's gestational age*. In other words, an infant born at a gestational age of 32 weeks is developmentally 8 weeks younger than a term baby born the very same day. In order to accurately assess the premature baby's developmental milestones, we use the *corrected age*: the age calculated from the expected or term date of delivery. During the first year of life for the premature baby, development equals or is only slightly slower than development of term babies *when corrected age is applied*. In most cases, correction is no longer necessary by the time your baby reaches 2 years of age.

The following list gives you some important milestones that your pediatrician will use in assessing your baby's development. *Remember to calculate your baby's corrected age when assessing the following skills:*

- *3 Months*
  pushes up on arms and holds head up
  beginning to bring hands together at the midline

- *6 Months*
  sits with support
  holds head up
  sits on his or her own with back rounded
  transfers objects from hand to hand

- *8 Months*

  sits without support

  grasps objects between thumb and forefinger

  responds to a simple verbal request, accompanied by a defining gesture ("May I have the ball?" as you hold out your hand)

- *12 Months*

  pulls up to a standing position

  responds to a simple verbal request without accompanying gesture ("May I have the ball?")

By 2 years of age, the healthy preterm baby has "caught up" with his term playmate as far as development is concerned. Some premature children reach developmental milestones early as a result of extrauterine stimulation, supporting the contention that your proactive attempts to manipulate your baby's environment in healthful ways play an important role in development.

A SUCCESS STORY

Zach and Diana are the busy parents of two sons, Terrence and Ryland, who were both born prematurely. Our talk with Zach took place at one of the Sunday Roundtable talks held at Dr. Klein's home. We were able to speak with Diana just a few days after Terrence had a successful wrist tendon surgery and made his mom very happy by not even having to spend one night in the hospital!

Zach: Our first child is now 8 years old... My wife was out Christmas shopping when she called me at work and said, "I think my water broke." She is not someone who is prone to overreacting, and she was upset. Fortunately, she was five minutes from a big urban hospital. I got there and was not at all prepared for any of it. Terrence was born at 29½ weeks. His lung burst and he had to have surgery. . . . He had hydrocephalus—swelling of the brain. When he was born, he cried briefly and they took him away. I remember thinking, "Don't cry, don't cry." But as I read and educated myself, I realized it was a good thing... that it encouraged breathing. He was on a respirator for weeks.

I read [medical] journals and books... we did allow a lot of treatment suggestions, but not everything that was proposed. He was born too early to know how to suck, but it was very important to my wife to breast-feed him, and so she pumped and eventually he did learn how to nurse. He's got cerebral palsy. He is phenomenal. He spent 3½ months in the hospital and we were there constantly. He came home before his due date. He is just great.

When Diana became pregnant with Ryland she was 37. She was on bed rest because of the risk. Without going into depth about the psychological effects of our first birth, we certainly never lost sight of the fact that if this was how it needed to go, how were we going to get through it. . . Ryland was born 6 weeks early. Diana had been on bed rest for about two months when her water broke. When we got to the hospital, there was a nurse on duty and the chemistry just wasn't there between her and my wife. Then the shift changed and a new nurse came on who was amazing—very positive and upbeat. Obviously, thoughts about Terrence and his 3½ months in the hospital were running through our minds. . . all the operations and the therapy and all the battles we had to go through. But I remember thinking how I wanted my wife to give birth while this great nurse was still on duty. . . . The shift was going to change at 8:00 and he was born at 7:55. When Ryland was born and started crying, it was just the opposite of what I did when Terrence was born. I was just telling him, "Cry, cry . . ." and the nurse must have thought I was crazy. I can't say that we knew everything was just fine, but we knew whatever happened, it was not going to be that bad. His color was good and he seemed to be moving. Ryland did have apnea and jaundice, and he needed to stay in the hospital for 3½ weeks. There were some ways in which it felt the same because we had our experience with Terrence under our belts. It was all kind of speeded up. . . . There were days that we actually didn't go in to the hospital to see Ryland because we had a 3-year-old at home. When I look at it now I think, *do we just ignore Ryland because Terrence needs all the attention?* But I don't think so.

My wife got pregnant again 2 years ago and we lost that baby—a daughter—at 18 weeks. It was sad and somber, and a very personal experience for my wife and me. But I think about all our experiences, each pregnancy, and the two children we have. I feel that everything Terrence has been through has helped Ryland in some way. Ryland will start kindergarten soon. Because of Terrence's continued therapy, we were able to mainstream him in school last year. He had been going to a specialized school and was by far one of the least handicapped children there. I went through my life ignorant of these kinds of problems for children and then all of a sudden, there it was, right there in front of me with my son. I learned that you can't get too negative. You just figure out the next step.

Diana: After Terrence was released from the hospital, we participated in a support group that Dr. Klein had put together. It was four or five families who had premature babies; it was so important because it builds your confidence, and I felt like I was in a situation where a doctor was treating the whole person... the whole family in a way. We'd talk about things we were going through, and it was just so comforting to have a safety net. I remember thinking, "Just let me get through the meeting without crying." That was the only *official* support group I participated in, but I became the vice president of the parent-faculty association (PFA) of Terrence's school when he began

preschool at a center for kids with handicaps. And the PFA meetings kind of turned into a support group. Our best attendance was always when we were able to discuss our frustrations and sometimes get some help from a professional, such as a school psychologist. I became very close with one woman in that group. Now Terrence is in another school with a more traditional PFA doing fund-raising and things like that and I want to say, "Hey, can't we just sit around and talk?" I feel like through the years I have developed a lot of faith, and that includes faith in my children. I remember in the early days in the NICU, when I'd hear a monitor go off and get frightened, the nurses always said, "Look at your baby... Is he breathing? Does he seem OK?" You have to look at and "listen" to your kids. Many times I ask Terrence, "What do you think?" He is so intuitive.... He has so much to offer. I feel like he can accomplish anything.

Now Terrence is mainstreamed into a regular elementary school. We were nervous at first, thinking kids might be mean, but they have been so sweet. If anything, they tend to sort of treat him like the class pet. . . . That has its own set of problems, because we want so much for him to be treated like any other kid. So I sometimes will bring things up to the kids in his class one-on-one, sort of playing down his differences. Some day I'd like to do a sort of presentation to the class explaining some things about Terrence, but it feels too emotional for now. Like most kids, he has a few friends and they have sleep-overs and love to play. But I'd have to say that while everyone is very friendly, the other boys don't really roughhouse with him. Terrence is 8 now and his comments and questions seem to be about his own physical characteristics. He doesn't really seem to talk about the way his friends may perceive him.

My boys are like all kids in the way they relate to each other. They love each other, but Terrence went through the stage of suggesting that we take his baby brother back to the hospital. Pretty typical, I think. They are so different from each other. Ryland is very physical, and he loves hanging around with his big brother and older kids in general. Last week Terrence had to go in for a surgery to transfer some tendons in his wrist from the back to the front. He did really well and was released the same day. Whenever my friends call and ask if they can do anything, I tell them to pray, so I'm not surprised by how well it is going. One thing I know for sure is that faith and fear cannot reside in the same house.

Chapter Eight

Caring for Your Baby's Nutritional Needs

When There Are Gastrointestinal Problems

The gastrointestinal system of the premature baby is likely to be affected by the same shared factor that may influence neurological and respiratory systems: incomplete intrauterine development. Our growing understanding of pregnancy and the intrauterine environment have guided our efforts to support premature babies in their extrauterine settings. From the neurological perspective, we make attempts to buffer a premie's interaction with the very different environment outside the womb; that is much of what NIDCAP has sought to do in recent years (see chapter 4). As for supporting the premature baby's respiratory system, synthetic surfactant—developed in research laboratories—is used to replace the naturally occurring surfactant the baby would have produced on its own in utero, had it been born at term.

When it comes to providing nourishment to the premature baby, we try to mimic what we know about the nutrition that crosses the placenta to the developing baby. In any individual baby the appropriate method for providing nutrition will depend on gestational age at birth as well as any clinical circumstances that may exist. Premature babies born with minimal problems after delivery may initially be provided with *glucose* (sugar water) by IV after birth and then started on *enteral nutrition*, which is any feeding that occurs via the gastrointestinal tract. *Parenteral nutrition* is the provision of nutrients through an intravenous (IV) or intra-arterial line, and is more likely to be established for babies with severe respiratory and/or circulatory problems after birth.

Let's say we have a little baby who is about 900 grams at birth. Typically, birth weight drops in the first week or so. Depending on the baby's clinical condition, the neonatologist may start enteral feeds anywhere from 1 to 7 days of age. If the baby's clinical course is particularly rocky, the onset of enteral feeding may even be later. Breast milk and regular formula each contains 20 calories per ounce (undiluted). However, for these babies initial feedings will be diluted, whether it is colostrum followed by breast milk, or formula. If tolerated, the amount given enterally will gradually be increased and eventually offered undiluted. Premature babies are born before they have had the time necessary to receive the full compliment of calcium and phosphorous that are so important for normal bone mineralization. Fortunately, there are commercially prepared human milk fortifiers that can be added to pumped breast milk to enhance its caloric content and add these vitally important minerals. There are also fortified formulas designed especially for premature infants that provide similar benefits and as much as 24 to 27 calories per ounce.

At the same time that enteral feedings are begun, the doctor may start a baby on parenteral nutrition. The parenteral nutrition can be provided in one of several ways:

- A catheter can be placed in the umbilical artery.
- An IV line can be inserted into a hand or foot or even the baby's scalp.
- A central line is often used when a baby is going to be on parenteral nutrition for an extended period of time. The central line may be placed by putting a catheter through the skin into the vein of the arm or another peripheral vein, and threading it all the way up until it reaches the *vena cava,* which is the large blood vessel in the center of the body that carries blood back to the heart. When a central catheter is inserted in this way it is referred to either as a *PICC (peripherally inserted central catheter)* or

PVCC (percutaneous venous central catheter) line. A central catheter may also be inserted by a surgical procedure referred to as a "cut down," when an incision is typically made over a vein in the neck or groin and a special catheter (called a Broviac or Hickman catheter) is inserted and then threaded into the vena cava. The proximal (outside) end is then tunneled under the skin to come out some place away from the vein used for insertion. This is often referred to simply as a *Broviac*. When a pediatric surgeon places a Broviac in the neck of a female baby, he will avoid tunneling the line to emerge in the front of her chest. This is to avoid any possible cosmetic disfigurement as she matures. Instead, he is likely to tunnel the line so that is comes out either under the arm or in the back.

Whenever it is necessary to place a central line that goes deep into an infant's body, there is always concern about the possibility of an infection taking hold and spreading throughout the bloodstream. The longer a central line stays in, the higher the risk of developing an infection. Your baby's doctors are continually balancing possible adverse effects of any procedure against the positive gain. This is yet another of the risk-versus-reward situations that often characterize neonatal care.

Some babies who are severely ill may require parenteral nutrition for an extended period of time and may be given *trophic feeds*, which are small amounts of enteral feeding. Trophic feeding does not supply sufficient calories for growth, but it is effective in stimulating gastrointestinal maturation and function. This means the mother who is pumping her breasts may be able to provide her baby with colostrum and then small amounts of breast milk for trophic feeds, even if parenteral feeding is required to provide much of her baby's nutrition. Mothers are likely to be encouraged to provide breast milk, which is usually very much in the best interest of mother and baby. However, the mother who by choice or necessity is not providing breast milk should have confidence that her baby can do well on one of the special formulas that are now available for premature infants.

Total parenteral nutrition (TPN) is a method of delivering total nutrition by IV rather than through the gastrointestinal tract. The intravenous feeding of TPN supplies a very high concentration of glucose for adequate calories, protein (sometimes in the form of individual amino acids), sodium, potassium, magnesium, vitamins, trace minerals, and lipids. Because of the high glucose concentration that is sometimes necessary for adequate calories, a central catheter is often used.

There are several possible complications of parenteral nutrition:

- *TPN cholestasis* or *cholestatic jaundice* is characterized by increased *direct bilirubin* (bilirubin after it is metabolized by the liver) in the blood that may appear after two or more weeks of parenteral nutrition. Normally, the direct bilirubin should pass out of the liver into the intestinal tract and out of the body. Although the exact cause of TPN cholestasis is unknown, there is evidence to suggest that the lack of enteral feeding and resulting nonuse of the gastrointestinal tract may cause the direct bilirubin to back up into the liver and the blood. It is best treated and possibly prevented with early and ongoing use of trophic feedings. Although this problem may get a little worse after parenteral nutrition is stopped, it eventually resolves within several months after the initiation of full enteral feedings.
- *Hyperglycemia* sometimes occurs when a baby receiving parenteral nutrition is unable to metabolize the relatively high concentration of glucose (sugar) quickly enough. Hyperglycemic babies may be given insulin to help metabolize the glucose that is so important to their growth.

Just as we cannot entirely replicate ongoing gestation to support neurological or respiratory development, we do not know how to precisely reproduce the concentrations of various nutrients in the mother's blood or the rate at which these nutrients cross the placenta to nourish a baby growing in utero. In neonatal units throughout the country, parenteral nutrition is given fairly continuously throughout the day at a rate and concentration designed not to overwhelm the baby's very young metabolic systems.

Necrotizing Enterocolitis (NEC)

The neonatologist will proceed cautiously with a feeding strategy because of concerns about the possibility that feeding may be a contributing factor in the development of *necrotizing enterocolitis* (NEC). Necrotizing enterocolitis occurs primarily in premature babies, affecting as many as 4,000 newborns in the United States each year. The increasing incidence of NEC in the past 20 years seems to be associated with improved survival rates for premature babies. The thinking used to be that occurrences of NEC were most likely to occur in the second week of life in an infant being cared for in the NICU. The current understanding is that NEC can occur in other settings, such as the intermediate care unit, and in recovering as well as sick premies. The following risk factors are most commonly associated with NEC:

- prematurity
- too much enteral feeding
- infection
- incidents of low oxygen or poor blood circulation

Necrotizing enterocolitis is usually defined as a disorder of sick premature infants that occurs when a section of either the small or large intestine is damaged. Necrotizing enterocolitis does not always kill all the tissue in a particular area of the intestine; although some tissue may become *necrotic* (die), there may be enough healthy tissue to allow that portion of intestine to become healthy again. When NEC does advance from the lining of the intestine, it often invades the several layers of the intestinal wall. Affected tissue may become distended and rupture, spreading its contents and infection into the abdominal cavity.

The medical experts are not yet certain about the causes of NEC; it may be due to poor circulation through the intestines as occurs with patent ductus arteriosus (see chapter 5), or periods of oxygen deprivation (hypoxia). When circulation is chronically poor or is interrupted, normally harmless bacteria may invade the intestine. Necrotizing enterocolitis sometimes occurs as an *outbreak* (several babies develop NEC around the same time) in a particular setting. When such an outbreak occurs, a specific organism may be to blame, but doctors have not found a particular organism that is always the culprit. When there is an outbreak, the least mature infant is most likely to have the most severe symptoms.

Another factor that is thought to play a role in causing NEC is an overzealous increase in the amount of enteral feedings. Doctors are therefore very cautious and will proceed slowly with any increase in enteral feeds. However, since it is clear that NEC also occurs in infants who have never been fed, the actual occurrence in any one infant does not in itself mean that feedings were advanced too quickly.

There are three levels that you might hear your doctor use to describe NEC: suspected; definite; and severe. The onset of NEC may be subtle, as is the case with many conditions in premature babies. Symptoms may include:

- intestinal distention resulting in abdominal distention and tenderness. Your baby's nurse may be measuring your baby's abdominal circumference in order to follow the progress of the abdominal distention.
- blood in the stool
- shock
- decreased activity
- a bluish appearance over the stomach
- low heart rate
- apnea

If NEC is diagnosed or even suspected (you may hear your doctor refer to a "NEC scare"), the following medical treatment is likely to occur:

- stopping enteral feeding and providing nutrition intravenously (TPN)
- prescribing intravenous antibiotics
- monitoring the patient with X rays and laboratory tests

After blood cultures are obtained, a decision will be made as to the antibiotic therapy. Careful attention should be paid to your baby's respiratory and circulatory status and appropriate support made available if needed. Since NEC has the potential to progress very rapidly, your baby's neonatologist can be expected to monitor her progress very closely.

When a Baby with NEC Needs Surgery

If NEC advances to the point where medical therapies are not sufficient to control it, surgical treatment may be necessary. One of the complications of NEC is that a baby may develop a perforation of the intestines. A perforation is a hole in the intestines that permits intestinal contents to leak out into the abdominal cavity. The usual course for treating a perforated intestine is surgery. The surgeon will attempt to remove any of the dead *bowel* (intestine) that he does not think will survive. The type of surgery performed will depend on which part of the intestines are damaged, what needs to be removed, and what part of the bowel needs to be taken to the abdominal surface. In a *jejunostomy* a hole is created in the abdominal wall to allow for direct emptying of the jejunum (the middle part of the small intestine, past the stomach and duodenum) through a temporary opening in the abdominal wall. When the opening is in the *ileum* (a section of the intestine closer to the colon), it is called an *ileostomy*. A *colostomy* is the surgical procedure that enables the colon (the large intestine) to empty through the temporary opening. The only time this surgery is not temporary is on those very rare occasions that the entire colon, down to the rectum, is involved. In that case a permanent colostomy may be required. Even more rarely, the surgeon will open up the intestines and see that the whole intestinal tract is involved and cannot be saved; in those cases the likely decision is not to proceed with any surgery. However, there is research into the area of transplants, and theoretically at some point in the future a child might survive on TPN until such time as an intestinal transplant could take place.

Temporary jejunostomy, ileostomy, or colostomy provides an opportunity for healing and growth. In time, the fragile gastrointestinal tract will become hearty enough to have its healthy ends reattached. The eventual goal is to have a healthy gastrointestinal system capable of supporting a growing baby's nutritional needs. After an ostomy takes place, the two things parents need to know are: How much of the intestines are left? At what point in the intestine did the colostomy or the ileostomy take place? The amount of enteral nutrition and how successful that nutrition will be in supporting the baby's needs is very much dependent upon the location of the procedure. If it's a fairly high jejunostomy, even though the baby's condition is improving and she can be fed, she may not absorb enough nutrition to provide adequate calories for growth and continued recovery. In the case of a colostomy, the whole small intestine is still likely to be intact, and is more likely to enable an infant to do very well on oral nutrition. You will likely talk about the fact that as your baby gets older, bigger, and stronger, there will be a follow-up surgery to reattach the healthy ends of the intestine to each other.

Typically, every attempt will be made to proceed with the follow-up surgery well before a baby goes home. If the ostomy is in the jejunum or ileum, your baby's medical team will be eager to get it reconnected as soon as possible, in order to facilitate use of the rest of the intestines for absorption of nutrients. If the ostomy has taken place in the colon, there is still ample opportunity for good nutritional absorption in the intestines, so reconnection is not a priority as regards nutrition.

Follow-Up Care for the Baby with Gastrointestinal Problems

As trying as it is for both you and your baby, by the time of discharge, most babies who have had an ostomy procedure are recovered and their healthy intestines are absorbing the nutrients they need for growth. Occasionally, even with the knowledge that their baby will have to return in a matter of months for follow-up surgery, the family of a baby with a colostomy will want their baby to come home prior to reattachment. Under certain circumstances the parents will discuss this option with their doctor, who may agree that such a move would be in the best interest of the family and the baby. Naturally, appropriate steps will need to be taken so that the family is educated in their baby's care. On rare occasions, so much of the intestines are damaged and need to be removed that even after they are hooked back up there are still nutritional problems that present themselves and make growth a difficult issue. These babies may require follow-up by a pediatric gastroenterologist to work at developing the strategies that can best supply adequate nutrition.

Some babies who have survived a severe incident of NEC are still at risk for poor nutrition and recurring gastrointestinal complications. Babies who required surgery are at additional risk for bowel obstruction. Call your doctor immediately if your baby shows any of the following:

- irritability with abdominal cramping
- a distended abdomen
- vomiting
- lack of any bowel movements

After discharge, most babies who have survived NEC will be followed by their primary care physician, who might recommend that a baby also be seen by a pediatric gastroenterologist should the need arise. The most common long-term complication of NEC is *strictures* (narrowing of a section of the intestinal tract, typically in the large intestine). Most of the time, strictures become evident during an infant's hospitalization, but in some cases strictures do not cause symptoms and may not become obvious for as long as 6 months after the onset of NEC. Strictures commonly cause gastrointestinal bleeding and may contribute to bowel obstruction.

While strictures are the most common long-term gastrointestinal complication of NEC, *short-bowel syndrome* is the most serious. Short-bowel syndrome occurs when the bowel's ability to absorb sufficient nutrition is diminished as a result of significant *bowel resection* (surgical removal). This results in a decrease in the absorptive surface of the bowel, a depletion of vital enzymes, and *hypermotility* (overly rapid movement of nutrition through the bowel). The ileum contains most of the vital transport sites for the absorption of nutrients, so babies whose ileum has been spared resection will fare the best regardless of what percentage of bowel has been lost. There are medications that may be helpful in controlling diarrhea and hypermotility. Antibiotics may be required to control overgrowth of bacteria, and in some cases surgery may be indicated to remove a stagnant (inoperative) section of the bowel.

Most babies with short-bowel syndrome will be able to tolerate small amounts of enteral feeding at the time of discharge, but parenteral feeding may be ongoing for an extended period of time. There may be very specific recommendations regarding the type of enteral nutrition these babies can handle. They may begin with elemental formulas or, in rare cases, special formulas without fat or carbohydrates may be recommended. Babies with short-bowel syndrome will require vitamin replacement.

Parents should recognize that this may be a long course, but TPN is very effective in improving the long-range prospects of babies who are unable to withstand enteral feeding. As these babies grow, enteral nutrition will increase in scope and amount. Very few babies continue to show signs of malabsorption after 2 years of age. Many babies with short-bowel syndrome will eventually come to do well on a liberalized enteral diet, with many foods that are appropriate to their age, but as many as 50% may remain intolerant to certain foods. Signs of food intolerance, such as diarrhea or undigested food in stools, should be discussed with the doctor.

Gastroesophageal Reflux (GER)

Gastroesophageal reflux (GER) is a condition that causes the contents (or some of the contents) of the stomach to go back up into the esophagus and sometimes all the way back up to the back of the mouth and down into the trachea. When this happens we say that a baby aspirates the gastric contents, and this can create a serious strain on the respiratory system. When GER occurs and is severe, the upper end of the baby's airway may close in an attempt to prevent stomach contents from going into the lungs; this may be a contributing factor to apnea and/or bradycardia in a baby (see chapter 6). Depending on the severity of GER, there are several ways in which it may be treated:

• Cisapride is a medication that enhances the ability of the intestinal tract to move its contents along, with the result that there is less food in the stomach for shorter periods of time. The less time there is food in the stomach, the less likely it is to come back up.

- Another alternative is H₂-blockers (such as Zantac). These medications decrease acid secretion in the stomach. When stomach contents goes back up into the esophagus, they are not acidic, so it's not as irritating to a baby's esophagus.
- Some families report success with thickening feedings with rice cereal to inhibit reflux.
- You may want to talk to your doctor about positioning your baby in an anti-reflux position so that the head of the bed is higher than the bottom. Speak with your doctor about the most appropriate sleep position for your baby.
- There is a technique called *transpyloric feeding,* by which enteral nutrition is provided through a tube that is inserted into either the nose or mouth and goes through the stomach and directly into the jejunum. This bypasses the stomach and gives the reflux the opportunity to resolve as the baby gets bigger.
- In the most severe cases, a baby may require a surgical procedure known as a *fundoplication,* which will partially close the lower end of the esophagus where it enters the stomach, thereby making reflux far less likely. After this procedure is done, many babies have a *gastrostomy,* which is a procedure that places a tube into the stomach through an incision in the abdominal wall. This tube enables a baby to take feedings directly into the stomach until mouth feeding is possible.

Oral Defensiveness

Many babies who have endured both respiratory and gastrointestinal complications that involve prolonged oral intubation of any type often learn to associate all oral intrusion with discomfort, and may refuse to feed by mouth. We describe these babies as being *orally defensive*. This problem often affects those infants who have had severe chronic lung disease; who have been on a respirator for extended periods of time; or who for various reasons have been intubated for long periods of time. There are feeding specialists, usually occupational therapists, who will work with babies and their parents to slowly decrease oral defensiveness and encourage babies to become comfortable eating by mouth. This is another opportunity to consider establishing a relationship prior to discharge with an occupational therapist who is expert in helping you to understand what your baby is experiencing. A battle of wills between you and your baby over mouth feeding can have no victors; the baby is likely to grow more and more resistant. Try to get guidance early on.

If the baby refuses to take oral feeding, a gastrostomy with or without a fundoplication may be necessary. A family's first reaction to having their baby receive a stomach tube is often quite negative. Yet in some cases, a baby may be discharged with a stomach tube in place if parents are adequately instructed in care and feeding under these special circumstances. Many parents have expressed feeling that this was just not what homecoming was supposed to be. But in retrospect, families often describe an unexpected sense of relief over knowing that their babies were able to receive adequate nutrition via tube without the intense and often unsuccessful efforts to feed them by mouth. In some situations where a baby is orally defensive, even if an anti-reflux surgical procedure has not taken place, some doctors may recommend the insertion of a nasogastric tube which goes through the nose and into the stomach. Unfortunately, this can create additional oral defensiveness because the baby has something sticking in her nose and the back of her throat. There is also the risk that the tube may get dislodged from the stomach and end up in the trachea, causing the baby to aspirate food. If such a procedure is necessary, it must be done with appropriate home health care. It may be necessary to have a nurse come into the home quite frequently to check the placement of the tube.

Chapter Nine

Understanding Vision and Hearing Problems in Your Premature Baby

Our Senses

Among the sensory systems of the human body that keep us in touch with the world around us, our capacities to see and hear are among the most significant to us as a species. Our survival has depended upon the ability to sense an approaching menace, and shift focus almost instantly to matters close at hand. Primitive humans could hear and see an approaching predator well before they could smell or touch it. A warrior, hearing the distant battle cry of his enemy, could rely upon his versatile sense of sight, first to seek out his enemy on the horizon, and then to focus quickly upon the fine work of aligning the gut string of his bow into the tiny notch on his arrow shaft. Just as these senses supported the survival of the species, they are instrumental in forging connections between us. We know that infants are fascinated by looking at faces, and current research supports the idea that the early experience of looking into the eyes of a loving parent supports neurological development in the brain of a young baby. The soothing quality of a mother's or father's voice, the soft cooing and singing that marks the beginning of love between parent and child is universal, transcending every social, economic, cultural, or linguistic barrier that divides the world today or the world of several thousand years ago. Today, a premature baby born at risk for vision or hearing loss has access to laser and microsurgical techniques, as well as ongoing systems of support that were unheard of when you were an infant.

Retinopathy of Prematurity—The Most Common Vision Problem for Premature Babies

Our precious sense of sight allows us to look at our babies as they look back at us. This mutual admiration society is universally perceived as one of the most important factors in establishing a connection with your newborn. It is understandable that of the many complications that may affect a baby born on the threshold of viability, a diagnosis of *retinopathy of prematurity* (ROP)—which can cause mild to severe visual impairment—may be one of the most frightening to new parents. If you do have a premature baby at risk of having a visual deficit, ROP is the most likely culprit.

Retinopathy of prematurity is a disorder of the developing retinal blood supply, which occurs in some premature babies. It is, at least in part, a consequence of our ability to save the lives of younger and younger babies. In the developing fetus the blood vessels supplying the retina appear at the beginning of the second trimester. The vessels continue to grow from the optic disc at the center of the eye out to the far periphery of the *retina* (the light-sensitive nerve tissue that lines the back of the eye) until the retina is fully vascularized. In the premature baby the retinal blood supply is incomplete. Stress to an infant at the time of delivery may cause injury to the developing retinal capillaries. Once damage to the delicate retinal capillary bed occurs, there is a variable delay before growth begins again toward the periphery of the retina. When growth resumes, it may complete the normal vascularization of the retina without any problem. In other cases the blood vessels grow abnormally and excessively through the retina. The surplus growth of these blood vessels may cause the retina to become scarred or to detach from the back of the eye, causing a range of vision loss from mild to severe.

Not all premature babies will develop ROP, and the precise cause of the disease remains unknown. Those most at risk are premature babies who are sick, have a low birth weight, and are born at 30 weeks gestation or less. Retinopathy of prematurity may regress on its own or improve with treatment. It is accurate to say that it occurs at least in part because a very premature baby has not had the gestational time to become completely physiologically prepared for its new environment outside the womb. There has been a great deal of discussion implicating fluorescent lighting in hospital neonatal units as advancing the progression of ROP. The harshness of such lighting makes it an easy target, but there has not yet been a conclusive study to prove this true or false. There is an ongoing study called the Trial of Light Reduction for Reducing Frequency of Retinopathy of Prematurity (Light-ROP), which is assessing the effect of nursery light reduction on ROP and its severity. The significance of external events in the neonatal unit (such as lighting and nursing care) are still in question.

The Relationship Between Oxygen and ROP

In the 1950s researchers sponsored by the National Institute of Health found that the level of oxygen routinely delivered to premature babies was a risk factor for ROP. Oxygen levels were reduced and the incidence of ROP decreased. Today we continue to learn about saving the lives and improving the quality of life for premature babies. Smaller and smaller babies are being successfully treated for respiratory complications. As the technology to keep very young babies alive has advanced (particularly in the area of respiratory support), ROP has reemerged as a complication. Parents of premature babies born today can be reassured that physicians caring for newborns now understand that oxygen, when needed, should be used only to restore oxygen saturation levels to the normal range and should be stopped as soon as it is no longer needed. In the modern neonatal unit, neonatologists and primary care physicians using oxygen therapy understand its relationship to ROP and are likely to consult a pediatric ophthalmologist to be sure that an infant's eyes are *fully vascularized* (have their full complement of tiny blood vessels to the periphery of the retina) and are no longer at risk for ROP before oxygen delivery is liberalized.

Stages of ROP

In the 1980s an *International Classification of Retinopathy of Prematurity* (ICROP) was created. This system utilizes the following three features to describe ROP:

1. Position The position of the disease is described by the use of three zones of the retina, which are divided into concentric circles around the optic nerve.

zone one—a small circle in the eye with the optic nerve at its center

zone two—a circle that completely surrounds zone one

zone three—the remaining crescent of retina in front of zone two

2. Extent Retinopathy of prematurity is described in clock hours, so as to distinguish between an eye that has only a small wedge of abnormal blood vessel growth (perhaps from twelve to two o'clock) and an eye which has a ring of wild vascular growth all the way around the retina.

3. Plus Disease This term is used to describe ROP where the blood vessels are more convoluted and dilated than normal. This is an indication of a more severe and active case of ROP.

The ICROP also describes the severity of ROP through the use of stages from 1 to 5, with 1 being the mildest and 5 the most severe.

Screening for ROP

Another study called the Multicenter Trial of Cryotherapy for Retinopathy of Prematurity (CRYO-ROP study) appears to indicate that a baby's postmenstrual age is innately connected to the progress of ROP. Additional results of the same study indicate that surgical treatment is definitely helpful in impeding the progress of ROP. In light of these findings, it is clear that early screening is a very important weapon. The following guideline for screening is adapted from a joint statement issued by the American Academy of Pediatrics, the

American Association for Pediatric Ophthalmology and Strabismus, and the American Academy of Ophthalmology in 1997:[1]

> *Screening is called for in infants with a birth weight of less than or equal to 1,500 grams or with a gestational age of 28 weeks or less. Also those babies weighing more than 1,500 grams who have been ill and are considered by their attending pediatrician or neonatologist to be at risk for ROP should be screened.*
>
> *This examination should be carried out by an ophthalmologist with experience in the examination of preterm infants.*
>
> *Screening should be performed between 4 and 6 weeks chronological age or between 31 and 33 weeks postmenstrual age as determined by the infant's attending pediatrician or neonatologist.*
>
> *Scheduling of follow-up examinations are best determined by the findings at the first examination using the International Classification of Retinopathy of Prematurity (ICROP).*
>
> *If the retinal vasculature is immature and in zone two but no disease is present, follow-up examination should be planned at approximately 2- to 4-week intervals until vascularization proceeds to zone three.*
>
> *Infants with ROP detected in zone one should be seen at least every week until involution of ROP occurs and normal vascularization proceeds to zone two or the risk of attaining threshold conditions has passed. Infants with ROP in zone two, or with immature vessels (without ROP) detected in zone one, should be seen at least every one to two weeks.*
>
> *Infants with threshold disease (ROP at a level of severity that is likely to benefit from surgical intervention) should be considered candidates for treatment of at least one eye within 72 hours of diagnosis.*
>
> *The attending pediatrician or neonatologist should refer the infants who fit the examination criteria for initial examination to the ophthalmologist. If a baby is transferred to another neonatal unit or hospital, a new primary care physician or neonatologist should ascertain his status so that any necessary ophthalmologic examinations can be arranged.*

Treating ROP

If the vessels continue to proliferate and place the eye at risk of retinal detachment and visual loss, treatment of ROP is indicated. Just as there have been advances in respiratory therapy, scientists working on developing new treatment for ROP continue to make progress. Today treatment for ROP is most likely going to be one of two types of surgery. A third surgical alternative may be called upon if other management has failed to arrest the progress of the disease. The surgical options are:

• *Cryotherapy* Normal tissue from the outer edge of the retina is frozen. Freezing effectively destroys healthy tissue, which in turn slows the progress of abnormal growth in blood vessels.

This procedure appears to show a significant reduction in the progression of ROP. Cryotherapy requires the use of narcotics for pain management.

• *Laser Surgery (also referred to as laser photocoagulation)* This procedure utilizes a laser light delivered to the targeted area of the retina. The laser light is absorbed by tissue and converted to heat, which breaks down cells and slows the accelerated growth of blood vessels. This treatment may have a success rate even greater than cryotherapy in stopping the progress of ROP. It is also less traumatic and has fewer complications than cryotherapy.

• *Scleral Buckling and Vitrectomy* If there has been partial retinal detachment, as may occur in stage 4 ROP, scleral buckling may be used to place a silicone band around the equator of the eye, which is tightened to create a slight indentation on the inside of the eye. This procedure allows the retina to flatten back down onto the wall of the eye, and good vision may be retained. The encircling band usually needs to be removed within months or years because of continuing growth of the eye.

In cases of stage 5 ROP, where there has been complete retinal detachment due to scar tissue on the retina, doctors may consider vitrectomy, which involves making several small incisions into the eye, and taking additional steps to attempt to allow the retina to reattach to the wall of the eye.

Both cryotherapy and laser surgery are now in use, but study into the prevention and nonsurgical therapies for ROP continues. The National Eye Institute is currently sponsoring a very interesting trial called the Supplemental Therapeutic Oxygen for Pre-threshold ROP (STOP-ROP) trial, which is designed to determine whether supplemental therapeutic oxygen given to infants with moderate ROP will lessen the likelihood that ROP will progress to a degree of severity that calls for surgical treatment. This trial is particularly interesting in light of the concerns throughout the medical community about excessive oxygen.

In cases where ROP regresses, which is to say it improves, your primary care physician may still recommend that your baby be examined by a pediatric ophthalmologist in the months that follow. Babies with regressed ROP may have *myopia* (nearsightedness), and early use of glasses may be warranted. *Strabismus* (a condition in which the two eyes do not work together in a synchronized fashion) and *esotropia* (crossed eyes) may also occur. If there is any residual scarring of your child's retina, there is a risk of developing a detached retina later in life. Your doctor will probably decide to schedule an annual exam with an ophthalmologist who is familiar with ROP in an attempt to provide early detection of retinal detachment.

While ROP is the most common disorder to affect the eyes of premature babies, there are other conditions that may occur. In rare cases babies can experience extreme vision loss due to a complication of periventricular leukomalacia in which the cortex of the brain is damaged, causing a condition known as *cortical blindness*.

When a Baby Is Visually Impaired

Visual impairment, particularly when it is severe, is a challenge for you and your baby. Infancy and early childhood years are equally important to the development of a sighted, partially sighted, or blind child. For the blind infant, developmental milestones—such as reaching and walking and even chewing—may be delayed. Each of these skills depends upon a baby's ability to see, whether it is the enticement of a toy to reach for, or observing the way family members place food in their mouths and begin to chew. There are certain behaviors that parents, siblings, caregivers, and physicians can utilize to initiate comfortable, rewarding interactions with a baby who is blind:

- Try speaking softly and soothingly to a baby *before* picking him or her up. Be very gentle. Your baby will learn to associate voices with touch and the possibility of motion.
- As mentioned throughout this book, learn to read your baby's cues as to his or her readiness for contact. The "body language" of the baby who cannot see will differ from that of the sighted infant. A baby who can see you may avert his or her eyes to indicate that he or she would prefer not to interact just then, or turn his head to say, "No more food right now." You will need to tune into the particularly sensitive frequency on which your baby is going to transmit his wishes, especially before he begins to speak.
- Support and guide siblings in their attempts to interact with their baby sister or brother. The whole family may benefit greatly from professional counseling in the matter of supporting each other, as well as the newest member of the family. (See the resource guide, Appendix E, for specific resources for the visually impaired and their families.)

Parents may be astonished to learn that visually impaired children do not usually become aware of a sensory deficit until they reach the age of 4 or 5 years and begin to understand that others have a capacity that they lack. The parents who are anticipating this question will do their child a service by responding honestly, but with as easygoing a demeanor as is possible. It may help to recognize that although your child may not see, he is more like his peers than unlike them. Your child has gifts and abilities that make him unique, just as sighted playmates have their own set of strengths and liabilities.

Sound, Noise, and Your Baby's Hearing

As the parent of a premature baby, your thoughts are far more likely to be on caring for your child than on remembering wild nights out on the dance floor, or wincing as your own parents entered your bedroom—where the speakers were blaring loud music—to plead with you to "Turn down that noise!" How could they call that incredible music. . . NOISE? For purposes of any discussion of "noise" as a factor in your baby's development, we define *noise* as *undesirable sound*. Sound has intensity (loudness), frequency (pitch), periodicity, and duration. The loudness of sound is measured in decibels. Although one person's sound is admittedly another person's noise, we do know that the ability to hear any given frequency can be damaged as a result of overexposure to noise. The federal government has established standards for noise exposure in the workplace, and a generation of aging rock-and-rollers are coming forward to discuss their own damaged hearing after many years of too much fun in front of giant speakers blaring too much noise.

Most of what is known about noise-induced hearing loss has been learned from studies of adults with occupational exposure to noise. However, we now know from evidence collected in studies over the past 25 years that fetuses and newborns exposed to excessive noise may also suffer noise-induced hearing loss. We've learned from ultrasound observation that a fetus responds to sound stimulation as early as 24 or 25 weeks gestation, and we believe that the auditory pathways of the central nervous system reach maturity by 28 weeks.

While studies are not conclusive, there is certainly strong evidence to suggest that prolonged fetal exposure to the roar of jet engines (as might occur in the case of an expectant mother working outside at an airport) can contribute to high-frequency hearing loss in a school-age child. Yet there is "noise pollution" much closer at hand for your premature baby in the NICU. Several studies have looked into the effects of minimizing exposure to noise for premature infants. In one such study, premature babies wore earmuffs and the effect on their sleep time was examined. It was determined that infants wearing the earmuffs had significantly higher oxygen saturation levels as well as less fluctuation in oxygen saturation. There were also increases in quiet sleep time when the earmuffs were worn.

In another interesting study, premature babies were offered individualized environmental care that included reducing exposure to the noise from standard NICU activities, such as a decrease in opening and closing of the incubator porthole doors. These babies needed significantly fewer days of respiratory support on a ventilator and required fewer days of oxygen administration. In a third study that offered premature babies prolonged respites from the noise of the NICU, their neurological development (as reflected by electrical impulses of the brain measured by EEG) more closely resembled the development that we know to occur in utero. These studies all seem to support decreasing noise for premature babies in the NICU, which appears to be very much in keeping with the principles of NIDCAP (Neonatal Individualized Developmental Care and Assessment Program), discussed in chapter 4. Many NICUs throughout the country are beginning the important work of developing anti-noise policies to reduce noise.

In 1994 the Joint Committee on Infant Hearing listed risk factors for identifying infants and young children at risk for hearing loss. Unfortunately, of the babies who will experience hearing loss, only 50% will be identified through screening due to known risk factors. It follows that this same committee went on to endorse the goal of universal screening for hearing loss as early as possible, stating that all infants with hearing loss should be identified by 3 months of age and receive attention by 6 months of age. Until the time the goal of universal screening can be realized in every hospital and birthing center throughout the country, the Joint Committee on Infant Hearing recommends audiological evaluation for *neonates* (newborn infants up to 1 month of age) showing any of the risk factors described below:

Neonates (0-28 Days) (For use when universal screening is not available)

- *Family history* of hereditary childhood sensorineural hearing loss.
- *In utero infection,* such as cytomegalovirus, rubella, syphilis, herpes, and toxoplasmosis.
- *Craniofacial anomalies,* including those with morphological abnormalities of the pinna and ear canal.
- *Birth weight less than 1,500 grams* (3.3 pounds).

- *Hyperbilirubinemia* at a serum level requiring exchange transfusion.
- *Ototoxic medications,* including but not limited to the aminoglycosides (a type of antibiotic), used in multiple courses or in combination with loop diuretics.
- *Bacterial meningitis.*
- *Apgar scores* of 0 to 4 at 1 minute, or 0 to 6 at 5 minutes. (The score is a method of assessing well-being in a newborn. A score of between 1 and and 10 is assessed, first at 1 minute and then at 5 minutes. See chapter 5 for a complete description of the score.)
- *Mechanical ventilation lasting 5 days or longer.*
- *Stigmata* or other findings associated with a syndrome known to include sensorineural and/or conductive hearing loss.

Anyone reading this list of risk factors is likely to think it applies to an awful lot of the premies in the neonatal units of our hospitals, and they would be correct. Almost all premature infants who are in the NICU will have their hearing tested before discharge. Be sure to ask your baby's doctor about the results of the hearing screen. Even if the screen is normal, it is a part of your baby's thorough medical history and you should be aware of its results.

What Is Hearing Impairment?

Approximately 1 in 2,000 newborn infants has a significant hearing loss; a large number of these are premature infants, many of whom fall into categories at high risk for hearing loss (as described earlier in this chapter). Hearing impairment in an infant falls into two categories:

Sensorineural hearing loss is a hearing problem that originates in the inner ear. It can occur if there is damage to the nerves that send and receive information from the brain. Such damage may be the result of infection; oxygen deprivation before, during, or after birth; or the use of drugs in doses large enough to damage an infant's hearing.

Conductive hearing loss originates in the middle ear. It occurs when sound waves cannot be effectively transmitted across the eardrum to the three tiny bones (hammer, anvil, stirrup) of the middle ear on to the cochlea, which is filled with fluid (an excellent medium for conducting sound) and lined with cilia, which are microscopic hairs that vibrate in response to sound waves. This type of hearing loss can occur as a result of a series of ear infections or an abnormal collection of fluid in the middle ear.

It is also possible for hearing loss to develop in older babies as a result of medical conditions that occurred after an initial hearing screening indicated that there was no impairment. If you have any concerns about your baby's hearing (even if his initial screening was normal), discuss it with your primary care physician so that another evaluation can be ordered. Even if you have not requested an evaluation, your primary care physician may recommend it. Premies are more likely than term babies to suffer recurrent ear infections or eustachian tube dysfunction, resulting in conductive hearing loss.

The Importance of Early Detection and Intervention

As advances in medicine enable us to send babies born at increasingly younger gestational ages out of the NICU and into the homes and lives of their families, the medical community is trying to keep pace with the ongoing tasks of evaluating infants at risk for hearing or vision deficits and promoting family awareness about how to best support their baby's needs.

Since a deficit in hearing can interfere with the development of speech and language, every effort should be made to detect hearing loss as early as possible. We know that *behavioral techniques,* such as observing whether the baby consistently responds to hand claps or the ringing of a loud bell outside its visual range, is not as reliable as a test of hearing capabilities. The two methods of assessment currently recommended by the Joint Committee on Infant Hearing are:

- *Auditory brainstem response (ABER)*, also referred to as *brainstem auditory evoked response* (BAER), which measures the brain's response to a sound.
- *Otoacoustic emissions (OAE)*, in which sound emissions from the inner ear itself can be measured and used as a means of determining an infant's hearing capabilities.

Of these two methods of assessment, ABER has been used for at least 15 years in both universal newborn screening programs and risk assessment evaluations. Typically an initial screening is performed shortly before an infant is to be discharged from the neonatal unit. Newborn screening is typically accomplished with a noninvasive automated hearing screening device when a baby is in an open crib. If the initial screen is abnormal, a more formal and extensive test will be performed. Otoacoustic emissions screening has also been used and appears to be successful in identifying hearing loss. Current medical literature has not yet shown one test to be preferable to the other in assessing hearing in newborns.

DR. KLEIN COMMENTS ON RETESTING BABIES AFTER AN INITIAL ABNORMAL HEARING TEST

Parents of babies whose hearing registers as abnormal on initial testing may (and should) be advised to retest in one to three months. If hearing is still abnormal at one to three months, I will refer my patient to a pediatric ear, nose, and throat specialist. As sophisticated as testing methods are, they are fallible, and many premature babies whose hearing register as abnormal on an initial screening will go on to have excellent hearing, with little or no deficit and no complications or developmental delay in their speech and language acquisition. In a similar fashion, there are rare cases of a baby testing normally who will go on to demonstrate some degree of hearing loss.

When Hearing Is Determined to Be Abnormal

The right to a hearing evaluation and follow-up intervention has been secured through the Individuals with Disabilities Education Act (IDEA), and if follow-up screenings indicate a hearing deficit, a team should be assembled to help you to develop an individualized family service plan (IFSP) that will outline an early intervention program tailored to the needs of your baby. Hopefully the full evaluation process should be completed within 45 days of referral.

Early intervention services that might be offered prior to the completion of a full evaluation might include information for the family regarding support in the community and the type of amplification that might be best suited to a baby's needs. The team members who may participate in assessing and evaluating your baby's hearing may include:

- Your *primary care physician*.
- An *otolaryngologist*, who is a doctor specializing in treatment of ear, nose, and throat disease. Some specialize specifically in hearing problems.
- An *audiologist*, who is trained to assess and evaluate hearing loss and can recommend appropriate amplification devices such as hearing aids, personal FM systems, vibrotactile aids, and/or cochlear implants.
- A *speech-language pathologist* with expertise in assessment and communication skills.

When an evaluation has taken place and hearing loss has been diagnosed, an individualized family service plan should be designed to maximize your child's particular set of strengths, while minimizing the impact of any hearing loss on subsequent development. Consistent with the principles of the family-centered care discussed throughout this book, there are several key elements to early intervention:

- *Support of the Family* Your active participation and ongoing education about hearing loss will be an important part of supporting your child. The professional members of your team should be able to direct you to state and community-based organizations, educational materials, and support groups.

- *Services* It is important that monitoring of your child's health and hearing be ongoing. It should include continued assessment of amplification needs and any other resources that will maximize your efforts to support your baby's hearing.

- *Activities* Participation in activities, possibly in a group situation, that encourage development and promote language acquisition and communication is helpful to you and your baby. Contact with other families experiencing similar challenges will help you to feel *and be* less isolated.

We know that our greatest strength in supporting the baby who has hearing loss is the earliest possible identification of the problem. The use of hearing aids in young infants, followed by speech and language therapy very early on, often brings excellent results.

Chapter Ten

Taking Your Baby Home

When Is Your Baby Ready to Leave the Hospital?

One of the first questions that most parents of premature babies ask their physician is, "When can I take my baby home?" The answer typically used in response to this question is, "The baby will come home around the time it was originally due." But in actuality, most babies born after 28 weeks come home somewhere between 35 and 37 weeks gestation. Those born between 24 and 28 weeks may have complications that require them to stay in the hospital for a longer time. To put it simply, discharge will depend on when your baby fits the criteria for discharge established by your hospital. This criteria will vary somewhat in individual facilities, but are fundamentally as follows:

- The baby must be able to suck, swallow, and breathe in a coordinated fashion in order to take all feedings by mouth. (Very rarely, a baby has a problem that requires tube feeding. But if it fits all the other criteria for discharge and the parents are prepared to take on the special challenges of tube feeding at home, this baby may be able to be discharged.)
- The baby must maintain body temperature outside the incubator at room temperature.
- The baby should be apnea-free for at least 5 to 10 days if not on respiratory stimulant medication, and 3 days or more if receiving respiratory stimulant medication.

- Weight gain should be consistent for 3 to 5 days prior to discharge. There is no standard weight to be attained, assuming all other requirements are met.
- Parents must be prepared to care for their babies in the home environment. This might include receiving CPR training, having child care scheduled, and being capable of using an apnea monitor and other equipment if needed.

Screening for eye problems and a hearing assessment usually take place before discharge. (See chapter 9 for a detailed discussion of possible vision and hearing problems.)

DR. KLEIN COMMENTS ON DISCHARGE OF PREMATURE BABIES

In the past it was common for most neonatal units to have specific weight criteria for discharge home (approximately 2,000 grams), and weaning from an incubator to an open crib at room temperature (approximately 1,800 grams). However, there was no scientific basis for the specific weights in either case. More recently, studies have shown an infant can maintain its body temperature at a much lower weight than was previously thought. As a result, some hospitals are sending babies home who meet all discharge criteria, even if they weigh less than 1,800 grams.

Discharge Planning

Discharge planning should begin at the time of admission. In the best-case scenario, the neonatologist and the primary care physician will work together, thereby streamlining communication, decreasing the likelihood of rehospitalization, and promoting a positive and smooth transition from the hospital to home. Family assessment, the process by which family readiness to care for their infant at home is determined, should begin as soon as the baby is born. Basics such as a safe home environment that includes appropriate bedding, telephone, plumbing, and electricity will be evaluated, usually through interviews with parents conducted by discharge-planning personnel (social workers and case managers, important members of the All-Star Team described in chapter 3). Appropriate questions regarding a family's financial situation and insurance should be initiated by discharge planners early on. If no one is asking those questions, ask a nurse or your doctor if they can direct you to the right person to speak with. Families are often surprised to learn that the most common delaying factor in the discharge process is funding. Financial planning and the involvement of discharge-planning personnel should begin as early as possible. It is very helpful in determining what home care expenses will be reimbursed by the family's health insurance carrier and what the family's eligibility for government assistance may be.

All members of the team, including physicians, nursing staff, occupational and physical therapists, parent advocate, and social worker, will add valuable insight to the family assessment. By meeting periodically with various members of your baby's team, you develop the lines of communication that are so important in acquiring the skill, confidence, and trust needed for successful home care when the time comes. Just as your baby's readiness for going home increases by increments, your own concerns will expand to include questions about how complicated home care is likely to be. Keep in mind that your team members in the unit have a great deal of experience with helping parents as well as babies. You will need to know some very basic "how to's" before you are ready to care for your baby at home.

- Are you confident about feeding, diapering, and bathing your baby? Although you have gone through this with your baby's nurse, a run-through prior to discharge may be just the thing to give you real confidence with the process.
- If your baby has gastroesophageal reflux, how will you elevate the head of the crib (if suggested) to a 30° angle? *A blanket roll under the crib mattress may do the trick.*
- If you have a family pet, have you considered that its freedom in the house may need to be temporarily curtailed when you bring your baby home? Are there likely to be jealousy issues with the dog who is used to

being the baby of the family? *Introducing your favorite pet to a new doll that is seen in your arms prior to your infant's home arrival may be helpful.*

- Are you prepared to limit the number of visitors your baby receives immediately after discharge? Are you prepared to tell even a doting grandma that she must wash her hands before holding or even touching the baby? *Tell her it's doctor's orders!*
- Have you (and anyone else who will be a caregiver to your baby) had infant CPR training?
- Are you confident in your ability to administer oral medication if any have been prescribed?

In the case of the uncomplicated premature baby, you may be lucky enough to go home with little or no durable medical equipment (DME), but you will need to provide all the basics for your baby's home care. As your baby nears homecoming, there will also be many practical considerations:

- *Car Seat* First on the "to do" list as you near discharge is the purchase and installation of a car seat. The safest place for your baby is in a rear-facing car seat that is carefully secured (following instructions from the car seat manufacturer) in the center position of the back seat of your car. Your baby is likely to need additional padding, such as a rolled blanket or covered foam pads, surrounding her on either side for head support while she is very small. There are additional concerns about oxygen desaturation in premature babies and low-birth-weight infants when placed in car seats in a semi-upright position. Use the following guide (adapted from a recommendation of the American Academy of Pediatrics) when placing your premature baby in a car seat:

1. Use infant-only car seats with a three-point harness system or convertible car safety seat with a five-point harness system for optimum comfort, fit, and positioning. Never place a small infant in a car seat with a shield, abdominal pad, or arm rest that could directly contact an infant's face and neck during impact. *Do not use a car seat designed for children weighing more than 20 pounds until your premature infant has reached or exceeded that weight.*

2. Use a car safety seat with a distance of less than 5½ inches from crotch strap to seat back to reduce the risk of your baby slumping forward.

3. Select a car seat with a distance of less then 10 inches from the lower harness strap to the seat bottom in order to reduce the potential for the harness strap to cross your baby's ears.

4. With your baby positioned with buttocks and back against the back of the car seat, use blanket rolls, placed vertically on either side of your baby, for head and neck support.

5. In rear-facing car seats, shoulder belts should be in the lowest slot until your baby's shoulders are above the slots.

   The harness retainer clip should be at the midpoint of your baby's chest. Be sure the crotch strap goes between the legs near the crotch. Use clothing with legs.

6. If needed to maintain your baby's upright position, a firmly rolled blanket can be placed under the seat to tilt it back to a 45° angle.

7. *Never place an infant or child car seat in a location that has an activated front airbag, and never have your baby in a moving vehicle unless she is securely strapped into the car seat.*

   All infants weighing less than 20 pounds and/or younger than 1 year must be in a rear-facing, secured safety seat.

8. Never leave an infant unattended in a car safety seat.

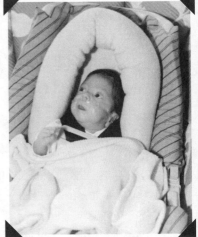

Premie with blanket roll in car seat.

In 1990, the American Academy of Pediatrics issued a statement[1] alerting us that premature babies and low-birth-weight infants may be subjected to oxygen saturation problems when placed in car seats in a semi-upright position. They then made specific recommendations regarding the safe transport of these infants at risk that included a period of assessment of apnea, bradycardia, and oxygen desaturation of each premature infant in a car seat before hospital discharge. Although this is done in many neonatal units, other units do not do the test because they feel the car ride home cannot be replicated in the hospital and that this time is better served teaching the family how to correctly place their infant in the car seat in such a way to avoid slouching forward and subsequent respiratory problems.

• **Crib and Bedding** Crib slats should be no more than 2⅜ inches apart, with end posts no higher than ⅟₁₆ inch above the crib's end panel. Don't let your sentimental attachment to an heirloom family crib get in the way of safety! The crib mattress should be a snug fit, and be securely surrounded by bumper pads that snap or tie into place. Pillows are not safe for babies and should never be included in the crib. Always trim any excess length from bumper ties. Unless instructed otherwise by your baby's physician, your baby should always be placed on her back to sleep.

• **Strollers** If your baby is coming home on a monitor, or using oxygen, check to make sure all necessary equipment will fit onto, into, or somehow be compatible with your stroller. This is an area where parents of older babies may be able to be very helpful. It is a good idea to get a stroller with a big basket, as well as a canopy that can temporarily hold something if you need to free up a hand.

• **Infant Carriers** The infant carrier you use will need to be washable and sturdy, and have adjustable padded shoulder straps. You will want a front pack with adequate head support. If possible, try several on for size and comfort before purchasing. If your baby is sent home on oxygen or is having respiratory problems, you may want to avoid the compromising position that results when you place your infant in a baby carrier.

• **Bath Seats** A portable bathtub or seat can help you to bathe your baby safely and comfortably whether in the tub or by sponge bath. Always consider your own posture while bathing your baby. Placing the bath seat in the sink or on a counter may be less of a strain on your back than kneeling at the tub. *Of course, you must never leave your baby unattended at bath time.*

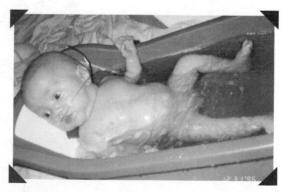

Bath time with nasal cannula in place.

• *Clothing and Diapers* You will find a resource guide in Appendix E that can direct you to great sources for premature baby clothes. Interestingly, finding clothing for tiny babies can be very emotional for a parent. Some parents are superstitious about baby clothes and make it clear that they do not want any until after the baby is born. Many premature babies are born before their mom was given her baby shower. The truth is that your baby's need for clothing is very basic, and it is both mentally and emotionally wise to get clothes that fit your baby when she comes home. The sight of your tiny baby in sleepers that swim on her is not psychologically beneficial to you, or comfortable to your baby. Get started with the basics and give friends and family the joy of giving you the little extras, like handmade sweaters or booties. Many parents of premature babies comment happily that their babies quickly began to outgrow their specially purchased premie outfits, so don't invest in an entire wardrobe of premature baby clothes. The list that follows should help you to get started:

- six cotton snap undershirts
- six one-piece, leg snap pajamas
- eight receiving blankets
- two hats (seasonal)
- three sets of socks or booties
- two blanket sleepers (seasonal)
- two one-piece leg snap snowsuits for a winter baby
- two soft, hooded baby towels for bath time

You may want to order (check the resource guide in Appendix E) premie cloth diapers or premie disposables, or combine the two. Check with manufacturers for any free samples they may offer, and wait to see what fits best before you stock up. Anticipate an average of 10 diapers per day, and always have a dozen extra cloth diapers on hand to protect your clothes from spit-up. "Accessorizing" takes on a whole different meaning to a new mom.

WHEN YOU NEED FOLLOW-UP CARE AFTER DISCHARGE: GETTING THE MOST FROM YOUR HEALTH INSURANCE

Nadine Vogel is an estate planning and private insurance specialist in Los Angeles. She is the mother of an NICU graduate with special needs, and is the founder, president, and executive director of Special Needs Advocate for Parents (SNAP), a nonprofit corporation that is a national resource for the parents of special needs children. (Look for the SNAP listing in the resource guide in Appendix E.)

Ms. Vogel's general insights into the workings of private insurance companies will be helpful to any parent, but they will be of particular interest to parents of those premature babies (most likely at the younger gestational ages) who are in need of follow-up care such as monitors, oxygen, or various therapies after discharge from the hospital.

The first thing I recommend to parents of babies who will be in need of follow-up care at home is to *read your health insurance policy!* Be careful not to confuse your *policy* with your *outline of benefits booklet.* The outline of benefits is perhaps 10 or 15 pages that seems to indicate all these wonderful benefits, but actually tells you nothing about the specifics of your policy. Typically, people who have purchased their own insurance have received a copy of the policy. For those who purchased health insurance through their employer, *the human resource office of your company must maintain a copy of the policy on file.* They won't allow you to remove it from the premises, but you can read and/or copy the policy. I recommend that you copy the policy so that you have it on hand for your own use. If you work for a very large corporation, it may take a little work to track down the policy, but be sure to put in the effort. It will be well worth your while.

Depending on the needs of your child, there may be very specific elements of the policy to consider. *Home Health,* for example, may be crucial to the child who needs nursing care, or one or more therapies (occupational, respiratory, physical, speech). If you read your policy carefully, you will realize that while your child may not need nursing care, your home health benefits may include therapy that can be pulled out of your policy in addition to the coverage that may already be available under the heading of the *specific therapy (such as speech or occupational)* that might also be cited.

Look into your policy under the name of the specific therapy you need. There may be headings for *occupational therapy; respiratory therapy; physical therapy; speech therapy.* If these therapies are covered, the policy will also tell you precisely the conditions and criteria that are covered: perhaps speech is covered only after surgery, or following an illness. So unless you are very clear on the specifics of your policy, you may be in for a great deal of frustration. The bottom line is: *Know your policy and what you are contractually entitled to.*

For the families who have a premie who is still in the NICU, I recommend that as they begin to comprehend what the continuing health-care needs of their baby are going to be, they highlight the pertinent information in their policy (being careful to look at the part of the policy that cites *limitations and exclusions*, to make sure you are requesting something that is contractually available). For the baby going home with, let's say, an apnea monitor. . . that is quite straightforward and may not be too complicated to arrange. But if your baby is going home with a lot of durable medical equipment and nursing care and the need for several therapies, then your case is complicated and you may need some help. You may wish to approach your primary care physician, one of the neonatologists, or the medical director of the NICU for help in communicating with your insurance company.

I advise parents to create a one-page summary of the criteria for what is covered on your policy, as well as a one-page summary of the limitations and exclusions. Give this concise information to the physician who will be speaking on your behalf with a representative from your insurance company.

For those families whose baby has complicated follow-up care and may need numerous services, there is another important point to consider: Many policies have what is called *utilization review,* and/or *case management.* In a complex case, your insurance company may assign you a case manager. *The case manager for the insurance company is almost always a nurse. If possible, request a case manager with pediatric nursing experience.*

The physician representing your baby's interests can speak with the case manager or medical director of the insurance company (who is also a doctor), and say, "This is what we need. . . ." In this way you establish a relationship with two medical people from the outset. On many of the occasions that we (as parents) get denied, it's because we don't ask the right way. . . we may not make our requests within the parameters of what is allowed on the specific policy. In situations where you need more than your policy appears to offer, your case manager may be able to design a package (for a particular time period such as 30 to 90 days) that will offer more benefits and services than you appear to be eligible for.

When you, as a parent, call your insurance company, it is not unreasonable to ask immediately to speak with a supervisor. You can simply say, "*I mean no disrespect, but my baby is in the neonatal intensive care unit with a fairly complex case and I think it best for all of us if I speak with a supervisor from the outset.*" If you feel that the supervisor with whom you speak is helpful, get her name and her phone number and try to speak directly with her every time. Having to repeat an NICU story over and over is needlessly frustrating. If you are assigned a case manager, that is the only person at the insurance company you are likely to need to speak with.

Generally, when you speak with a representative of the insurance company, document everything. If you've made particular agreements, fax them a letter to that effect and always keep a copy for yourself. I always advise parents that if they mail anything to their insurance company (reports, statements, letters) everything should be sent certified return receipt, *and keep a copy of everything*. Some companies are just so large that things have a way of getting lost and you need to have a way to track your case. Also, clarify *in writing* a specific time frame for your insurance company to respond to your requests. (If, for example, you know by your certified return receipt exactly when your letter was received, you can reasonably request that they respond within 15 business days.) This gives you a specific follow-up date.

It is also very important to know that if you are ever denied a service or benefit, your insurance company is legally obligated to inform you in writing of the denial, and the reasons for the denial.

Finally, there may be options, benefits, and services available to you from the state, county, or even your local school system. The discharge planner or other team members at your hospital may be able to direct you to these resources, but if not, keep looking on your own: talk with other parents, call state agencies such as the Department of Children's Services or the Department of Health and Welfare, and generally leave no stone unturned until you've located every possible resource that may benefit your child.

Insurance companies and hospitals may assign your child a case worker, but you too are your baby's case worker. . . . You are your child's voice. I realize it is a lot of pressure to put on a new parent, especially a new parent whose child needs special medical care, but doing things the right way can literally change your child's life. After all, this is about giving your child the very best possible quality of life.

DR. KLEIN ANSWERS FREQUENTLY ASKED QUESTIONS

"Can we continue kangaroo care at home?"

Kangaroo care can be a very helpful support system for you and your baby. I encourage parents to continue "skin-to-skin" care at home for as long at the baby seems comfortable and responsive. If you and your baby did not try kangaroo care in the neonatal unit of your hospital, you may be pleasantly surprised to see what an asset it can be to helping mother and baby to establish vigorous feeding at the breast. (See chapter 4 for a detailed discussion of kangaroo care.)

"Can we keep the baby in bed with us? How about in the same room?"

Understandably, parents often want their baby as close to them as possible. After all, you have been separated from your child for weeks or maybe even months, and finally you have your baby at home. However, I think the babies and parents sleep a little better with some distance between them. If the mother is right next to her, the baby is more likely to wake up and sense or even smell the mother and become completely wakeful. This is especially true if they are breast-feeding. A baby who is breast-feeding is very alert to the scent of the mother and of breast milk, and the mother who is nursing is likely to have her milk *let down* (milk begins to leak from the nipples at the sound of her baby's whimper or cry) if her baby is right there. Although this may sound just great to the mom who

has waited an eternity to have her child with her, it can soon turn into a sleep-deprived situation for all. You might try a crib on the other side of the room, or bedding the baby in its own nursery if you're comfortable with that. If you're concerned that you won't hear an important cry, try using a nursery monitor turned down low. Infants wake up in the night, just like we all do. A big part of their development is to learn how to get themselves back to sleep.

If you have another young child at home, having the baby in your room can compound that child's already difficult situation. Your attention has already been diverted as you spent hours at the neonatal unit each day, and now the baby comes home and gets the prize spot in your bedroom. Not a good scenario for a positive sibling relationship. Consider instead putting the baby's crib in the same bedroom as your other child. Your three-year-old will sleep right through the infant's changings or feedings and will feel happily invested in their big brother or sister role.

"My baby makes so much noise. Is there something wrong?"

Babies are noisy, plain and simple. I've had parents bring tape recordings of their baby to the office, convinced that there was something wrong. They snort and snuffle and snore and gurgle and chortle and breathe loudly through their noses. And all of that is just fine. But it points again to the wisdom of creating a little distance between parents and baby in the family sleeping arrangements.

"Our twins, born at 32 weeks, are coming home from the neonatal unit. Is it wise to co-bed them?"

Some nurseries co-bed (placing twins in the same crib) in the unit before the twins even go home. If you want to put your twins in the same crib, go ahead and try it. I usually tell families that co-bedding is just fine. But when the babies get so big that they are disturbing each other's sleep, then it is time for separate sleeping arrangements. Although we don't yet have the data that proves it absolutely, some people think there is less apnea and less bradycardia when you co-bed twins in the neonatal unit. They seem to eat more heartily and gain weight faster.

"Are there special steps to take to guard against infection once our baby comes home?"

Infection control, whether in the NICU or in your home, is vitally important to your baby's health. You have waited so long for your baby to be discharged from the hospital, the last thing you want is to have to readmit her with an infection. But it is a fact of life with premature babies that they are vulnerable to infection. The most important thing to remember is that being vigilant about something as simple as hand washing is your first and best defense against infection. As soon as you leave the neonatal unit, you become the

front line in your baby's campaign to remain healthy. The good news here is that really close attention to hygiene can be a pivotal factor in keeping your baby healthy. You need to have antibacterial soap at every sink, and you (as well as anyone else who is touching your baby) need to use it. The house rules are simple:

- No visitors come in if they have a cold.
- Anyone who holds or even sits with the baby needs to wash their hands.
- Siblings, where it is age appropriate, should be encouraged to hold or touch the baby as long as they follow the same rules.
- Any caregiver (mother or father) who has a cold and *must* care for the baby has to wear a mask—the inexpensive type you can buy at the drugstore.

"We've only had my son home for a week, but he seems to be starting to wheeze. My husband has asthma. Could the baby be allergic to something?"

Sometimes a baby who appears to be free of respiratory difficulty in the hospital begins to have breathing problems after going home. In my practice, I do a thorough family history that will alert me to any allergies and/or asthma or chronic bronchitis in members of the family. The tendency toward allergies can run in a family, and the most frequent allergic reaction is to dust. You may delay the onset of dust allergies by keeping the baby's environment as dust-free as possible. A dust-free environment is most important for very premature babies who may have an overt or sub-clinical mild case of chronic lung disease (see chapter 5 for a discussion of chronic lung disease). You may want to purchase an air purifier for the room in which the baby spends the most time and run it 24 hours a day. You can and should talk with your pediatrician or with an allergist who can give you information on creating a dust-free environment before your baby comes home.

Of course, no one should smoke in the home, whether or not the baby is there at the time. In fact, you should avoid having the baby in any environment where people have been smoking, even if it has been "aired out" before the baby arrives. This includes your car, your parents' home, *any place that you take your baby*. I usually suggest to families that if someone is a smoker, they smoke outside and wear a designated jacket to protect the rest of their clothes from smoke, as well as a hat to protect the hair from becoming infused with the smell. After smoking, they must wash their hands and face to try to rid themselves of this particularly noxious odor. I know I am not likely to have a serious impact on anyone's long-term smoking behavior, but parents really must be vigilant about protecting their babies from smoke and its noxious odor.

Chapter Eleven

Follow-Up Care for Your Baby

A Visit to the Doctor

Premature babies, just like their term counterparts, are vulnerable to the colds, flus, and infant and childhood diseases that bring thousands of babies in the United States to the doctor each day. Yet not every visit to the doctor is due to illness. The complete checkup is your pediatrician's opportunity to assess your child's general health on a regular schedule of visits. Every doctor has an individual approach, but the underlying reason for the visit is to enable your doctor to maintain an ongoing picture of your child's health.

DR. KLEIN COMMENTS ON THE PREMATURE BABY'S SCHEDULE OF VISITS, IMMUNIZATIONS, AND THE COMPLETE CHECKUP

After discharge, I often see healthy premature babies in a few days and then every week until they reach their actual due date. Then, as long as they are thriving and growing well, they go onto the same schedule that I use for term babies, but based on a premie's *corrected age,* which is the "age" calculated from their expected date of delivery. I see them at the following corrected ages: 2 weeks, and 1, 2, 3, 4, 5, and 6 months. After that the schedule be-

comes somewhat variable, but I frequently see babies again at 9 and 12 months, based on actual age.

Immunizations

The immunization dose and schedule for a premature baby is the same (with one exception) as for a full-term baby; beginning at 2 months of age these are based on actual age, not age-corrected for prematurity. The exception to the standard immunization schedule is the hepatitis B immunization, which—following the guidelines of the American Academy of Pediatrics—should not be given to premature babies born to hepatitis-B-antigen–negative mothers until 2 months of age or a weight of 2,000 grams, whichever comes first. Premature infants born to hepatitis-B-antigen–positive mothers should be treated the same way as full-term babies and receive HBIG (Hepatitis B Immune Globulin) within 12 hours of birth, as well as simultaneous hepatitis B vaccine in the appropriate dose. Immunization and HBIG for a premature infant whose mother's hepatitis B status is unknown is the same as it would be for a full-term infant. Premature infants born to hepatitis-B-antigen–positive mothers who are under 1,500 grams at birth should receive three additional hepatitis B immunizations, for a total of four doses. (See the immunization schedule in Appendix C.)

The Complete Checkup

A complete checkup for a baby born prematurely is not unlike a term baby's examination. Any differences due to this particular baby's "different beginning" may mean we are following up on a clinical course that may have had more complications than for the term baby. A baby is weighed and measured, and head growth is noted by measuring head circumference. Weight, height, and head circumference are plotted on a *growth chart* for both actual and corrected age. (See Appendix D for an example of a growth chart.) The growth curve offers parents a visual impression of their baby's growth, relative both to the individual infant and to other babies. I show parents that the curves differ for boys and girls, and as time goes by, we get to see various patterns of growth emerge. The plotting of the growth curve is a jumping-off point for discussion of many aspects of a baby's life, including feeding and sleeping habits. It can be very exciting for parents to watch their premie's growth curves begin to "catch up" with the normal curve for term infants. It may be helpful for parents to recognize that while their baby may indeed be catching up, he may still grow along his own curve. We may talk about continued normal head growth for corrected age and how the movement toward the normal curve is such a reassuring sign for a positive developmental outcome.

Usually the measurements for height, weight, and head circumference of a baby will have been completed by my nurse by the time I come in to the examining room, and I will record them on the baby's growth chart. I like to have the opportunity to observe a baby in his parents' arms. I usually ask the mom or dad to sit in a chair while holding their baby. If the mom needs to stand so she can rock her baby, that's fine—we do what is comfortable. Since I like to begin the visit with the baby on his parent's lap, I tell this to my families at their first visit so they become familiar with the routine. As we talk, I put the appropriate notes in the baby's chart. I ask parents if there are any questions or concerns that they want to address, and we may go into detail right then unless their question involves the physical exam. If it doesn't happen to come up in the course of the conversation, I'll always ask about how the baby is feeding and sleeping and about the life of the family in general.

Then we go on to discuss development. We talk about what the baby has done so far and what to expect in the future. I describe my assessment of developmental milestones such as smiling, cooing, rolling over, etc., at appropriate visits. We always talk about the importance of understanding that the age at which milestones are expected should be based on corrected age and not actual age. I evaluate a baby's muscle tone and reflexes and explain that reflexes also appear and disappear based on corrected age, and variations in muscle tone often resolve by 7 to 9 months of age. For most babies born at less than 30 weeks gestation, I also inquire into whether the child is participating in an early intervention program and whether the child has been scheduled to be seen at the NICU developmental follow-up clinic.

I may make suggestions about feeding or sleeping. Although it has been suggested that preterm infants have more nighttime sleeping problems and more episodes of irritability compared to full-term infants, I have not found this to be true. Parents of premies are sometimes surprised to learn that I receive as many, if not more, phone calls about these types of problems from parents of full-term babies as from parents of premature infants. If the baby is on oxygen or if there is an apnea monitor being used, we'll talk about how that is going. It is not unusual for me to ask about what kind of support is available to the family. If I feel there are unexplored options as far as help for tired parents, we may talk about looking into how to work that out.

We discuss what immunizations, if any, are going to be given at the visit, and what the complications might be. I have parents sign forms giving permission for their baby's immunization. If the baby is on medication, we review that and talk about any past medical history that is relevant. If there was some problem or issue discussed at a prior visit, I will bring it up to see what resolution, if any, there has been. Of course, each progressive visit encompasses additional elements of the baby's development.

I talk about safety issues at almost every visit. Sometimes I think I may repeat things too frequently, but I feel it is important to stress everything from car safety to pool safety to baby-proofing the house. I begin to talk about baby-proofing at the 4-month (corrected age) visit, because that is when babies will usually start to reach for things that they invariably put in their mouth. I like to give parents stickers with the number of the local poison control center to place on their telephones. By the 9-month visit, when babies are likely to be crawling around, I am really hoping that all the baby-proofing of the house is complete.

Then I move on to the complete physical examination of the baby: top to bottom, stem to stern. As I describe these visits, remember that with premature babies I am always talking about their corrected age. At 4 or 5 months, and sometimes before that, I begin the exam with the baby on his mother's lap. I like to take a little time to play as we start the physical. When the baby is old enough, I may hand him one or two tongue depressors to hold, and then we'll play with them. Play is instructional for me and tends to be calming for the baby. I begin the exam by listening to the chest, because I want to make sure I get to that, even if the baby becomes restless or upset during the exam. I listen to the lungs to make sure there is no wheezing—no questionable sounds. If the baby has chronic lung disease (CLD), I make sure to count the respiratory rate and enter it in the chart. As these children outgrow their CLD I expect to see a decrease in the respiratory rate over time. I listen to the heart to make certain there are no abnormalities. I then listen to the abdomen and examine it with my hands. While the baby is on the parent's lap, I remove the diaper and examine the baby's genitalia, and also the hips to make sure they are moving correctly. I stretch out both legs to make sure they are of equal length, and put the diaper back on. I ask parents to hug the baby by placing their arms over the baby's arms. While the baby is comfortably restrained, I look at the ears, nose, and throat. I look in the mouth to see if teeth are coming in. Depending on the age, I may hold the baby upright in order to make sure that his legs can support his weight. In an older baby, I may ask to see how he is walking. I will examine the baby's tone (muscle tension) in both the upper and lower extremities. At this point, the typical examination of the baby is pretty much completed.

If this is the first visit after discharge, I will start the breast-fed baby on supplemental vitamins and iron. If the baby is receiving formula with iron, additional supplementation is probably not necessary. I have found that waiting until the first office visit to discuss vitamin and iron supplementation is far more relaxed than adding yet another element to the busy process of discharge. We will discuss any problems that are the result of prematurity, any laboratory tests that need to be performed, and any referrals to specialists when needed. I usually like to measure calcium, phosphorus, and alkaline phosphatase (an enzyme involved in bone formation) levels anywhere from 4 to 8 weeks after discharge from the neonatal unit in babies born at less than 32 weeks gestational age. If these levels are abnormal, the infant may need extra calcium, phosphorus, and vitamin D supplementation. At this point in the office visit I usually leave the exam room and my nurse will follow up with the appropriate immunizations, hemoglobin measurement, or tuberculosis testing as needed.

Sleeping Problems and Irritability

When premature infants reach a postmenstrual age of 36 to 38 weeks, they often seem to become more alert and spend less time sleeping. Parents may begin to complain that their babies are crying more. In this situation, parents of premature babies need precisely the same type of reassurance that might be offered to parents of full-term infants. If after examination your doctor finds the baby to be in generally good health, it is time to begin the process of encouraging your baby to sleep more at night than during the day. In order to encourage nighttime sleeping, try keeping the lights off and using a very dim night-light only when necessary for feeding or changing your baby. When you go in to feed or change your baby during the night, resist the temptation to talk or play. Time-honored methods such as rocking, holding, singing, or giving a bath may do wonders in helping a baby to prepare for sleep. Many of the complications of prematurity have the effect of putting parents on a sort of heightened level of alert. While this is certainly understandable, it may be wise to give the baby his own room as soon as you are comfortable with that idea or even willing to consider the possibility. Separate rooms are often the start of a better night's sleep for all. Consider using a one-way audio monitor to decrease your fears about not hearing your baby. Putting the effort into establishing nighttime sleeping is great for your baby and no small bonus to sleep-deprived parents.

Home Safe Home: Baby-Proofing

You may have taken some initial safety steps (such as posting emergency numbers near the phones) as you planned for discharge before bringing your baby home. But as your baby has grown, so have the needs for making the home environment safe. The weeks will race by and before you know it, you will have a baby who is exploring his crib and looking a lot like he will soon be able to circumnavigate the whole house. If you haven't done so yet, now is the time to take additional baby-proofing steps in your house or apartment:

- Have the telephone numbers of your pediatric office, poison control, the fire department, and of course 911 posted at every telephone.
- Be sure that your baby's bed is not next to any curtain cords or electrical wires that he or she might grasp or become tangled in.
- As your baby grows more independent, consider any special arrangements that you may want to make regarding your pets.
- Check with the local nursery to be sure that none of your houseplants are potentially dangerous to your baby.

It may seem a little early to be worrying about these next steps, but if you can manage to get them done before your baby is mobile, you'll be glad you did:

- It is not too early to count the number of electrical outlets in your home and purchase safety caps to cover them from exploring baby hands.
- Even if you don't yet have them installed, start thinking about safety latches for cabinets and safety gates at the tops of stairs and between rooms you won't want an adventurous baby to enter.
- Store all poisons, medications, or any dangerous or toxic substances in high, locked, inaccessible places.

Early Intervention/Infant Stimulation Programs

Many premature infants qualify for and probably benefit from early intervention (sometimes referred to as infant stimulation) programs. Whenever possible, it is important to arrange for these programs prior to discharge from the hospital so that the lag time between discharge and the onset of services is minimal. Your doctor may be likely to recommend an infant stimulation program if your baby is significantly premature—usually under 30 weeks. These programs are offered by occupational or physical therapists, or other health-care professionals who specialize in the developmental needs of premature babies. It can be very rewarding for parents to work with a specialist who is trained to teach gentle exercises and positioning and other ways to interact that will help to advance the physical development of young, premature babies.

Weight Gain

An optimal rate of weight gain is 20 to 30 grams per day, as weight and height measurements plotted for corrected age gradually approach the normal curve during the first 6 months (corrected age). If your baby's weight is below the growth curve, your doctor may recommend a 24-calorie formula, such as those described in chapter 8. Many healthy preterm infants are discharged from the hospital on high-calorie formulas. These formulas may be continued until an infant's weight for corrected age reaches the 25th to 50th percentile, or her measurements have entered the normal area of the growth curve and are tracking along their own curve. If your doctor has any concern about your baby's growth rate, she may suggest that you keep a record of the baby's feeding so that fluids and calories can be calculated during a subsequent office visit. In some cases, as mentioned earlier, extra calcium and phosphorus should be given either by special premature infant formulas (which already contain extra calcium and phosphorus) or by direct administration of calcium and phosphorus preparations by mouth. Your doctor may recommend that you follow the feeding schedule that was used in the hospital during the first few days of transition from hospital to home. After your baby has become accustomed to the new environment, more liberal feeding may be successful. It can be helpful in establishing a pattern of nighttime sleep to try feeding every 2 to 4 hours during the daytime (when it is light outside) and only when your baby awakens at night. Most premature babies are ready to start on solid foods at 4 to 5 months (corrected age).

Feeding Strategies

As described earlier, a healthy premature baby develops the ability to suck, swallow, and breathe in a coordinated fashion between 34 and 36 weeks gestational age. Until this age, enteral feeding is accomplished by gavage. Because some infants can coordinate feeding by mouth when breast-feeding at an earlier post-conceptual age, breast-feeding can first be attempted between 32 and 33 weeks. It is important to not become discouraged if initial attempts at breast-feeding are unsuccessful. The nurses at the hospital may have been able to offer you useful advice as you pump your breasts and then attempt to breast-feed. Many mothers of premies who were still struggling to establish breast-feeding at the time of their baby's discharge have had excellent results by working with lactation counselors. (See chapter 4 for an additional discussion of pumping and breast-feeding.) It is possible to offer pumped breast milk by bottle while aiming toward an initial goal of nursing your baby once a day. Because most premature infants have a relatively high arched palate, a long, narrow nipple often works best. Short nipples do not reach far enough into the mouth to touch the roof of the mouth and stimulate sucking. Again, try to maintain a confident but patient attitude, knowing that your baby is receiving the necessary amount of nutrition, even if it is not yet breast-feeding. Try nursing again in 3 to 4 days. If your baby successfully takes one full feed by breast, try slowly increasing the number of breast-feeds until your baby is nursing at every feed. This can often be accomplished over 3 to 5 days, but don't worry if it takes a longer time. Bottle feeding with pumped breast milk will continue to supply the nutrition your baby needs for growth. Any mother attempting to breast-feed a premature infant may need to continue to pump her breasts four to five times a day, because the premie often does not nurse vigorously enough to maintain her milk supply until a post-conceptual age of approximately 38 weeks. A breast pump with a "double set-up" that allows her to pump both breasts at the same time often works best.

One possible transitional strategy that has worked for many families is to have the mother nurse every other feed, while the father or other caregiver gives the baby either breast milk or 24-calorie formula by mouth during the alternate feedings. Eventually the infant may be totally breast-fed as long as your pediatrician is convinced that adequate growth is being maintained. By this time a full feed should take from 30 to 45 minutes, allowing for ample cuddling time between mom or dad and their baby.

ONE DETERMINED MOM AND ONE BREAST-FED BABY

Louisa was set on breast-feeding her baby, and she shared her success story with us:

I really wanted to breast-feed my son. He was born at 34 weeks and had a hard time latching on. I was ready to give up, and I asked at the hospital if they knew a lactation counselor who might be able to help me. They told me about a woman who they said was really good. I went to see her and she said, "It's going to take a couple of months, but you'll be able to do it eventually." I used a supplemental nursing system where the baby gets additional milk from a tube next to the nipple while he sucks. I did it all. . . and finally 3 months later, I was breast-feeding! It was something I really wanted to do, though I had no idea it would be such a hassle. But it was well worth it. At one point my husband was saying, "Why are you doing this to yourself? Let him have a bottle." But the woman who got me through this was a godsend to me. She had a breast-feeding clinic on Tuesdays and Thursdays; I would go there religiously and meet other people and hear about the problems they were having. I'd realize I was not the only one. People might break down crying sometimes. . . But it was a lot easier for everyone there, knowing we were all going through it.

Infection Control After Leaving the Hospital

We've mentioned this before, but it merits repeating: Hand washing before touching or holding the baby is your very best practical safeguard against the spread of infection. This means Mother and Father and Grandma, and siblings and any other friends or caregivers. Certainly, no one who is obviously ill should hold or go near your young baby. Any necessary caregiver, such as a parent or home health-care worker, who has even the hint of a cold or any other illness should wear a face mask in addition to rigorous hand washing with antibacterial soap. You can buy several inexpensive face masks at any drugstore and keep them on hand. As much as you may want to celebrate being home with your beautiful new baby, it is probably wise to limit the number of visitors to your home. You can even tell friends and family that it is "doctor's orders" that you have no more than four visitors at any time, so as to be certain you are giving your baby an opportunity to avoid any casual contact with someone with the sniffles who may want to "drop by."

Support Groups

After leaving the hospital, it is not unusual for parents to experience an unanticipated sense of isolation. The team that had assembled for the days, weeks, or even months of your baby's hospitalization is no longer at your constant disposal: your almost reflexive reaction to ask a question of a nurse or doctor, or solicit an opinion from another parent, comes to a sudden end. Couples turn to each other and may be confused about feeling let down. The day they have awaited may not surge along with the confidence and optimism they expected would characterize the time of their baby's discharge. Fortunately, the range and scope of support for families with premature babies is quite extraordinary. The resource guide in Appendix E is evidence of the number of dedicated and valuable support groups for families with almost any issue pertaining to their premature baby. A support group, or sometimes participation in several support groups over time, can go a long way in dispelling the sense of isolation or powerlessness that many parents experience. If you do experience difficulty in adjusting to being at home with your baby; if your baby has a complication of prematurity that has longer-term implications in growth or development; or even if you'd simply like the opportunity to speak with parents whose experiences raising their babies is likely to mirror your own, there is support out there for you. Many parents who have said they never would have described themselves as "joiners" were nevertheless delighted to have found a support group that served their needs. More than one parent who joined a support group in search of help has turned around a year later to be the one to offer the voice of experience in the unending cycle of support for families with premature babies.

Taking the Pulse of the Family

If you have children at home, the premature birth of your baby may not have been the experience you had prepared them to expect. Instead of meeting the chubby bundle in a parent's arms just in time for the first big snowfall, a sibling may have had to trick-or-treat with a friend's parents because Mommy and Daddy were at the hospital with the new baby who came too soon. And to further confuse things for a preschooler, Mother may have been on bed rest in the hospital for many weeks, seeing her four-year-old for only a scheduled play date each afternoon. Hopefully, an age-appropriate explanation provided comfort and reassurance that Mom would be fine, but it still was not like having Mommy home to tuck a young child into bed each night.

Depending on your child's age, you may have made an initial explanation about why the new baby had to stay in the hospital, or why he was so tiny compared to a classmate's new baby brother. Or, if your daughter is a young teen, she may have had to jump into family life in ways not yet experienced—suddenly called upon to learn how to use the washing machine and make her own lunch. Maybe she had to go to a friend's house every day after school because Mom was at the hospital with the baby and Dad was going there right after work. Regardless of your child's age, he or she will need to be reassured in age-appropriate terms that you are still there—caring about the stuffed animal that is missing; telling the story at bedtime; or sympathizing about the algebra teacher *"who is sooo unfair!"* or the best friend who ate lunch with someone else.

There is no doubt that the rigors of caring for a premature baby can be enormously stressful on family life. Back in the days just after your baby was born, you may have encouraged your children to visit the hospital after preparing them for the sight of their new baby brother or sister. Perhaps it was helpful to encourage siblings to draw a picture for the new baby, make a tape of favorite music, or record their own voices reading a cherished story for the newest member of the family. Slowly you may have worked to integrate your children into the life of your baby, just as you encouraged your children to accept this new tiny brother or sister into their busy lives.

When the time comes to bring the baby home, it is very important to find ways to retain as much "normal family life" as is possible. Look for age-appropriate ways to include your children in the life of your new baby: very young children might enjoy a colorful chart mounted on the refrigerator door that rewards them with a sticker every time they remember to wash their hands before coming to cuddle the baby. A teenager might enjoy being asked to search the Internet for information about caring for premature babies. A mother with a 13-year-old son said she was amazed and deeply touched when he chose "My Premature Baby Sister" as the topic for his semester's science report, even before her baby girl (born at 30 weeks) was released from the hospital.

It may be difficult for parents of a baby who may be at home after an extended hospital stay to recall the time before their baby's birth when they ran out with their five-year-old for a picnic in the park on a moment's notice—or the mother who took an hour every afternoon to take turns reading aloud with her third-grader. Yet some form of balance is the magic carpet that will carry your family through this trying and complicated time. Constancy is vitally important to your other children—whether it is a promise to play chess with your 12-year-old every Sunday morning, or the knowledge that Mom or Dad will read a story every night before bed for a preschooler. This is not the time to set unattainable goals, such as a big family vacation to a far-off island; this is the time to settle in and establish your own individualized version of family-centered care. Don't expect your children to be as immediately invested in their new sibling as you are. Love and caring will blossom for them at its own stately pace. Instead, give your children the gift of having reasonable expectations of them, and making sure that they continue to have designated opportunities to have your undivided attention and the constantly reassuring presence of your love.

Chapter Twelve

Supporting Your Baby with Chronic Lung Disease at Home

Discharge Planning

A baby with respiratory problems may remain hospitalized for a prolonged period of time, and it may be difficult to predict the timing of discharge. For a baby with CLD to be considered for discharge, she must have stable oxygen requirements, be receiving complete enteral nutrition either by mouth or gavage, and be gaining weight (at least 20 to 30 grams per day for 3 to 5 days). Many babies who require prolonged oxygen therapy will be sent home with an apnea monitor, not because of apnea risk, but so that in the event their oxygen supply is interrupted (resulting in bradycardia or apnea), the alarm will sound to alert parents.

While the personnel may vary depending on what hospital your baby is in, discharge planning can be greatly facilitated by having a meeting that is attended by the following members of your team: primary nurse, neonatologist, primary care physician, case manager, and the discharge planner from the hospital. Such meetings usually occur on a regular basis to provide ongoing discharge planning for all babies. If home nursing is anticipated, then a representative from the home health-care agency should also be included. Hopefully this team will also be working with you to evaluate your readiness to care for your baby at home, and as discharge draws near, you may participate in subsequent meetings.

One of the most important issues to examine will be the level of care needed to successfully care for your child at home. The potential need for additional caregivers depends on many factors which include:

- the level and intensity of care needed by your baby;
- the number of caregivers living in your home;
- your employment status (this will have an impact on your availability);
- your willingness and ability to provide the care that is needed.

In general, an infant who is stable; is on oxygen by nasal cannula; tolerates feeding by mouth; receives oral diuretic therapy twice a day, every other day; and is getting inhalation treatments with a handheld nebulizer every 6 hours can be cared for in the home by a mother and father (two adult caregivers) without home nursing—assuming both caregivers don't work at the same time. If possible, you may be asked to identify additional caregivers, such as other members of the family or baby-sitters, who can also be trained to care for your baby. Skilled nurse assessment visits may also be needed to provide continued in-home assessment, answer any questions, assure the quality of in-home care, and provide you with some relief.

If inhalation treatments are required more frequently than every 4 to 6 hours, and/or additional medications and/or procedures are needed, then home shift nursing may be warranted. Occasionally, 24-hour nursing may be required in the beginning to facilitate a particularly complex discharge, though this can usually be decreased after several days to one 8- or 12-hour shift per day, usually to provide care at night. Further decreases in nursing care will be possible as the infant's condition improves. Although many families and physicians initially think that home nursing sounds like a good idea, it can be very difficult to have an additional person in the house. Some families actually request that the home nursing time be cut down or eliminated completely. As we have discussed many times before, one of the basic tenets of family-centered care is to encourage a family to be justifiably confident about their skills in providing for their baby. The continuous availability of nursing care in the home has the potential to interfere with a competent family's ability to take over complete care of their baby. Ongoing communication with the primary care physician will be very helpful in providing the balance of support and independence for these families.

Most babies with CLD will need to come home with DME and supplies. It is best if these needs (including oxygen) are seen to by one supplier who is also familiar with your baby's particular requirements:

- *Oxygen* can be supplied either in tanks as liquid oxygen or by an oxygen concentrator with small tanks available for travel. The equipment provider should assess the physical environment and take into consideration the particular individual needs of the family and patient to decide what type of setup is best.
- *An event-recording apnea and bradycardia monitor* should be used for all infants sent home on oxygen. Alarm settings should be ordered to be set as described previously. As stated earlier, this provides a safety net in case there is a malfunction in the oxygen delivery system when the infant is not being observed.
- *An intermittent pulse oximeter* (a device that makes individual measurements of oxygen saturation) is also helpful to have at home for the caregiver to use in case there is some question about the baby's respiratory status.
- *A handheld nebulizer* will be needed for infants who are on bronchodilator treatments.
- *Tubing, syringes, and other consumable supplies.* For those infants receiving gavage feeding, all the necessary syringes and tubing will be required. If the baby is on overnight continuous feeds, then a continuous infusion pump will be needed.

A home assessment may be a part of your family evaluation prior to your baby's discharge. The physical layout of your home environment should be evaluated by your DME supplier for space and electrical availability. Try to arrange this in the week or two before your baby comes home. You should make every effort to produce a dust-free environment for your baby; this includes an air purifier. Your primary care physician, the manufacturers of the air purifier, and the National Lung Association are all possible sources for pamphlets and handouts on providing a dust-free environment.

Your Baby at Home on Oxygen Therapy

Clearly a significant part of the discharge procedure for you and your baby is your familiarity with any equipment and procedures that are necessary to your baby's well-being in the home environment. Home oxygen therapy for babies with CLD (chronic lung disease) has the very substantial benefit of enabling parents to have their baby at home with them while they continue a course of continuous oxygen therapy.

Education of parents and other caregivers of babies on home oxygen therapy is key to its success. Hopefully any parent with a baby on home oxygen therapy will feel confident about the following vital areas of care:

Baby at home with oxygen tank and nasal cannula.

- Are you able to describe those physical characteristics of your baby that could help a medical professional or paramedic to assist you over the telephone if needed?
- Do you understand the diagnosis of CLD (chronic lung disease) and acknowledge the need for oxygen for your baby's growth and development?
- Are you able to identify an increased need for oxygen?

- Can you clearly identify problems with your baby that indicate a need to contact your doctor or to call 911?
- Do you understand the oxygen delivery system, and do you know the safe procedure for using it?
- Can you demonstrate infant CPR?
- Have you thought about your family's needs, and do you have the resources to meet those needs during the weeks or months that you are using oxygen therapy?
- What medications does your baby need; what is the purpose of each medication, and do you know how to deliver it?

Parents who still have a baby in the NICU may find it helpful to share these questions with the nursing and discharge staff in order to identify any area in which they would like to receive additional education and support. If you already are lucky enough to have your baby at home, consider this a sort of refresher curriculum and ask your pediatrician or home health-care company for any specific information that will fill out your growing expertise at caring for your baby.

In addition to the criteria above, parents who have "been there, done that" can be an invaluable resource in helping you and your baby through this important time. You may find some of the following tips very useful:

- Make sure that you (and everyone who will be caring for your baby alone) has received adequate instruction in infant CPR.
- Call your local fire department (the paramedic squad) to make sure that they have equipment, such as an infant-size bag and mask, that might be needed for a premie in an emergency. If you are in a rural area, make sure they know you are at home with a premie and that they know how to get to your house.
- It is important to make every effort to have all oxygen supplies (tanks, tubes, monitors, etc.) in place before your baby comes home. This includes portable oxygen that you will use in the car. *Try several practice runs on your own.*
- Always keep a full complement of extra supplies (tubing, nasal cannula) in the house and car.

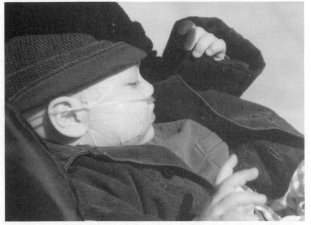

Restore used to secure a nasal cannula.

- Restore is an excellent product for keeping a nasal cannula in place, especially for babies who will need the cannula for an extended period of time. Restore is a paraffinlike substance that comes in paper-thin sheets, protects an infant's tender skin from being damaged by tape, and can easily be cut into any shape you need. You can cut the Restore and place it on your baby's cheeks so that it follows the outline of the cannula's edge. It is very soft and molds to the shape of the face. The cannula is placed over the Restore, and silk tape can then be used to secure the cannula to the Restore. One parent who discovered the product only after her baby had suffered for months with bleeding cheeks and very tender skin called it "a lifesaver." Call a medical supply store or pharmacy to inquire about this product.

- You may find it most convenient to use one very long (50-foot) tube attached to the main oxygen tank in your home. If you prefer this to shuttling back and forth between tanks, make certain that the tubing is always unkinked and is not blocked by a closed door or any other obstruction.

- In order to avoid worrying about the tubing becoming wrapped around your baby's neck (particularly once the baby starts rolling over), run the tube underneath a one-piece sleeper, and out one of the sleeper legs.

Out and About with Your Baby on Oxygen

As is usually the case with family-centered care, it is in your baby's best interest to understand and comply with those elements of care that are really up to you to control. If your baby has been quite ill, your doctor may recommend that you make a slow entry into the world beyond your home. Under ideal circumstances, you should be introduced to the possibility of home oxygen therapy at least 2 to 3 weeks prior to discharge. This is the opportune time to talk about your expectations for your baby's improved health. Your doctor may want to speak frankly with you about the chronic nature of your baby's respiratory problems. It may be very helpful to know that while there is indeed cause for celebration when your baby is finally discharged from the hospital, you may be fantasizing about a rate of recovery that is not realistic. Many families, eager to get their babies home, become convinced that once they do get their child home, she will get better and be off oxygen in a matter of a few short weeks. Although you may be correct in believing that having your baby at home will improve her quality of life, it is important to realize that you may be dealing with the outward signs of respiratory difficulties (oxygen, the nasal cannula, apnea monitors) for quite some time. Parents often have more of a problem with this obvious visible sign of illness then with many other aspects of home care. Many families whose babies are recovering from serious respiratory complications will recognize themselves in the following words:

Our daughter Eva was born at 29 weeks gestation and came home from the hospital with an apnea monitor and oxygen when she was 9½ weeks old. To tell you the truth, the way we handled going out with her was—we didn't go out. Not because of what people might say about the cannula or her being small, but because she had been so ill and I was determined that she not be exposed to a lot of people and potential infection. It was the middle of RSV (respiratory syncytial virus) season and I wasn't taking any chances. When we did go out, it was for a Sunday drive and dinner. We chose restaurants very carefully and even would ask them to open an otherwise empty section for us. People were so accommodating. They were great. We'd just explain right out that our daughter had

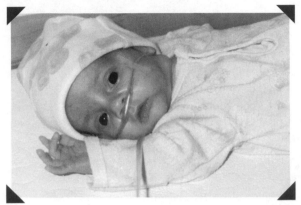

been very ill and we were trying to take every precaution. . . it just wasn't wise to expose her to a lot of people. I found that when I did talk to people, I had an almost compulsive need to tell them everything that had happened to her. . . if they said she was tiny, I wanted them to know what an incredible baby she is, and look how great she looks! I would almost give her entire discharge summary any time anyone said a word to me. That felt much better to me than giving her corrected age. That felt like lying. . . and I am so proud of what she has accomplished.

—DAVID AND TRACY (PARENTS OF TWO DAUGHTERS EDEN AND EVA, BOTH PREMATURE, WHO WERE BORN 11 MONTHS APART)

Follow-Up Care

A recovering baby with CLD just discharged from the hospital should be seen by her physician within 2 to 5 days after discharge in order to:

- discuss all your immediate concerns
- review any records of home nursing personnel that may exist
- begin to assess outpatient growth
- assess your baby's general well-being
- discuss all current treatment issues
- begin to receive general guidance about well care for your baby

DR. KLEIN COMMENTS ON THE FIRST VISIT TO THE DOCTOR'S OFFICE AFTER DISCHARGE FOR BABIES WITH CLD

I often ask parents to bring all their infant's medications with them to the first visit. I can then make sure they have the "right stuff," that the directions on the bottles are correct, and they understand how and when they are to be given.

Subsequent routine visits may be scheduled weekly until a post-conceptual age of 40 weeks. After this initial period of weekly visits, if your baby is growing well, routine visits may then be scheduled every 2 weeks. Less frequent visits, such as every 3 to 4 weeks, may be sufficient after the first 3 or 4 months after discharge, as long as your baby's condition is stable and she is growing well. Your baby may need to be seen more frequently if there are changes being made in her medication or any other facet of her therapy.

You will be introduced to the standard growth curves for full-term infants as you take your baby to see the pediatrician. Because of their tremendous significance to your baby's medical plan, weight and length and head circumference should be carefully measured at each visit, and plotted for both the chronological and the *corrected* age (the age calculated from the expected or term date of delivery). You can expect to discuss your baby's recovery with your doctor, who will want to know if you are complying with whatever therapies have been established for your baby. Honest discussion, which includes your happy feelings about good progress and your worries about any lack of progress, is an important tool in managing your baby's recovery.

Feeding at Home

The feeding strategies mentioned in chapter 8 may be followed once you have your baby at home. Initially the optimal rate of weight gain is expected to be 20 to 30 grams per day, with your baby's weight and height measurements plotted for corrected age gradually approaching the normal curve. High-calorie solids such as avocado, rice cereal, and cooked egg yolks may be introduced at a corrected age of 4 to 6 months. High-calorie diets are not usually discontinued until oxygen is stopped. If a gastrostomy tube was placed and gavage feedings were required prior to discharge, then they are usually also continued at home until oxygen therapy is no longer needed. (See chapter 8 for a more detailed discussion of follow-up care for babies with gastrointestinal problems.)

Weaning Your Baby from Respiratory Therapies

While on diuretic therapy, your baby will probably have her electrolytes monitored every 4 to 6 weeks, and potassium and/or sodium supplements should be supplied as your doctor prescribes. Many babies are likely to be weaned from diuretic therapy before oxygen is discontinued. (See chapter 5 for a detailed discussion of diuretics.) If on exam your baby's lungs are clear without wheezing, your doctor may stop diuretics before criteria are reached for stopping oxygen.

As your baby grows heartier, you may find that you are very eager to discontinue oxygen. However, your doctor will probably not withdraw oxygen until it is clear that your baby has demonstrated sufficient growth and lung repair to survive with minimal respiratory symptoms and continued growth once oxygen has been removed. Increases in weight are very encouraging, and your doctor will monitor weight as a measure of adequate nutrition. *However, lung growth correlates better with increases in body length, so it is your baby's length that your doctor is likely to follow to assess the adequacy of growth.*

Once a baby's weight and length reach the 25th to 50th percentile for corrected age, or both of these measurements have entered the normal area of the curve for corrected age and are tracking along their own curve predicted by parental height, your pediatrician may begin to consider stopping home oxygen therapy.

DR. KLEIN COMMENTS ON HIS CRITERIA FOR STOPPING OXYGEN THERAPY

My criteria for stopping oxygen are similar to those mentioned previously for determining how much oxygen is needed. If the oxygen saturation is over 95%, more than 95% of the time while in room air, and lower than 90% saturation less than 1% of the time, then oxygen can be discontinued during the day. For infants who meet the above criteria for oxygen saturation in room air, oxygen therapy is continued at night for another 4 weeks. If the infant's clinical status and growth rate remain stable, oxygen is then completely discontinued. Clinical symptoms, such as tachypnea, retractions, and poor air entry should also be taken into consideration. I prefer to make these measurements in the home with a four-channel instrument that records respiration (measuring both chest wall movement and air flow), heart rate, and oxygen saturation. Infants are monitored over an 8- to 12-hour period at rest, while feeding and during sleep. This type of evaluation is often referred to as a "state change study" and can be requested by your baby's doctor through a home health-care company that specializes in pediatrics. These studies often need to be done late at night so that sleep can be observed.

The decision to stop bronchodilator therapy, if required, is usually made after the decision to stop oxygen. Treatments can be decreased from every 6 hours to every 12, and then completely discontinued if tachypnea, coughing, and/or wheezing does not reoccur.

If Your Baby Gets Sick

When an illness such as respiratory syncytial virus (RSV) occurs, it is likely to bring on an increase in pulmonary symptoms and respiratory decompensation. In that case all of the previously mentioned modes of therapy, including corticosteroids, may need to be aggressively restarted and/or increased. Respiratory syncytial virus is responsible for many infections to which premature babies may be particularly vulnerable. It can be spread by the airborne spray of a cough or sneeze, or by hand-to-hand contact with anyone or anything that harbors the virus. If the virus comes in contact with the mucous membranes of the nose or eyes, the infection can take hold. Although RSV can occur at any time, it tends to be particularly common during the winter months. In otherwise healthy adults or older children, RSV can manifest as a cold with stuffiness, nasal discharge, a cough, or other coldlike symptoms. But in a young premature baby, particularly one with BPD, respiratory syncytial virus can cause serious breathing problems and result in rehospitalization. If your pediatrician feels your baby is at risk for serious problems from RSV, he may recommend a medication called Respigam, to be given throughout the RSV season in the form of monthly intravenous infusions. Influenza immunizations are also indicated for all family members, caregivers, and babies with chronic lung disease who are over 6 months of age.

Families with a recovering baby at home must be particularly careful about allowing exposure to anyone who may be ill. It is wise not to allow more than four additional people in your home at any one time during the winter months when the incidence of all respiratory illnesses is at its peak. *All caregivers must be careful to meticulously wash their hands at all times before handling the infant and to wear a mask at the first sign of an upper respiratory infection (URI). Be particularly careful not to touch the outside of the front of the mask, where organisms are concentrated.* Common sense should be coupled with extra vigilance about exposing your baby to smog, dust, illness, or cigarette smoke. To be the parent of a baby who is recovering from respiratory problems is an enormous responsibility and an inspiring experience.

Chapter Thirteen

Caring for the Premature Baby Born Between 34 and 36 Weeks Gestation

The Baby Who Is Not Quite Term

When we talk about babies who are born prematurely, we are discussing those born anywhere from the threshold of viability at 23 to 24 weeks postmenstrual age (PMA), to those who are at 36 completed weeks PMA, and the weeks in-between. (For purposes of this chapter, when we use 36 *weeks* to describe an infant's gestational age, we always mean 36 *completed* weeks.) Infants born between 34 and 36 weeks PMA are unlikely to have the significant problems that affect infants born earlier. These 34- to 36-weekers may spend their total hospital stay in the "well baby" nursery, never needing to go into the neonatal unit. Some are ready to go home just a day or two after delivery, while others may have problems that delay their discharge home for a week or two, but are not so serious as to require a transfer to the NICU. Occasionally an infant experiences more severe problems, such as respiratory distress or sepsis (blood infection), that delay discharge for several days or weeks and require transfer to the NICU.

It is fair to describe the period from 34 to 36 weeks as a sort of gray area as far as discussions of prematurity are concerned. Although these babies are very unlikely to have the health problems of much younger babies, there are still significant conditions that can delay their discharge. Let's look at some of the health issues that you may need to understand.

Regulating Body Temperature

Most healthy premature babies born between 34 and 36 weeks don't seem to have much of a problem maintaining body temperature. All babies born in the hospital, whether full-term or premature, are initially placed on a warming bed while they transition from the warm intrauterine environment to the relatively cold room-temperature climate. Depending on their size, most infants are then placed in an open crib. There are some babies born at this gestational age who will need to be placed in a temperature-controlled environment in an incubator. The incubator is an enclosed, temperature-controlled, infant-size bed. Today's incubators are not as frightening to look at as those we may recall from old movies. An incubator (or isolette) in the modern neonatal unit is typically made of Plexiglas to allow your baby to see out, and you and the medical staff to see in. Porthole openings allow for gentle hands to reach in to touch and care for your baby.

A baby born between 34 and 36 weeks may need to be in the incubator from several hours to several days. At this age, infants are often taken out of the incubators for brief periods of time in order to be fed (either by breast or bottle) and held by their parents.

When Your Baby Has Jaundice

Infants born prematurely (as well as those born at term) often have a high bilirubin count and the resultant yellowish discoloration of the skin that we call *jaundice*. Jaundice is the result of the liver's inability to metabolize the yellow-colored bilirubin that is produced as the baby's red blood cells break down. The baby's liver processes the bilirubin, which is then passed out through the intestines as waste. As the production of bilirubin exceeds the liver's ability to process it, the characteristic yellow color appears first in the eyes and face, and then moves down to the trunk and legs. It may be quite obvious to you, or it may be more discreet and be brought to your attention by a doctor or nurse. Although jaundice can also occur in term babies, the less mature systems of premature babies leave them more vulnerable.

In a baby born between 34 and 36 weeks, peak levels of bilirubin in the blood occur from 5 to 7 days after birth. Bilirubin levels are measured by milligrams per deciliter (mg/dL) of blood. For a baby born between 34 and 36 weeks, over 2,000 grams in birth weight, and healthy, phototherapy (special lights that help your baby's body to clear the bilirubin) may be introduced when levels reach 15 mg/dL. The bilirubin levels for a healthy term baby can be higher, depending on age, before phototherapy is introduced, but phototherapy is a sort of preemptive strike against the likelihood of rising bilirubin levels in the premature baby. Your physician may have started phototherapy as soon as the telltale yellow color spread to your baby's belly. If your baby was discharged within a few days, your pediatrician may be monitoring your baby's bilirubin count as an outpatient, and also relying on you to be observant of your baby's skin color. Phototherapy is usually very effective in combating jaundice, and can be introduced in several ways:

- In the hospital, the baby may be placed under a bank of fluorescent lights designed for this purpose. These lights can also be rented for home use from a company specializing in durable medical equipment (DME).
- The use of fluorescent lights may be combined with placing the baby on a *fiberoptic blanket* so that he is exposed to light from both sides. The fiberoptic blankets can also be used separately. If your baby is otherwise ready for discharge, you may be instructed in the use of these blankets (which can be supplied by the hospital or a medical equipment company) for home care. The fiberoptic blankets are very effective and have the additional advantage of allowing you to hold, feed, and cuddle your baby during phototherapy.

Phototherapy at Home

If your infant is feeding well, is active, and doesn't show any indications of other medical problems, home phototherapy is likely to be an appropriate choice. A representative from your home health-care provider should do the following:

- assess the degree of clinical jaundice;
- draw blood for bilirubin determinations;
- weigh your baby;
- set up and explain all aspects of the phototherapy system that your doctor has recommended for your use;
- arrange follow-up clinical assessments and blood drawing as directed by your pediatrician.

The clinical follow-up is important because very high levels of bilirubin can cause brain damage. If bilirubin levels are not decreasing

DR. KLEIN COMMENTS ON HOME PHOTOTHERAPY FOR PREMATURE INFANTS

Preterm infants less than 37 weeks gestation are more likely to have elevated bilirubin values when compared to term infants. They still may be managed at home if otherwise ready to be discharged from the hospital. It is important for parents to note that bilirubin levels in preterm infants peak later, at 5 to 7 days of life, compared to 3 to 5 days in full-term infants. In healthy preterm babies (34 to 36 weeks) with jaundice after the first 24 hours of life, phototherapy should be started when the total bilirubin level reaches 15 mg/dL. Phototherapy can be provided at home as long as the premature infant is feeding heartily, is active, and appears well, and the total serum bilirubin level is less than 18 to 20 mg/dL. Assessment by a home health-care nurse is critical for an outpatient approach to work, although some physicians may want to assess the infant in their office initially. The home health-care nurse must be available for follow-up clinical assessments and blood drawing as determined to be necessary by the responsible physician, based on changes in bilirubin levels. It is important for parents to know that once phototherapy is started, skin color is not a usable indicator of serum bilirubin levels. In healthy preterms over 5 to 6 days of age, phototherapy may be stopped when the TSB (total serum bilirubin) reaches 12 mg/dL or less. In a preterm infant less than 5 days old, phototherapy may be stopped cautiously at a TSB of 10 mg/dL, remembering that close follow-up is needed until after the predicted peaking of bilirubin at 5 to 7 days of life. If levels do not respond by stabilizing (±1 mg/dL) or declining, then hospitalization, intensive phototherapy, and possibly exchange transfusion is warranted.

in response to home phototherapy, your baby may need to be readmitted to the hospital for intensive phototherapy. If bilirubin levels do not respond to this treatment, then an exchange transfusion may need to be performed. In this procedure, the baby's blood and circulating bilirubin are withdrawn slowly and exchanged for donated whole blood with low bilirubin levels. This is an effective and rapid way to lower bilirubin levels.

Hypoglycemia (Low Blood Sugar)

In utero, prior to delivery, blood sugar (glucose) is transferred via the placenta from the mother's blood supply to the baby in order to provide a ready source of energy to the unborn infant. At birth, this supply stops abruptly when the umbilical cord is cut. This results in a temporary decrease in blood sugar, followed by a rise after the baby's own blood-sugar-regulating system takes over. Occasionally, especially in infants born between 34 and 36 weeks who are not routinely supplied with intravenous sugar immediately after delivery, the regulating system does not work adequately to keep the blood sugar in the normal range. If the blood sugar level stays too low for a long time, brain damage may result. Because of this, blood sugars in most premature infants are often measured after birth. If a single blood sugar level is below normal (40 mg/dL), as measured with a *glucose reagent strip* (a way of measuring glucose), the baby may be fed immediately by breast, or by tube or mouth with sugar water or formula. Usually when the blood sugar is measured again, it has risen into the normal range (>40 mg/dL). If the blood sugar doesn't rise, an IV may be started and the baby will be given IV sugar in order to maintain a normal blood sugar level. The intravenous sugar will be continued as the baby starts to feed. Gradually the volume of IV fluid will be reduced in such a way as to make sure the blood sugar level stays in the normal range. This may delay discharge, because sometimes it takes several days for the baby's own blood-sugar-regulating system to take over.

Feeding Your Growing Baby

We see a broad range of feeding ability among babies born between 34 and 36 weeks. Although it is possible for a baby born at 35 weeks to appear and behave much like a term baby, it is just as likely that a baby born at this gestation will share characteristics of the less mature infant. The final weeks of fetal development do not follow a terribly precise course. We know that a healthy premature infant develops the ability to suck, swallow, and breathe in a coordinated fashion between 34 and 36 weeks postmenstrual age. With all the extraordinary advances made in medicine, we still cannot predict whether your baby born at this age will definitely have accomplished this mission while in the intrauterine environment, or if he may need a little "help from his friends" to turn into a vigorous feeder.

It's safe to say that most babies born at this time will be ready to nurse at the breast or take formula from a bottle immediately after delivery, but there are some infants who will need assistance in the form of a tube that goes into their mouth or nose and down into the stomach. Tube (gavage) feeding is not easy for parents to see in the early days of their baby's life, but it is an invaluable method for providing nourishment to the baby. Talk with your doctor and perhaps with other parents whose children braved similar circumstances. This is a situation where a picture can be worth a thousand words. Many parents have scrapbooks or photo journals of their child's journey from premature baby to rollicking three-year-old. We have included many such pictures in this book and hope you find it reassuring to look at them. There may even be pictures on hand in the neonatal unit.

We've talked a lot about how mothers who cannot feed their babies at the breast can still begin to pump their breasts with an electric double set-up breast pump. The first efforts of pumping will yield colostrum, and that will be followed within a day or so by milk, both of which can be fed to your baby by tube. It is important to recognize that many first-time moms may have received some misinformation about the appropriateness of breast milk for their baby with jaundice. You may hear your doctor refer to jaundice in the first week of a nursing baby's life as *breast-feeding jaundice*. Breast-feeding jaundice occurs because during the first few days of life there is not enough breast milk to stimulate the excretion of bilirubin from the body. Once the breast milk, which is rich in fluid and calories, comes in, it serves to jump-start the function of the liver and intestines to excrete the bilirubin. This differs from *breast milk jaundice,* which occurs in over one-third of all (premature or term) breast-fed babies after the first week of life, when an as-yet-to-be-determined factor in breast milk interferes with the metabolism of bilirubin by the liver. This type of jaundice may last as long as 3 months. Neither of these forms of jaundice is a reason to avoid breast milk for your baby.

Within a relatively short time your baby will be able to begin to feed at the breast or the bottle; it may only be once a day at the start. The mother who wants to breast-feed should continue to pump both breasts at least eight times per day to build up her milk supply. Slowly increase the number of breast-feedings, while continuing to have your baby feed by tube or on a bottle. Any family who has gone through this experience will tell you support from the baby's dad is incredibly important in helping a new mother make the commitment to successful nursing. This is another situation where it can be very useful to speak with families who have "been there." Eventually your milk supply will be plentiful enough to replace alternative feeding methods.

It is important for new parents to be aware that the first few days after birth is a very dynamic time for a newborn's shifting body fluids. Even infants who are ready to feed (either by breast or bottle) immediately after birth take in only a small amount on the first few days. Their weight decreases for several days, and then as their fluid intake increases (and the mother's milk comes in, if she is nursing) they begin to regain their birth weight. In fact, if a baby doesn't lose a little weight after birth, the doctor may be concerned that there is some fluid retention.

Discharge Criteria

Discharge criteria for this group of premature babies is similar to those stated previously, with some minor modification:

- Your baby must be able to take all feedings—whether breast or bottle—by mouth.
- Your baby must be able to maintain body temperature in room temperature.
- As long as your baby is feeding well, weight gain is not a particular criteria for discharge. Your pediatrician, however, will either want to see your baby back in her office in 2 or 3 days for a weight check, or she may schedule a nursing home visit to have the baby weighed and assessed.
- Your baby should have stable vital signs and be free of apnea.

Parents of babies born between 34 and 36 weeks should read the discussion of *discharge planning* in chapter 10. Even though your baby may not be as small as an infant born at a younger PMA, you should still pay particular attention to the details about the purchase, installation, and use of car seats for the premature baby.

Parents' Emotional Response to Their 34- to 36-Week Premie (the Nearly Term Baby)

The emotional response to the birth of a baby 4 to 6 weeks before expected is quite variable. Many women will tell you they were very ready to stop feeling like a baby motel and felt elated to get an early reprieve from the last few weeks of pregnancy. Others, fearing that they have not "come through" for their baby, were uneasy about having had an early delivery. Some of these responses, of course, correspond to the health of the newborn and how long the baby may need to stay in the hospital. It also depends on whether the parents were able to get everything ready before the delivery—this includes getting to their last childbirth and breast-feeding classes.

The parents of all these babies are likely to ask their physician about when they can expect their baby to "catch up" with a full-term infant. There is no simple answer to that question, no absolute gauge, table, or chart that will tell you your baby is all caught up. This is a question we touch on several times throughout this book, because there are many perspectives from which it is asked. For the parents of a baby born between 34 and 36 weeks, their baby may catch up on structural, physical, and medical levels quite early, but this baby still will not fit the fantasy the parents may have had of delivering at term. From an emotional perspective, these parents may first have had to deal with their baby's unanticipated complications, however mild. Then they are confronted with *not necessarily feeling ready* to care for this infant, and *not being prepared* with some of the basic physical aspects of caring for their baby at home.

It can be very helpful for parents to acknowledge that although their birth experience was not what they expected, it is not a condition from which they or their baby need to *recover:* it is a set of circumstances to which they need to *adapt*. This is where the term *a different beginning* can be so helpful. If you are continually asking or even silently worrying about when your baby will be normal, the inevitable implication is that until that time comes, your baby is abnormal. That definition is neither accurate nor advantageous for you or your baby. Often for the baby who is born from 4 to 6 weeks prematurely, the significance of any health problem is going to depend on the parents' perception of whether or not there is a problem. This goes back to the earlier discussion of the wisdom in speaking with your baby's doctor and gaining as much accurate information as you can; you may find that you can alleviate unnecessary stress. Your positive approach will have an impact on everything from a mother's ability to successfully nurse her baby, to your other children's emotional security, to strengthening your marriage. Kangaroo care (see chapter 4) has been a very gratifying aid to new mothers and fathers bringing home their babies born between 34 and 36 weeks. Be sure to ask the members of your nursing and medical team about this simple but very effective way to help you and your baby to thrive. Kangaroo (or skin-to-skin) care can be especially helpful to help mother and baby establish successful breast-feeding.

ROUNDTABLE TALK

Couples with Babies Born Between 34 and 36 Weeks Tell Their Tales

Dr. Klein: What everyone here today has in common is that you all have babies who were born between 34 and 36 weeks. Technically, babies born under 37 weeks are considered less than term, but while most babies born at this time may have some mild problems, some have no problems at all. We're hoping you'll tell us about your experiences with babies born at this slightly premature gestational age.

MARIE AND TOM

Marie: My pregnancy itself wasn't particularly difficult. There were some concerns in the beginning about miscarriage, so they put me on minimum activity at about 3 months, and I stayed that way throughout the pregnancy. I was very calm during my pregnancy. It was fine. The most difficult thing for me was limited activity. I probably tended to do more than I should have.

Jill: At what gestational age was your baby born?

Marie: Let's see Eliza . . . was born at 36 weeks. At about 34 weeks I called the doctor because I'd had some pain in my side for a couple of days. My doctor told me to meet him at L&D [Labor and Delivery] . . . Just as they put me on the fetal monitor, I started to have contractions and had to be admitted to the hospital. After 10 days or 2 weeks in the hospital on the fetal monitor, my doctor came in and said, "Okay, we came up with a time slot. It's going to be at 3:30." I said, "On what day?" He said, "In about 15 minutes." That was it! My doctor was waiting until my daughter's lungs were mature enough, then he came in the door and said, "Okay, that's it."

Dr. Klein: Do you know why they did the C-section?

Marie: I was a high-risk pregnancy because of some preexisting medical conditions, so they watched me throughout the pregnancy. In addition, there were several really thin spots on my uterus. But the C-section went fine. The only problem was that Eliza had low blood sugar. They said they were going to put her in the NICU for probably just one night and then move her to the nursery the next day. And it turned out her blood sugar was fine after that.

Tom: But she had one apnea episode that night.

Marie: That's right. . . they decided to keep her in the neonatal unit. So she was born by C-section on Friday, and we were both discharged the following Monday. We went home with an apnea monitor that we kept for about 6 weeks. She weighed 5 pounds, 14 ounces at birth. She is 7 weeks old now, growing like a weed. She gained 21 ounces in 2 weeks.

Dr. Klein: How was it having her on the monitor at home?

Tom: We had no problems with that. During the day we'd be walking around with her and feeding her and putting her down in front of us. It really didn't get to be any kind of hassle at all. I'd lug it from one place to the next. She didn't mind having the belt around her at all.

Jill: Any apneic episodes after Eliza came home?

Tom: Just one in the first couple of weeks, and then that was it. She's been fine ever since.

Dr. Klein: Let me ask you one question. Another option in caring for Eliza could have been to keep her in the hospital for another week, and if she hadn't had any alarms in the hospital, we would have sent her home without the monitor. Which option do you think would have been best for you?

Tom: I think I would rather have her home. The monitor was actually kind of nice, because so many people are just constantly jumping up to make sure the baby was fine. All we had to do was look, and the lights were blinking and we knew she was fine.

Marie: Eliza is our first baby, so we're obviously going to worry about what is normal and what isn't normal. So we didn't really have to worry about her not breathing at night; we had the monitor. She's in our room. Now she's sleeping longer—most of the night.

Tom: After the birth everything has been pretty uneventful.

Dr. Klein: Do you feel like you were prepared for her?

Tom: I think so. The only thing we got caught short on was the first night when there weren't any bottles for milk. So I was out at 11 P.M. at night, trying to find bottles and nipples and this and that.

Marie: We had bottles, but the nipples we had were too big. So he was out late that night looking for tiny little infant nipples, because she was so tiny she needed the little ones. She couldn't even get her mouth around them. So that's how we were not prepared. We weren't prepared for her being so small.

WINNIE AND BILL

Winnie: I should say that this was my second pregnancy. And I can also tell you that even though I worked in the ob-gyn field, being the one who is actually pregnant was completely different. In my first pregnancy with my older son Jason, who is now 22 months, I was having full-blown contractions at 28 weeks. . . . You just don't think it is going to happen to you, but there I was in the hospital for 7 weeks prior to his delivery. We did everything possible to hold off my labor so that his lungs would have time to mature. Finally, we knew his lungs had matured sufficiently. . . it was New Year's Eve and I said, "Let's take him." And he was fine. . . everything was fine, and he was able to come home.

Bill: We had no understanding when the early labor was happening in the first pregnancy of what was going on. Even though we had taken classes. . . . And with all that, we got pregnant again.

Winnie: With the second pregnancy we knew that preterm labor could potentially be a problem again, so I wanted to take it easy from the beginning. For quite awhile I was so sick I could not do anything anyway. I actually had to be in the hospital because I was dehydrated from vomiting so much. At 6½ months it finally stopped. I thought, "I can breathe now and go out and do a little bit. . ." *Wrong!* I started to go into preterm labor at 6½ months with the contractions. I was back to the hospital twice and placed on bed rest at home. Eventually I stayed at home with a monitor system that was hooked up to the obstetrical ward at the hospital. This was my second baby and I was more relaxed this time. They would ask about my condition, if I had any discomfort, vaginal bleeding, back pain, stuff like that. I wasn't as fearful as I'd been in my first pregnancy—I just had confidence in my doctors that they would make everything okay.

Bill: It was a lot easier having the monitor at home on Winnie, because we felt safer. There were several occasions when things came up that would have meant a trip to the hospital.

Winnie: But being on bed rest with an 18-month-old at home is hard to do. No matter how much help you have, he wants his mommy. And he knew there was something wrong with me because I was not able to get up and play with him. And I was going back and forth to the doctor weekly, going in and out of the hospital. It was a little rough on our son. No matter who was there, he always wanted Mommy.

Bill: I was advocating for holding off as long as possible, but once Winnie's water broke, that was it.

Winnie: Our daughter Tess was born at 35½ weeks. It had been a difficult pregnancy from the beginning, but Tess was fine. She was put on an IV to give her some glucose. They gave her some formula, and the next day she was fine and we went home. I felt she was going to be okay.

Jill: What was Tess' birth weight?

Winnie: She weighed 5 pounds, 9 ounces, which seemed so small. She was kind of jittery. Her nervous system didn't seem to be quite as developed as I expected, and she was always just shaking and jittery. She startled easily. She liked to be held—still to this day she wants Mommy to hold her all the time. It's hard to get her to sleep sometimes. Part of that is my fault; she was so delicate and tiny that I wanted to make her safe.

Bill: This is kind of a joke, but I used to sing to Winnie's tummy when she was pregnant with Tess. And so now, I don't know if there is any connection, but when nothing seems to work, I'll pick her up and carry her and sing, which most people can't stand, but it seems to put her back to sleep.

Jill: How is feeding going?

Winnie: She had a real hard time latching on to me. She did not want to take the breast at all. She took the bottle just fine, and she preferred that so much that she would just scream and carry on. Finally Bill was just so upset with that, he said, "You have to have a lactation counselor come out and help you with this." So finally we did. We realized after 2 months that we both had thrush; my nipples were bleeding and cracking, but I didn't know that was what it was. After Dr. Klein prescribed some medicine, it worked, and then she went back onto the breast and now she won't take a bottle. It's a lot easier.

Bill: Once it became pleasant for Winnie, the baby sensed that comfort and she wanted to latch on. So she started feeding really well at the breast, and now that's all she does. Oh, she has also tried to breast-feed from my nose.

CELESTE AND MATT

Celeste: My pregnancy went very well to begin with. When I was about 6 months pregnant. I had been way overactive. . . I was planning a big charity event. I went to the charity event from 8:00 in the evening till midnight. At 2:00 in the morning I woke up with contractions that calmed down, but they scared me. I called my doctor, and she told me not to worry about it.

Matt: You could say that up until 6 months it was picture-perfect.

Celeste: At 34 weeks I woke up and I felt this weird liquid feeling. There was no question that it was my amniotic fluid; I knew that. I called the doctor. . . I was in kind of a weird zone. . . I went to the doctor. I remember the thing that stood out in my mind was the nurse saying to me, "If you feel any contractions let me know." And I kept thinking, "Contractions?" I don't know where my brain was. I was having the same kind of tiny contractions I had been having. The perinatologist came in; she looked at the monitor. She said, "You know, I told you he was going to come early. He looks fine to me, I think he's ready to go." They didn't want to induce until the amnio came back to say his lungs were developed. They had talked for a few minutes about trying to keep him till term—I was at 34½ weeks. They talked about holding him off, but he was really doing very well. I'm allergic to antibiotics, so nobody was eager to try waiting. I had quite a bit of amniotic fluid, so it wasn't really a problem, and they could have kept me for awhile except for the antibiotic issue. So they did an amniocentesis, and they gave me a shot. At midnight the test came back and they said we really ought to wait till morning. This is kind of funny: We thought they said that everyone was going to get together again in the morning and discuss it. So I was all excited; I didn't sleep. They had offered me a sleeping pill, and I didn't want to take it 'cause I thought I could be here for awhile anyway; I don't want to get into the habit. So I didn't sleep all night. At 6:00 in the morning, in came the nurse to induce labor. Every 2 minutes I would have a contraction, but I just wasn't dilating enough. The nurse, the respiratory therapist, they all came in and tried to cheer me up. My son kept going down and floating back up, which was why I wasn't dilating. He never dropped. I'm a little bit small in the pelvis, but there was no clear reason as to why he couldn't drop and why my amniotic fluid broke. Finally the next morning they did the C-section. When they pulled him out, he was screaming. So I knew he was fine at that point. He nursed 2 hours later. . . latched right on.

Matt: After birth, what happened was they pulled him out, then they took him over to this table. After they cut the umbilical cord, they put him on this table where they suctioned out some mucus, rubbed him off, then they put him on oxygen; I'd say no more than 10 seconds, and he was fine. He was 4 pounds, 15½ ounces.

Celeste: The first night, my family was so excited. They tried to kick my mother-in-law out of the hospital. We let everybody hold him that first night. And he had a little episode that night, where they had to put him under a warmer; they said he got too cold. After that we made a point of limiting the number of people who could hold him. Now he's 13 weeks.

Jill: Did you feel like you were ready to bring him home from the hospital?

Celeste: We were not prepared, we did not have anything. We were not planning to have a shower until afterwards.

Matt: We were planning on getting a few things a week or two before he was due, so we didn't have any clothes, we didn't have any receiving blankets; then we had to get premature diapers, 'cause the diapers were too big. They came up to his neck. . .

ROUNDTABLE TALK

Some Advice from the Group

Jill: Are there things that you have learned that could be helpful to parents in the same situation?

Marie: I would not worry about so much; things will fall into place. Don't worry if you have to change your baby on a table or a bed. Don't worry about clothes, 'cause they don't need clothes. They grow so fast.

Tom: I think that just not being surprised at all the things they throw at you so quickly. All of a sudden there's an apnea episode and low blood sugar. Things I never heard of and they're thrown at you like, "Decide,

decide, decide . . ." Those decisions sound terribly important, but they really aren't. The doctor knows what he's doing.

Celeste: The one thing I would recommend more than anything else is the breast pump.

Marie: I'm sure that's true. . . . The reason why I had such a hard time breast-feeding was that nobody helped me, and I knew nothing at all.

Celeste: I think the suddenness of having a premature baby can be a real shock. I would tell every parent to try to get information. I had a lot of information that [Dr. Klein] gave me: I knew the first thing I needed to know was that he was breathing on his own. As soon as I saw him screaming, I knew he was breathing on his own. Then the next step was, would he latch on to the breast? He latched on. So I kind of knew what I needed to look for. . . "Okay, you've done that; now you need to know this . . ." I felt like I got information that made it easier for me to ask questions of the nurses.

Matt: In fact, originally when we went in, they gave a tour of the NICU and introduced us to the respiratory therapist, who explained what he does, and so that way we felt more comfortable with the birthing process. I think the best thing we did, though, is get help when we got home. We got professional help, a person to help out.

Celeste: One of the things I would recommend is get a lactation con-sultant in the hospital and pump, because that first week is horrible when they don't quite know how to latch on and they're crying, and you have to try to relax while they are crying.

Matt: This was our first child, so we didn't know if this was appropriate, or is this right, does this sound good, we had no idea. I've got to say our overall experience was phenomenal. With a few exceptions. . . everything went perfectly. As far as the prematurity is concerned, when you feel your child might have a few more problems than normal because of the early start, because of the concerns you have. . . I think that really having access to somebody who has a lot of medical expertise and knowledge is very important.

Celeste: You have to feel like you can really talk to your doctor.

Dr. Klein: Do you have any feeling that you've missed something because you didn't go to term?

Winnie: Oh no, I'm glad it's over with.

Celeste: I was kind of in pain from about the fifth month on, so it was a big relief for me.

Marie: I felt guilty for wanting it to come early. I felt guilty wishing my baby to be premature, but I did.

Dr. Klein: Now that you have a baby who was born prematurely. . . Do you still think about your babies being a little bit different than term babies?

Bill: I felt our daughter was not as developed as our son was when he was born. I was used to a certain level of development, and her size was a lot smaller.

Winnie: But for me, when it came to the day when she was supposed to be born, she was more mature than a one-day-old [term] baby would be. She was somehow more aware of the world around her than you would expect of a one-day-old baby; it was very interesting.

Marie: Once she got home, I was comfortable. From the first day I felt very comfortable with her at home. It was in the hospital that I felt out of control.

Celeste: I'm comfortable too, especially now that I see that he's meeting all the milestones at the age he is, not at the adjusted age and weight on the growth chart. At this point I really don't pay that much attention to it. But for several months people would walk up to me and say, "Oh my, he's so small." And I would have to say, "No, we actually think he's big. Don't tell me he's small." So I think that now I don't really pay any attention to that. For several months I was definitely aware of the fact he was smaller and maybe a little bit behind.

Matt: I didn't really think of that.

Celeste: Everything is going well. Look how big he's gotten—now he's the size of a normal child his age.

Dr. Klein: They *are* normal babies born early. There's a wonderful term that describes premature babies as having *"a different beginning."*

Marie: I just say she was born a month early, and she's doing great.

Celeste: I find that people say, "Wow! This baby was premature?"

Winnie: I was very comfortable with her right away. I just wanted to pay more attention to her, because she was so fragile and so tiny. Maybe because she's a girl I can identify with her; I don't know, but I know I was different with her than I was with my son.

Bill: I had a strong feeling of really waiting for her actual due date to came around. In the beginning I felt a little bit uncomfortable. . . plus we had a hard time with our son because of the time Winnie spent in the hospital.

Matt: My mom always asked if he smiles yet, like he's supposed to be behind, not catching up as fast.

Dr. Klein: The best way to look at your babies and their development is to use their "corrected age." If a baby is born 4 weeks before she was due, we say she was born at a gestational age of 36 weeks, and plot her on her growth curve for her *actual age*. But when her due date arrives, we begin to plot her *corrected age,* which is calculated from her expected date of delivery. The same *corrected age* comes into play as you watch your baby attain developmental milestones. I always tell my families to remember that *it is correct to correct*. But it is also important to remember that all babies, whether they are premature or term, do not all do things at the same time. There is a very broad time frame when we talk about normal development.

Celeste: I actually just had a big milestone. I went to a baby shower and somebody said, "Oh, you have a pudgy baby." It was wonderful.

Chapter Fourteen

When a Baby Is Very Sick

Difficult Decisions

Early on in our own childhoods, well before the first signs of puberty, we begin to imitate being the mothers and fathers many of us are destined to become. On the road from childhood to adulthood we are driven to play with baby dolls, to flirt, to imitate the rites of love, to seek a mate and a more serious version of love, and finally to create new life. All of this has been played out by so many for so long that it appears predestined, and biologically speaking, it is. But sometimes something goes terribly wrong, and a life is created and brought into the world before it is fully equipped to take up its part. None of the years we spend in subconscious preparation to become parents prepares us for having the baby who may not be destined to survive.

When a baby's life is in jeopardy, brand-new parents find themselves at an unexpected fork in the road that was supposed to lead them unerringly to a lifetime of parenting. Which way do they turn? Sometimes a very young, very sick baby dies regardless of every attempt made to save its life, but other babies develop serious problems and linger for hours, days, or weeks with the aid of life support. Of the many consequential decisions that may confront the parents of a premature baby, the decision to withdraw life support from a gravely ill infant resonates from within the deepest reservoir of human experience.

For as long as technological advances in medicine have pushed back the threshold of viability for premature babies, medical ethicists have voiced doubts about doing so. Nevertheless, the person who questions the wisdom in pushing the limit of current technical advances in the care of very premature babies today might consider that the babies who were considered borderline 20 years ago are the routine success stories in today's NICU.

Advances such as the use of surfactant treatment and assisted ventilation can be very effective in maintaining life in very premature, seriously ill, or even terminal infants. We know that appropriate medical treatment should be defined as being in a patient's best interest, *but what is "in the best interest" for a very sick premature baby, and who defines the term itself?* The following comments are adapted from guidelines of the American Academy of Pediatrics:[1]

> *The American Academy of Pediatrics believes that physicians should provide life-sustaining medical care in conformity with current medical, ethical, and legal norms. Physicians should remember that two broad principles guide the implementation of therapy. First, beneficial treatment suggests that clinicians should justify the use of treatments based on the benefits they provide, not simply on the ability to employ them. Conversely, physicians need to consider potential harm to patients. Harm includes obvious physical problems such as pain, but may also include psychological, social, and economic consequences. Second, self-determination or autonomy accepts the likelihood that different persons may judge benefits differently. Our social system generally grants patients and families wide discretion in making their own decisions about health care and in continuing, limiting, declining, or discontinuing treatment, whether life-sustaining or otherwise. Medical professionals should seek to override family wishes only when those views clearly conflict with the interests of the child.*
>
> *If intervention in any form (ventilation, surgery, or some other procedure) would guarantee life and quality of life to a newborn*

at risk, withdrawal of treatment would never be in question. Sadly, this is not the case, and some very sick babies who are afforded every possible medical opportunity for treatment will die; some will have their deaths delayed by a matter of days or weeks; and some will survive with profound neurological or other tragic complications that will leave them without any possibility of living "a normal life."

In a very real way, the extraordinary capacity of modern neonatal medicine to sustain life in an extremely premature baby can seem to stand in direct opposition to the wisdom in doing so. Every day in the United States, parents are confronted with the devastating news that their baby cannot be expected to survive if life support is withdrawn, or they are told that life-saving measures may spare their child's life, but with devastating consequences. Imagine Justice holding her scales and trying to effect a balance between the sanctity of life on one side, and a quality of life on the other; but instead of being in the hands of the traditionally blindfolded Justice, in this case the scales are held aloft by parents with their eyes wide open to this most personal crisis. If we look carefully at the statement from the American Academy of Pediatrics, we see a clear attempt at a balanced approach to this very difficult dilemma. Nevertheless, there can be occasions when there is conflict between the physician, who is acting on his assessment of appropriate care, and parents who disagree with his treatment or approach. Parents should have the reasonable expectation that their voices will be heard, but not necessarily at the expense of the physician's commitment to his standard of care. The area for disagreement may be one of either overtreatment or undertreatment.

Strategies for Care

When there is disagreement between parents and their health-care team, either a physician or a parent may recommend bringing in an independent medical consultant. There will be occasions when there is more than one appropriate medical approach, and parents have the right to expect their physician to make these options clear and be prepared to discuss their possible consequences. A parent may want to see data that discusses outcome for various approaches that are under consideration. Sometimes another physician brought in as a consultant will be willing to provide the type of care that is consistent with the wishes of the family, and the decision is made to transfer a baby's care to the second doctor.

If parents and the physician cannot come to a mutually acceptable course of action, it may be appropriate to consult with the hospital *bioethics committee*. The members of a bioethics committee are likely to differ in each hospital, but the membership might be expected to include medical and nonmedical personnel from the hospital, as well as patient representatives, clergy, or business people from the community. A bioethics committee, as described in an article by William R. Sexson, MD, and Janet Thigpen, RN, MN, CNNP, performs four major functions:[2]

- to educate
- to enhance communication
- to address the ethical tensions that surround the health-care interaction through consultation
- to perform some specific administrative functions

The committee can serve as a venue in which everyone participating is presumed to have gathered with the intention of "doing the right thing," *even though there is no mutual agreement as to what that right thing is*. In the same article, Sexson and Thigpen go on to describe the review process of a bioethics committee at a major hospital:

> *The review process requires the presence of at least five, and preferably more, members of the committee (three of whom must be physicians); the person bringing the consultation; the patient, family or both; other physicians caring for the patient; and other support staff. The consultative process is separated into an information sharing portion where all the above persons are present si-*

multaneously and encouraged to share their perspective about the case. Frequently we find that this open sharing of opinions may resolve those problems in which communication and interaction still remain an issue. At the end of this portion of the review, all persons, except committee members, are invited to leave, and the case is discussed. The purpose of the discussion is to arrive at a set of ethically acceptable options and rank these options in order of preference. It is rare that there is only a single ethically acceptable option identified, but there is frequently a unanimous opinion about which option is most acceptable.

Once the formal consultation is accomplished, acceptable options are written down, reviewed within 24 hours by the committee members, and forwarded verbally to both the person initiating the request and the patient's attending physician. The reasoning behind the 24-hour delay in forwarding the committee opinion is important; it is to be certain that there has been no reconsideration or change on the part of any committee member.[3]

The debate over life-prolonging intervention for high-risk premature babies, and the equally complex decision to refuse or withdraw treatment for these infants, is likely to continue forever. There are as many "right answers" as there are parents hoping and often praying for the guidance to do what is best for their baby. All parents with critically ill premature babies need the support of their medical team in facing the challenge of their lives. Although it is unreasonable to expect consensus among all doctors and all parents on how to best handle the care of a critically ill or dying baby, it is completely reasonable to expect that every possible effort will be made to have honest, respectful communication when it is needed most.

WHEN A BABY DIES

Lila and Daniel are the parents of triplets: Maggie and her brother Jeremy are about 2½ years old—their brother Steven was removed from a respirator and died 11 days after he was born. Lila and Daniel have agreed to share their difficult story in the hope that it may be helpful to other parents. The startling honesty of Lila and Daniel's remarks is a testament to the love with which they honor the memory of their son Steven, as well as the courage and enthusiasm they bring to their daily roles as parents of Maggie and Jeremy.

Lila: I had been at home on bed rest and on a monitor. I went to the hospital leaking amniotic fluid and having contractions. . . I knew something was not right, and I was admitted on a Monday and delivered by cesarean section on Friday. Maggie and Steven were born at the same moment, and Jeremy came 4 minutes later.

Daniel: I got to see the babies as soon as they had been stabilized and brought to the NICU. Maggie was 1 pound, 8 ounces; Steven was 1 pound, 8½ ounces; and Jeremy was 1 pound, 10½ ounces. The urgency to deliver the babies at that point was because Lila went into pulmonary edema and there was concern that her life was at risk.

Lila: When I came out from under sedation, I was put in the ICU, and I was there for 2 days. I couldn't see the babies, but Daniel brought me a picture and they didn't look that bad. . . In the picture they did not look so small. But when I got out of the ICU and went to see them, I was just shocked. I had never seen anything so small. They were like aliens.

Daniel: This sounds really terrible, but my first instinctual reaction was to want to turn away. . . it was just very, very foreign and not at all the experience I'd anticipated. But that initial reaction didn't last, and I bonded with them very quickly. The first horrified reaction didn't last. I think there were a lot of factors—part of it is being robbed of what I imagine most men would expect to be the greatest part of a man's life, when a kid is born. . . to give out cigars and just do the whole thing. I expected to have kids and I was faced with fetuses. It didn't feel like they were really babies. . . . Obviously they were babies, but they were so different than what anybody would be expecting.

Lila: I was terrified. They seemed creature-like, and I didn't want to have anything to do with them. . . . They seemed to be suffering, and they had all these tubes. I wanted to walk away.

Daniel: For me, after my initial shock, probably after the first hour or so, I had a very strong feeling that we had to name the kids. I felt it was very important that we bond with these kids if they were going to have any chance. It felt very, very important that they have names.

Lila: We had already chosen two out of three names—Steven and Maggie. We debated over Jeremy or Matthew for the third name, and finally decided on Jeremy.

Daniel: Lila was discharged 5 days after the babies were born, and 2 days after that we went to a meeting at the hospital to talk about Steven.

Lila: It felt overwhelming, because there were all these people. . . several nurses and doctors. The neurologist began to talk about the diagnosis   I only really remember talking about Steven, because his condition was the most serious I remember the neurologist saying Steven had a grade 4 brain bleed. . .

Daniel: We were being given a very grim prognosis for this boy. . .

Lila: He would have no quality of life.

Daniel: The doctor described the pressure on his brain and his concerns about how Steven could be suffering.

Lila: Then I said, "What are you saying. . . that we should take him off life support?" He said

he could not tell us what to do, but that he would support our decision.

Daniel: Initially we went with a DNR—a "do not resuscitate." I just couldn't make a decision that quickly. He was still intubated. The big deciding factor—and that was the fight within myself—was what quality of life could possibly exist for this child. . . whether it was right to keep him on a ventilator, to prolong his suffering, versus taking him off the ventilator and not giving him a chance at life. I had to do my best to make as pure a decision for him as I could. To this day, I still don't know how much, if at all, it was a rationalization to take him off life support. I go over and over it, and I'll probably be going over it for the rest of my life. Was I self-centered in taking him off, because I didn't want to go through the obligations and responsibilities if we kept him on life support. . . having to take care of him. As of right now, I feel like we did the right thing, and I know I made the best decision I could at the time. But I still don't exactly know how pure it was.

Lila: For me, it was the idea of the quality of his life. . . that he would suffer; he would be in a wheelchair; he'd be blind; that he could spend the rest of his life in an institution. . . When you put them all together, what kind of life is that?

Daniel: When I was able to put myself in Lila's position, by taking out the religious factors that influence me, I was able to see her thinking: OK. . . He is suffering, and it is better to take him off life support right away. I recognized that were it not for religious issues that I felt so deeply, I could have argued just as adamantly to take him off life support as I was fighting to keep him on life support at that time. I remember thinking that if he stayed on life support, I could continue to gather information and at least feel I was making the best decision I was capable of.

Lila: We met with all the doctors on Friday and on Tuesday we took him off life support. The night before Steven died I refused to go to the hospital, and I'm sorry that I didn't go. I wish I had. Daniel went to be with him the night before he passed away. . . I just couldn't go.

Daniel: I did get to hold Steven the night before we let him go. When they took him off life support, I held him from that time until he died.

Lila: I was able to hold him while he was still on the respirator. I couldn't hold him after he died. . . I don't even remember them taking him out of the room after he passed away. We knew that we were going to have a funeral for Steven. The social worker had given us a number of places to consider and I made a definite choice. The day before his funeral, we were getting ready to bring

Steven's clothes to the funeral home when I got the call that our daughter Maggie's grade 3 brain bleed had resolved. . . she was getting better.

Daniel: One thing that was very important was that the nurses were great. . . That's one of the things that kept me sane. . . and my friends, and the fact that I'm an open book. . . Any feelings I had, I talked about, and the nurses were really great at listening.

Lila: Each of our babies had a primary nurse, and Steven's primary nurse even donated blood for Jeremy and Maggie. I got so much comfort from that. Our social worker was also a pretty big help. And I have a friend who was a premie born at 2 pounds 44 years ago. After Steven died, we still had two babies who were very premature. . . My friend was a big inspiration. . . If she could do it, my kids could do it. She really helped me go on. . . and photographs. . . The nurses took a lot of pictures of Steven while he was alive, and I am so thankful to have them. A few years ago I met someone whose baby was stillborn. She passed out pictures of the baby and everyone thought she was crazy to do that, but I understand now. This child is a part of your life. You want people to know this baby existed.

Daniel: We have one picture of Steven that is very important to me now. He is looking at the camera, and I see his eyes. They say the eyes are the window of the soul, and it is so evident in this picture. Having this picture of my son with his eyes open as opposed to being closed makes all the difference to me.

Lila: It is incredible to know now that many people have gone through this. I'm actually on the Board of Mothers of Super Twins (MOST). . . I have made so many friends who also had three babies and had to take one of them off life support. I don't know really if I'll ever fully make peace with the decision to withdraw life support from Steven. . . you do think maybe there would have been a miracle. . . maybe he would have been OK. I'm so deeply grateful for my children—Jeremy and Maggie are true miracles.

Daniel: You can't help but think "what if . . ." with Steven. The decision to take a child off life support is pretty much unresolvable on that level. Hopefully it was the right decision, or a decision that was more right than

wrong. But ultimately it is better that we suffer with our decision than Steven suffer any longer than was necessary. It is so deeply personal for any individual confronting this decision. For me personally, I prayed a great deal and came to believe that God knows what is in my heart even more than I do, and I can't keep anything from Him even if I wanted to. I've examined every side of myself, and I think it is the healthiest thing you can do. I've learned to try to be as honest with myself as possible. Not only as regards Steven, but with my life in general. . . my career, my marriage. Steven has a very important place in my life and he always will. I would tell any parent not to feel pressured into making a quick decision, and also to have the courage to look at yourself. It is very, very healing. All my thinking has helped me to get rid of a lot of emotional baggage so that I can honestly say now that I don't feel I wallow in sad feelings, but I have become even more reflective as a person.

DR. KLEIN COMMENTS ON ACKNOWLEDGING YOUR BABY'S LIFE BY FORMALLY RECOGNIZING HIS OR HER DEATH

As a physician who has practiced for many years, I still have not and don't ever expect to become inured to the tragic loss of a baby's life. Time and again I am touched by the courage and wisdom that parents bring to this very sad event. While every family, every individual, who loses a child will experience it in a highly personal way, I do believe that the impulse to mark the passing of life should be encouraged and supported for anyone whose baby dies.

It is very, very important to name your child and mark his or her passing with a funeral or service of some kind. You may find comfort in your religious faith, or you may have a very private secular service. You may plant a young tree or a flower garden to represent your baby's very real presence in your lives. Some parents find strength and have come in time to offer their strength to others in support groups for those who have lost a baby. We know that grief is not a static emotion: it is about process, and marking the rituals of mourning—whatever that may mean for you—can help the grieving process to begin.

Epilogue

A Few More Tales

When we met on Sunday mornings to speak with the parents who contributed their stories to this book, it was extraordinary to see the kinship among people whose only absolute link was the premature birth of their children. We all sat riveted as each person spoke, and while the details of every pregnancy and birth were unique, at the heart of every story were very courageous parents determined to make a go of their baby's different beginning

Many of the parents who met with us to share the stories we've included throughout this book made it clear that they had found comfort in speaking with other parents of premies—whether they had babies in the NICU at the same time, or joined support groups, or met in the waiting rooms of their children's doctors. There is clearly something very powerful in talking with someone who "has been there." It is in that spirit that we choose to end this book with a few more stories from parents. We are thankful to all the parents and children whose stories are told throughout this book, and hope you find them as inspiring as we have.

TWO BEAUTIFUL BABIES AND ONE EXTRAORDINARY FRIENDSHIP

Ellen's experience as the mother of premature twin daughters is significantly different than the experience of our other parents of premies: Ellen's beautiful girls were born to a surrogate and conceived with the help of donor eggs.

Ellen: I struggled with infertility for 7 years before having children. I was diagnosed with cancer, and I survived that. It's been 5 years, and I'm fine. Then I had a second cancer scare and had to have a hysterectomy. So we got through all that and decided we were still going to have children. After going through many embryo transfers of my own eggs, we realized I needed an egg donor. In all, I had three egg donors and two surrogates.

My first surrogate became pregnant and lost the baby during the 1994 earthquake. She and her husband ended up moving out of state, but we had frozen embryos in storage. It was absolutely clear that I could not conceive a child; it was out of the question for me. So I called a friend of mine and I said, "You always said that if you could do anything for me you would. Would you consider being a surrogate?" And she said to give her a little time and she would call me back. She discussed it with her entire family. A week later she called me back and said, "We'll do it. The whole family is going to do it."

My surrogate got pregnant on her second try. . . . We went for the first ultrasound: there was this little embryo, and the doctor said, "There's a pregnancy," and then, "There's another one." And I thought, "Please don't let there be any more." We didn't want a situation of our surrogate carrying a high-order multiple birth. It's one thing when it's your body and it's your choice, but when you are asking this of someone else, her health becomes an issue. But it was only two babies. In fact, our surrogate had twins of her own who were born at term. We were thrilled at the prospect of twins, because we could not imagine going through this again. It's too complicated, finding the donor and the surrogate. . . so much time and so much money.

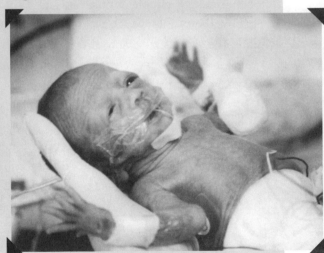

Photo by Stephanie Waisler.

So her pregnancy went along, and the only problems I ever felt were with the obstetrician who had never before had a patient who was a surrogate mother. Maybe he did not understand that this was a family arrangement between my surrogate's family and my husband and me; but my surrogate liked him, and I came to understand that although these babies were my children, it was her pregnancy. That was a very tough distinction for me to make, because I felt so clearly that I was the mother of these children, even though somebody else was carrying them for me. I could not really intervene; I could only hope for the best. We ended up staying with the obstetrician.

It was in April that we got a call from our surrogate: "We're going to the hospital." The babies were due July 17. We had just seen her several days before, because her daughter had her first communion; we had been with the whole family, and everybody was fine. . . Everything was terrific. Initially, when we got the call, I thought they would give her some medication and she would be fine. Maybe she would spend a few days in the hospital and go home, and then the babies would be born in July or maybe even a little early. . . but my husband is a doctor and he said, "No, we have to go to the hospital." I was still in a fog; it just never occurred to me that they were going to be born at this point. We got to the hospital at 3:00 in the morning. It was stressful. . . I felt the attitude toward my surrogate was so negative. It was as if everyone had given up. . . here is a woman who is carrying twins at 26 weeks. . . they were obviously very small, and the feeling I got from people was that they were not going to survive. And the whole delivery went like that.

Dr. Klein: This is hard to talk about, but it is vital because one of the most important things we hope to address in this book is the attitude of all the people that are taking care of parents and babies who are born early. Pessimism serves no purpose whatsoever. A positive attitude is as motivating when a mother is about to deliver as it has been throughout the whole pregnancy.

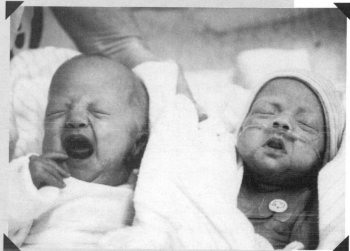

Photo by *Stephanie Waisler.*

Ellen: People kept coming in and out, and everybody looked very worried. So there I was after all these years—7 years trying to get these children—how could this be happening? The OB came in and his comment was, "It's in God's hands," which of course it always is, anyway. But by then I think her labor was 4 or 5 hours and it could not be stopped.

We found out that the babies were in two separate placentas and that there was an infection in one. . . . Then we went from the labor

Photo by Stephanie Waisler.

room to the delivery room. After 15 minutes our first child was born. Her name was Elizabeth, and she weighed a little over 2 pounds. Her head was the size of a little lemon. Nobody knew quite what to do—they had this woman who was giving birth to somebody else's children, and no one appeared to have any preparation for dealing with the situation. Our two families had always planned that we were going to be there, just as we had been together through the pregnancy. I remember the doctor said, "Would you like to cut your daughter's umbilical cord?" and I didn't know if I wanted to do that. . .

It was my surrogate's second set of twins; she had three children of her own. One singleton, which was a cesarean, and her twins, who were born vaginally at full term. Both my daughters were delivered vaginally, with Claire following Elizabeth in 15 minutes. Claire was blue and she made no sound whatsoever. She

was described as being desperately ill. I had a real problem here: I had two very tiny, very premature babies who were born very sick and needed to go to the NICU, and I had a dear friend who gave birth to these babies, and she felt as though she had let me down because it was happening in a way that had never been planned for or anticipated, and wasn't supposed to happen. It has been so interesting sitting here today and talking to other parents. . . listening to everyone's stories and questions about where do you go when the baby is born. . . I found myself identifying with the father in the birth situation, because I was an observer and I didn't give birth. They were my children from the moment they were born, but when I hear the men talk I know how they feel. Do you go with the baby? Do you stay with your wife? I can really understand the father's position on that. I chose to go with my surrogate, because I knew that she needed me. The babies had to go to the unit and I knew I would get to them, but first I had to be with my surrogate because she was so angry and upset. . . . The pregnancy had been fine, but she had tremendous guilt and I needed to be there to reassure her. Yet it was very difficult because I wanted to be with the children, so I stayed with her until she was calm enough and then I went to the girls.

As you know, at 26 weeks there are respiratory complications. So that was a big issue with the girls. Elizabeth weighed 2 pounds, 4 ounces, and Claire, who was born second, weighed 2 pounds, 9 ounces. Elizabeth had virtually no problems with her lungs after about a 24-hour period of time, but Claire had severe problems with her lungs—she was put on this ventilator and had to be paralyzed in order to tolerate it. I remember the first 22 hours in the parent's room... going in and seeing that little tiny baby attached to all this machinery... During the next week she suffered a brain hemorrhage, and for me, that seemed to be the most devastating thing. Now I realize that I didn't understand the gravity of her respiratory problems. When she had the brain hemorrhage, I thought it was the worst thing that could happen. You say to yourself, "These are my children, they are who they are, and I am going to take care of them." Brain hemorrhages are graded 1 through 4, and hers was a 2. But she got through it okay, and as of now we don't see any problems.

Jill: Was it easier to understand your daughters' medical information since your husband is a physician?

Ellen: I looked to my husband for clarification, but after awhile, because I spent so much time with the babies, I developed my own sense of how they were doing. My husband would look at their charts and see what the numbers said, and sometimes he would go crazy. But I was with them all the time, and at

a certain point I just knew they were doing okay. I knew we had a long road and we were not going to walk out of there right away, but I knew the babies were going to be okay.

Dr. Klein: One of the things we've heard now many times is how parents hear differing opinions from many sources and don't know whom they should listen to. Often people come to me saying, "Well I heard this or that..." And he [Ellen's husband] would get information saying, "Well, it could be this and it could be that." But he would persevere, looking for a definitive response. "If that's what it is, shouldn't we be doing antibiotics?" Your husband was understandably inclined to be as much the doctor as he is the father. It can be a very tough position for both people when there is a doctor caring for the child of a physician. For my own children's health problems I've usually tried to defer to the physician I've chosen, but I can't say I've ever been in a life-and-death situation with my children.

Ellen: As I said, I just knew we were going to bring our daughters home. Claire was in the hospital for 100 days. Elizabeth came home a week before her due date and Claire came home a week after her due date. There were major differences between the two of them. Elizabeth basically was never sick; she just started growing. I used to have this dream that my one child wasn't growing at all; she was getting older, but she wasn't getting any bigger... But of course she has grown, and both my daughters seem to be fine, and everything we went through eventually became a memory. I've kept a diary—I look back at it now, a year later, and see that after awhile I just kind of tuned out the negative stuff... I just took my girls to see my surrogate the week before last. She's an angel... She was a wonderful person to have done this for us.

Photo by Stephanie Waisler.

FOUR BABY GIRLS

Naturally occurring quadruplets are an extraordinary event. When they occur in a family with three young children already at home, it is an event that is staggering even to other parents of multiples. Antonia delivered her babies at 32 weeks and has never looked back. This is a story of a remarkable family.

Antonia: My babies were quadruplets—four girls born at 32 weeks.

Jill: Were you on bed rest?

Antonia: Yes, and that is one thing I would like to share with any mother who is told to go to bed: If your doctor tells you that your baby can be born prematurely, I think that you should take it very seriously, which I did, and really stay in bed. I don't care how bored you are or how much you want to walk down the hall, or if your child is nagging you to get something. It was my 15th week when my OB said he wanted me to go on bed rest, and then at 5 months he told me to go into the hospital and just stay in bed. I think people sometimes don't take it seriously when the obstetrician says to stay in bed. I took home bed rest very seriously, but it was very difficult, with, "Mom, I want this . . ." I mean, when your children are begging you for something, it's very difficult.

But I consider myself very blessed because our daughters were only in the hospital for a short period of time, and they are very healthy. I feel that has to do with my obstetrician, who kept me in the hospital and made it really clear that I had to stay in bed. So I did, and I really believe my body took the pregnancy as far as it could have gone. I really believe that if I hadn't been on bed rest, the babies would have been born probably at 25 or 26 weeks, because carrying four is really a heavy load.

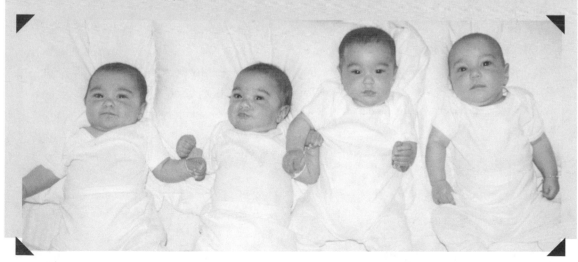

Jill: Don't you have other children as well? How did you manage?

Antonia: My three other children were 5, 3, and 2 when the babies were born. My husband, John, was taking care of the children. He was very, very good. Of course, I'm lucky that I have a very wonderful husband and he's a wonderful father—the kids didn't lack for anything. It was very hard on him—he was grouchy—but in the long run it was very worth it. We had a nanny from Austria for awhile. She was great; she could drive, and the children really got along with her. . . . She had to return to Austria; in fact, her sister is pregnant with triplets. . . . We don't have any family here.

Jill: At what point in your pregnancy did you get your diagnosis?

Antonia: First they told me I was pregnant with twins, then later quadruplets. I think it was probably 2 to 3 weeks, and I walked in my doctor's office and he said he only saw two sacs. Then later they saw three in one sac and one in the other. That's when they realized there were four hearts. . . four babies.

Jill: Your children were quite young. How much about your pregnancy did you share with your children?

Antonia: We told them, and they just walked around town saying mom was pregnant with four babies. And people said, "No, you mean one baby." And they said, "No! Four babies."

John: Our boys are pretty close. After they were born, Ben said, "Oh mom, I'm tired of people talking about the girls." Even when he went to the karate studio, people sort of came right at him. The second time I took him to karate, I just came right out and asked people not to say anything about the babies.

Jill: People were not sensitive?

John: They weren't. It was hard, because we were having quads and it was all over the news. People were pretty sensitive about Antonia being in the hospital. . .

Antonia: It was real hard for our other kids, because it's an unusual thing. It was very hard. John is a very good father. He did what he had to do.

John: And not just out in the world. . . what happens inside your home too. The help is the help, but when Mommy and Daddy are home, that is who everybody wants. Our kids do everything with us. If we go to the beach, everybody goes.

Antonia: They're 5 months old now and I want to try to treat each one equally. They're

very different in personality. It's really a big challenge, 'cause there are seven of them.

Jill: Can you tell us about your feelings when you and John first learned you were pregnant with four babies?

Antonia: When I first became pregnant with them, they told me that the odds were against me. The triplets were attached to one nutritional source and they had to share everything. . . it was not just a normal pregnancy or even a regular twin pregnancy. So I had to reach inside myself and ask myself, "What is it that I can live with?" And I decided to go for it. You really have to follow your own heart.

Dr. Klein: I wanted to go back and ask you about one comment you made. You said peo-ple were telling you that "the odds weren't good." What did that mean to you?

Antonia: One doctor told me that this would be a disaster. He even got angry at me, and I said, "I don't want to hear it." I walked out of there.

Dr. Klein: What was he telling you could happen, that would mean it was a disaster?

Antonia: He said that there were three babies in one sac and they were attached to the same placenta, and they're feeding off the same things and urinating in the same fluid. Apparently they didn't have a membrane separating them. . . I think one of them did have a membrane, but the other two didn't. And Lily did have a knot in her umbilical cord, but it was loose. He said the odds were against

John: This also may be why people thought that she might have Down's syndrome, because she had heart problems too. They said her tongue was a little large.

Antonia: No one knew if that baby had Down's syndrome until the baby was born, so it was like a big drama.

Dr. Klein: I remember John specifically asking a number of times if I was sure the baby didn't have Down's syndrome after she was born, after I looked at her and everything, so it really seemed to have stuck in there, a fear.

me, and it would be a disaster. He even pushed me to talk to another doctor. I said I didn't want to. I said I could deal better with it spiritually.

John: You had a lot of specialists, too, and they came in and saw different things—like on the ultrasound. I was going crazy.

Antonia: At 27 weeks, they told me Tara might have Down's syndrome—can you imagine what I felt? But Tara was the one they wanted me to keep, and to terminate the other three. I said, "No. If I terminate one, I terminate all. If I keep one, I keep all." That's what I could live with. Tara had a heart condition. She had a hole in her heart, and her pulmonary artery was smaller than it was supposed to be. And I said, "Well, can you fix it?" And he said, "Yes, we can fix it."

Antonia: Well, for me it was worse because I already have a special needs child at home, and they were telling me I'm going to have another one. Nikolas, he's a very normal child, extremely bright, but there's certain medications I have to give him. He has to take hormones.

John: There was stress, really. With the kids it got a little difficult. . . . They had their little moments, but it wasn't major. It was more like, "Where is Mommy?" and they'd cry a little bit and that's it. They got over it. They'd go see Mommy and everything would be fine.

Dr. Klein: I'm sure it was made even more stressful because you were talking with so many doctors. . . Sort of not knowing whom you should be listening to about what. . . In your situation, you know, no one doctor can say, "I've delivered five quads, six quads . . ." It is too unusual. Most physicians have never done it before.

John: Remember what I did with you [*talking to Dr. Klein*] when I kept on asking a question over and over? I did the same thing with our other doctors. I'd call and ask, "Did you see this, what do you think?" They might say, "Well, I don't see it." And I'm all for getting different opinions, but when you're dealing with your family—when you're dealing with your kids—opinions go out the window, really. You just want *an answer.* Some people can handle uncertainty, but with me, I need to know. I say, go with your heart, and go with the one that's done you right. I remember one time [our doctor] came in and said, "Look, you don't want to do anything crazy." He said, "Go with your heart. People see different things." And that's what I say, trust your intuition.

A TALE OF THREE BABIES

In our talks with the generous families who shared their experiences with us, one constant stood out: that individuals, marriages, and whole families were incredibly committed to providing the very best possible outcome for their children.

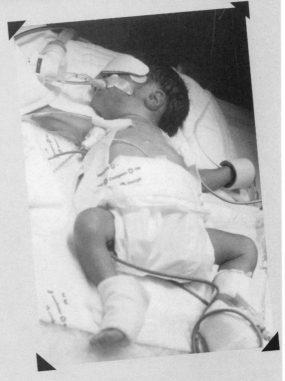

I'm Sarah and my son was born at 28 weeks, and he's now going to be 9 years old. It's kind of funny to go back in time; when we moved here I thought we had three months to settle in and unpack. Ten days later, I'd given birth to my first child. I went in to my OB, whom I had met a few months before we moved here. I told him I was having contractions; then I had one right there. He said, "Just lay low, stay in bed and relax, do nothing. I don't want to examine you, because I don't want to start anything, if nothing is happening."

I was too embarrassed to tell him that the furniture hadn't arrived and that I had no bed. But we had a sofa, and I did take it easy. I didn't take the idea of bed rest seriously, even though I was in the medical field and had told parents to really believe it when they say, "Do nothing." Before the next appointment, my water broke. We got in the car and my husband was not saying anything. It turns out he didn't exactly know where the hospital was. We saw a policeman, and my husband stopped in the middle of the street and asks for directions, and I'm freaking out now. We get there and they call the doctor, and I can't believe this is happening. A nurse came in. . . I wish I knew her name. She held my hand and said, "You're here. It's going to happen, whenever it's going to happen. There's nothing you can do about it. Just keep your faith and stay as calm as you can." I have to say, her words really helped. My OB came by, and his partner came by, and hours passed, and I'm thinking that I'll stay here for the next few weeks, and just be on bed rest and take whatever drugs they say I need. Then Dr. Klein came in and we talked about my due date. We talked about how far along I was. "I am 29 weeks!" "No, you're 28 weeks . . ." Finally I said, "It doesn't matter, 'cause I'm not going to have

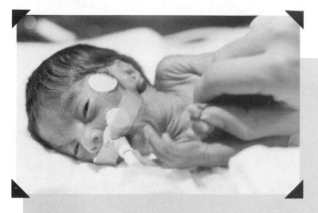

the baby for about 2 weeks." And Dr. Klein said, "I'm afraid I just don't think that is going to be the case." I was so angry at him. I thought, "This man wants me to have this baby now." I was in total denial. I just didn't want to face it.

Then my husband called. He'd gone to pay the movers, because while all this was going on, they had arrived, and had been sitting at our front door for hours. He said, "Should I go to the bank? I've got to pay them." I said, "You know what, I feel really good, go to the bank, pay them, come back and see me, whenever." Then, just as I hung up, my doctor's partner came in. He checked me and said, "This is it. We're going." I couldn't believe it. I guess I knew that Dr. Klein had been right, but I wanted so much to believe I could hold off for the next 2 weeks. He said, "The baby is coming, the head's down." Thank God my husband didn't go to the bank after all. He came back to the hospital as we were wheeling into delivery. The doctor said, "It's time to call the anesthesiologist if you want it." And I said, "No, no, no." Then I had this really bad contraction and I heard the nurse say: "The next contraction, push as hard as you can." And I'm

holding on for dear life, and she seemed to throw herself on me and she pushed my belly. I said, "Oh God, do I have to push again?" And she said, "No, it's all out." He was 3 pounds. When they put him against me I felt like I was holding nothing but a blanket—but I did get to hold him. He looked perfect, he was lusty and red and crying. And then I looked at him and I said his name, "Owen." It sounded really funny to me. He had these eyes, he was all eyes, and I really felt like he had intelligence. His face looked like he was a person already.

I thought I knew what I was in for because my godson had been born premature, but it was worse, 'cause you're living it, and it's your child. When you're going through it, you don't even want to hear about anyone else's normal life. There is no getting your mind off what you are going through. I didn't know anyone in my neighborhood. When I brought Owen home about 2½ months later, even though everyone said you need round-the-clock nursing—he had oxygen, medicine, monitor, and this and that—I couldn't stand having them live in my house. It felt so intrusive. And 2 weeks into it I said to Dr. Klein, "I want to do it all. I know what I'm doing." I was exhausted, but I didn't know it. I just wanted to get rid of everyone and have the baby and me, or my husband and me and the baby, but if I am honest about it, really just me and the baby.

I wanted to start over and say, "Okay, this is my normal new baby and I just want to have him for myself." Now, of course, I can see that it was not a healthy, realistic response. Unfortunately, a couple of weeks later I had to call all the nurses back. I needed the help all along, but I denied it. I just wanted that time with the baby—to pretend, I guess, that I had a normal baby, and I just wanted to be a normal person with that baby. It took a long time for me to sort it out. Still, it's an ongoing thing about having that premie and always needing all that special care; you just want to say at some point, "I don't want any more special care."

After Owen, I wanted a full-term baby. If I could have put Owen back in the womb, I would have, and done it all over again, just to do it right. So I got pregnant again when he was about 2½. This time my husband was not thrilled; he was scared. He didn't want to go through it all again. But I was sure it was not

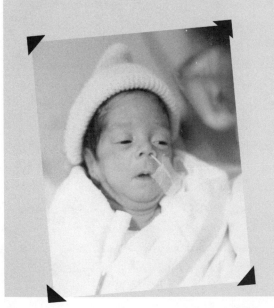

going to happen again: "We will have this perfect, normal baby. I just want to experience that, like other pregnant women." He said, "We have Owen, he's finally off everything, let's just leave it the way it is." I refused and I got pregnant. Then about 19 weeks into it I was put on bed rest. I really stayed in bed, and my sister came out and helped a little. But my husband really did it all—taking Owen to the sitter, going to work, coming home, doing the cleaning and cooking. I stayed in bed and only got out to take a shower.

Around 34 or 36 weeks, I was told effective in 2 weeks I was going to get off the medicine and be able to have the baby. It was around Mother's Day and the doctor said, "Since we're so close, you can go out for Mother's Day." So we went out for Mother's Day and everything was fine; I came home and went back to bed. My husband had finally come around to being happy about the pregnancy. I could hear his tone had changed, and he was telling all his friends on the phone, "The baby's coming." Then, on Memorial Day weekend, I suddenly realized that I couldn't remember the last time I had felt the baby move. My husband was talking on the phone to this friend of his, and I waited and waited, and then I said, "I've got to call the doctor." I didn't even tell him what was going on. I think he thought I felt contractions or something. So I called the OB and someone else was on call. I explained who I was and I said, "I don't remember when I felt the baby move, but I

heartbeat." And I said, "I want [my obstetrician]," and she said, "Let me call. I think for you he'll come out."

And he did. He was wonderful. He sat with us for 3 hours and told jokes and told us about growing up in New York. And when the baby came, it was just the doctor and the nurse with us. And that was so strange, 'cause when I had Owen, there were 11 doctors in there. And it was so quiet. Our baby was a boy and he looked just like Owen. I held my baby, [and our doctor] cleaned him and everything.

And I remember this guy came in the door. I knew he was from the morgue, but he was really nice. And he walked in and said, "Oh, I'm sorry." I said, "That's okay, can you wait? I'm not ready." And I held my son for a long time, and finally I gave him to the nurse. We named him Eric. Then I said to my husband, "You know, you didn't really want him." And he said, "That's not true; I just didn't want you to know I wanted him." He was mad at me for putting myself in danger, but he had never said any of that.

And then I had my daughter. That was the thing about having Eric. He gave us a lot of answers as to why Owen had been premature and why I went into labor early. When Eric's placenta came out, the doctor said, "You know, there are so many blood clots in there." When he saw the blood clots, he said he was going to draw some blood to see what was going on. Eight weeks later when I went back for a checkup, he had the answers.

think it was Thursday." I thought he was going to say, "Have a cup of coffee and get that baby moving." But he said, "Meet me at Cedars." I thought, this is not really happening.

We got a sitter and on the way to the hospital I finally said to my husband, "I don't remember when I last felt the baby move." But all this commotion was making me have a lot of contractions, so I thought, "Maybe that's the baby moving." We drove in silence all the way to the hospital. The nurse who took us in labor and delivery remembered us from 3 years back. That was amazing to me. She said, "How's your boy?" Then she introduced us to another nurse who was going to do the ultrasound. The poor nurse; she was really young and not prepared for this. She said, "There's something wrong with the machine; I'll be back." And she brought the first nurse back with her. That nurse just held our hands. She showed us the baby and she showed us the heart. She said, "There's no

"The reason you have contractions early in pregnancy is because the blood clots cause you to go into early labor. It caused the baby to have less oxygen." There were so many clots that the baby couldn't breath. I asked what we could do about that. He said in future pregnancies I would need a baby aspirin a day, and that would be enough to make the clots go away. Still bed rest, still early NSTs (nonstress test) to see how the baby's doing. So I was determined to get pregnant again.

Three more years went by, and my husband continued to say no. Then one day I said, "I'm doing it, with you or without you." And I meant it. I didn't know how I was going to do it, but I really meant it. I knew he didn't want Owen to be an only child, and I was willing to risk my marriage to make sure I had another pregnancy—a normal, regular pregnancy. Luckily he gave in. This time I thought, "Okay, I'll take that baby aspirin and maybe I won't even go into early labor." I'm thinking it's going to be perfectly normal.

At 20 weeks, the contractions started and I couldn't believe it. But I carried this one for 36 weeks, and she was fine: 6$^{1}/_{2}$ pounds, a girl. I know my husband is a wonderful father and loves his children, but he's fearful of fatherhood, and I know in my heart that if Eric had survived, I wouldn't have Emily. Eric gave us a world of knowledge, and that was his reason for being here. When Eric died, somebody said to me, "You'll always have pain about it, but someday you'll find out the meaning of his life, then you won't hurt so much." And I thought, "How stupid is that. What does that mean?"

But as time went by and I thought about it for a long time, I realized it was true, because if I hadn't had that experience, we wouldn't know about my blood problem and we would not have had Emily. When people ask me how many children I have, I always stutter and then I say, "I had three pregnancies and I have two children." I don't want to say I have two children or I had two pregnancies, because it

minimizes that child. And he's a person, and I acknowledge his bonding in our lives.

Before I had this experience it used to bug me to hear my grandmother say she had 11 children, 2 of whom had died. She would talk about those two other babies, like 9 was not enough. She would tell me that one day when I was a mother I would understand. When I lost the baby, my grandmother was still with us and I said, "Now I know." I wanted to know everything she went through, and she told me every little thing about her babies who had died. I was finally able to say to her, "I totally understand now why that was so much a part of you."

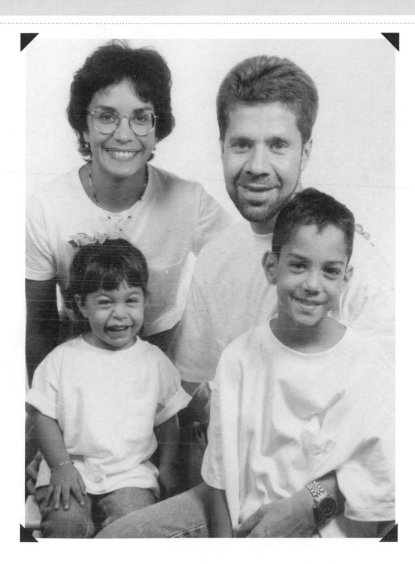

Glossary

ABER
see AUDITORY BRAINSTEM RESPONSE

ADRENAL STEROIDS
Chemicals that are similar to naturally occurring substances produced by the adrenal glands, which may be given either to a mother prior to birth to promote surfactant production or to a premature infant to improve lung function. Not to be confused with the steroids associated with bodybuilding.

ALVEOLI
Bubblelike air sacs in the lungs that form at the end of the bronchioles.

APNEA
Temporary cessation of breathing. See IDIOPATHIC APNEA OF PREMATURITY.

AUDITORY BRAINSTEM RESPONSE (ABER)
A method of hearing assessment that measures the brain's response to a sound. It is also referred to as BRAINSTEM AUDITORY EVOKED RESPONSE (BAER).

BAER
see BRAINSTEM AUDITORY EVOKED RESPONSE

BETA-ADRENERGIC AGENT

A synthetic or natural drug used to relax smooth muscle in the lung, which results in bronchodilation. Often used in the treatment of chronic lung disease.

BIOETHICS COMMITTEE

A hospital committee convened at the request of a parent or medical staff member to discuss and make suggestions regarding ethical/medical decisions that are a part of medical care. Such committees are likely to differ in each hospital, but the membership might be expected to include medical and non-medical personnel from the hospital, as well as patient representatives, clergy, or business people from the community.

BLOOD GAS

A measurement of the oxygen (O_2), carbon dioxide (CO_2), and acid level (pH) of the blood. Analysis of this information is important in determining appropriate medical therapy.

BRADYCARDIA

An abnormally low heart rate.

BRAINSTEM AUDITORY EVOKED RESPONSE (BAER)

see AUDITORY BRAINSTEM RESPONSE (ABER)

BRONCHIOLES

The smaller tubes in the lungs that extend from the bronchus.

BRONCHODILATOR

A drug that is used to relax bronchial muscle, allowing the bronchial tubes to expand.

BRONCHOPULMONARY DYSPLASIA (BPD)

A syndrome characterized by lung damage, seen in premature infants whose treatment for respiratory problems may have required an extended period of mechanical ventilation. May be referred to as CHRONIC LUNG DISEASE (CLD).

BRONCHO-TRACHEOMALACIA
An abnormal softening of the tissue of the bronchi and the trachea, commonly referred to as FLOPPY AIRWAYS.

BRONCHUS
The two smaller tubes in the lung that extend from the trachea.

BROVIAC
A specific type of catheter (tube) that is inserted into a vein and then threaded into the vena cava. The proximal (outside) end is then tunneled under the skin to come out someplace away from the vein used for insertion.

CARDIOPULMONARY RESUSCITATION (CPR)
A method of ventilating a person who has stopped breathing, by providing oxygen to the lungs that will then circulate to the other vital organs of the body. It is most frequently a combination of mouth-to-mouth resuscitation combined with externally applied chest compression. Cardiopulmonary resuscitation training is vitally important for parents and other caregivers of infants discharged from the hospital with a history of breathing control problems.

CEREBRAL PALSY (CP)
A term used to describe impaired muscular power and coordination from brain damage that presents itself as abnormalities in muscle tone (tension) and movement. It is what doctors refer to as a static neurological condition, which means that the brain damage does not change as a child gets older.

CHOLESTATIC JAUNDICE
A liver problem that is characterized by increased direct bilirubin in the blood. It is a possible complication that may appear after two or more weeks of parenteral nutrition. Also known as TPN CHOLESTASIS.

CHRONIC LUNG DISEASE (CLD)
Progressive and possibly severe respiratory problems that develop gradually during the first few weeks of life in some premature babies, usually with birth

weights under 1,000 grams. It may develop whether initial respiratory problems were severe or minimal. Your doctor may refer to this condition as CHRONIC RESPIRATORY INSUFFICIENCY OF PREMATURITY. BRONCHOPULMONARY DYSPLASIA also may be included under this general heading.

CHRONIC RESPIRATORY INSUFFICIENCY OF PREMATURITY
see CHRONIC LUNG DISEASE (CLD)

CLD
see CHRONIC LUNG DISEASE

COLOSTOMY
A surgical procedure that brings a portion of the colon (the large intestine) through the abdominal wall, enabling the colon to empty through the temporary opening.

CONGENITAL HEART DISEASE
Any of various forms of heart disease that may be present at birth.

CONTINUOUS POSITIVE AIRWAY PRESSURE (CPAP)
A continuous flow of oxygen and air delivered to the lungs that keeps them well aerated and prevents them from collapsing.

COR PULMONALE
Failure of the right side of the heart.

CORRECTED AGE
The age of an infant calculated on the basis of its expected date of delivery. A 5-month-old baby born 4 weeks prematurely would therefore have a corrected age of 4 months.

CP
see CEREBRAL PALSY

CPAP
see CONTINUOUS POSITIVE AIRWAY PRESSURE

CPR
see CARDIOPULMONARY RESUSCITATION

CRYOTHERAPY
The use of extreme cold to freeze tissue for a therapeutic purpose. Cryotherapy is used to reduce the progress of retinopathy of prematurity.

CT SCAN
A radiographic imaging technique.

DECIBEL
A unit of measurement used to describe the loudness of sound.

DIRECT BILIRUBIN
Bilirubin after it is metabolized by the liver.

DIRECTED DONOR PROGRAM
A program designed to allow patients or their families to request that blood needed for surgery or other therapies be donated by a known person, such as the father or a friend of the family.

DME
see DURABLE MEDICAL EQUIPMENT

DUCTUS ARTERIOSUS
A blood vessel in the fetus that connects the pulmonary artery to the aorta, which is the large artery coming from the heart that supplies the body with oxygen-rich blood.

DURABLE MEDICAL EQUIPMENT (DME)
Equipment, such as a home apnea monitor, that is supplied by a home health-care equipment company.

EARLY INTERVENTION PROGRAM

A course of therapy to support the particular developmental needs of an infant. Usually overseen by physical therapists, occupational therapists, or other specialists. Also known as INFANT STIMULATION PROGRAM.

ECHOCARDIOGRAM

An ultrasound evaluation of the heart.

ENT

Ear, nose, and throat. Also see PEDIATRIC EAR, NOSE, AND THROAT SURGEON (ENT).

ENTERAL NUTRITION

Any feeding that occurs via the gastrointestinal tract.

EXCHANGE TRANSFUSION

A procedure in which an infant's blood and circulating bilirubin is withdrawn slowly and exchanged for donated whole blood with low bilirubin levels. This is an effective and rapid way to lower bilirubin levels.

FIBEROPTIC BLANKET

A flexible material made of glass or plastic that transmits light. It may be used as an element of phototherapy to treat infants with jaundice.

FLOPPY AIRWAYS

see BRONCHO-TRACHEOMALACIA

FRACTION OF INSPIRED OXYGEN MIXED WITH AIR (F_iO_2)

The amount of oxygen, expressed as a percentage in a mixture of oxygen and air, that is given through a mask or nasal catheter.

FUNDOPLICATION

A surgical procedure used to treat GASTROESOPHAGEAL REFLUX (GER).

GASTROESOPHAGEAL REFLUX (GER)

A condition that causes the contents (or some of the contents) of the stomach to go back up into the esophagus, and sometimes all the way back up to the back of the mouth and down into the trachea.

GASTROSTOMY

The surgical introduction of a tube inserted through an incision in the abdominal wall directly into the stomach in order to provide a direct infusion of nutrition. This tube will enable an infant to take feedings directly into the stomach until mouth feeding is possible.

GAVAGE

A method of feeding liquid or semiliquid nutrition with a tube into the stomach.

GER

see GASTROESOPHAGEAL REFLUX

GE REFLUX

see GASTROESOPHAGEAL REFLUX

GERMINAL MATRIX

A layer of cells that surrounds the ventricles of the brain.

GERMINAL MATRIX HEMORRHAGE

A hemorrhage which is either contained in the germinal matrix layer next to the ventricle and does not extend into it, or does so only slightly, resulting in less than 10% of the ventricle area becoming filled with blood. Also referred to as a grade I PV-IVH.

HB

see HEMOGLOBIN

HCT

see HEMATOCRIT

HEAD CIRCUMFERENCE

One of three measurements, along with an infant's height and weight, that are entered on an infant's growth chart and used to determine adequate growth at checkups at the pediatrician's office.

HEAD ULTRASOUND

A diagnostic tool that outlines the shape of tissues within the skull with sound waves to look for evidence of intracranial hemorrhage or other conditions occurring within the cranium.

HEARING SCREEN

A test of hearing acuity that should be performed on most infants who are to be discharged from the NICU. Methods of hearing assessment in infants and children include AUDITORY BRAINSTEM RESPONSE (ABER), which is also referred to as BRAINSTEM AUDITORY EVOKED RESPONSE (BAER) and OTOACOUSTIC EMISSIONS (OAE).

HEMATOCRIT (HCT)

The amount of red blood cells present in a given volume of blood.

HEMOGLOBIN (Hb)

A combination of a simple protein and an iron-containing pigment in red blood cells that carries oxygen from the lungs throughout the tissues of the rest of the body.

HUMAN MILK FORTIFIER (HMF)

Either a liquid or a powder that can be added to breast milk to enhance its mineral and caloric content.

HYDROCEPHALUS

An increased accumulation of cerebrospinal fluid within the ventricles of the brain resulting from interference with normal circulation and inability to adequately absorb fluid. It may be caused by infection, developmental anomalies, blood in the ventricles, injury, or a brain tumor.

HYPERGLYCEMIA
An elevated level of glucose (sugar) in the blood.

HYPOGLYCEMIA
A deficiency of glucose (sugar) in the blood. Also known as LOW BLOOD SUGAR.

HYPOXIA
Periods of oxygen deprivation.

ICROP
see INTERNATIONAL CLASSIFICATION OF RETINOPATHY OF PREMATURITY

IDIOPATHIC APNEA OF PREMATURITY
Temporary cessation of respiration of the premature newborn, which is neither induced nor related to another disease.

ILEOSTOMY
A surgical procedure that brings a portion of the ileum (a section of the intestine closer to the colon) through the abdominal wall, enabling it to empty through the temporary opening.

INCUBATOR
see ISOLETTE

INFANT STIMULATION PROGRAM
see EARLY INTERVENTION PROGRAM

INFLUENZA
An acute respiratory infection that is caused by a particular group of viruses and is contagious. It is typically characterized by fever and chills and is usually most common in winter and spring. Influenza immunizations are indicated for parents, other siblings, and caregivers of young premature infants, and for those infants with chronic lung disease who are over 6 months of age.

INTERNATIONAL CLASSIFICATION OF RETINOPATHY OF PREMATURITY (ICROP)

A system developed in the 1980s that uses three features—position, extent, and disease—as well as stages of vascular development to describe the progress of RETINOPATHY OF PREMATURITY (ROP).

INTUBATION

The insertion of a narrow tube into an infant's nose or mouth and into the trachea in preparation for delivering additional respiratory assistance.

ISOLETTE

An enclosed crib for premature infants in which temperature and humidity can be regulated. Also known as an INCUBATOR.

IVH

see PERIVENTRICULAR-INTRAVENTRICULAR HEMORRHAGE (PV-IVH)

JAUNDICE

The yellow color of the body that is the result of the liver's inability to metabolize the yellow-colored bilirubin that is produced as red blood cells break down. Jaundice is characterized by a yellow color, first in the eyes and face, and then down to the trunk and legs. Although jaundice can also occur in term babies, the less mature systems of premature babies make them particularly vulnerable to jaundice.

JEJUNOSTOMY

A temporary surgical opening in the abdominal wall to allow for direct emptying of the jejunum (the middle part of the small intestine, past the stomach and duodenum).

KANGAROO CARE

A natural, nontechnological technique for the care of newborns and infants originally developed in South America, where there was a shortage of incubators. Susan Luddington, a nurse/midwife, is credited with bringing kangaroo care (also known now as "skin-to-skin care") to the United States, where it is being embraced by nurses, doctors, mothers, and fathers as a safe, beneficial way for either parent to provide comforting touch to their premie. Kangaroo care, as practiced in the United States, brings a mother or father together with their premature baby, who is held upright, dressed only in a diaper, next to a parent's bare chest. It is particularly helpful in helping mothers of premature infants to establish successful breast-feeding.

LASER PHOTOCOAGULATION
see LASER SURGERY

LASER SURGERY
A procedure used to treat retinopathy of prematurity by utilizing a laser light delivered to a targeted area of the retina to break down cells and slow the accelerated growth of blood vessels present in ROP. Also referred to as LASER PHOTOCOAGULATION.

LOW BLOOD SUGAR
see HYPOGLYCEMIA

MCT
see MEDIUM CHAIN TRIGLYCERIDES

MEDIUM CHAIN TRIGLYCERIDES (MCT)
Triglycerides are fatty acids. The medium chain triglycerides differ from others in that they are digested and absorbed differently than usual dietary fats, making them particularly useful in treating malabsorption problems.

MENINGITIS
An inflammation of the membranes of the spinal cord or brain.

NASAL CANNULA
Small plastic tubing fitted to the face with two small nipples that are inserted into the nose and connected by tube to an oxygen delivery system.

NASAL CONTINUOUS POSITIVE AIRWAY PRESSURE (NCPAP)
see CONTINUOUS POSITIVE AIRWAY PRESSURE (CPAP)

NASAL OXYGEN CANNULA
see NASAL CANNULA

NASOGASTRIC TUBE (NGT)
A tube that enters the body through one nostril and extends down into the stomach for feeding.

NEBULIZER
An apparatus used to produce a fine spray or mist by passing air through a liquid or vibrating liquid at a high frequency to produce extremely small particles.

NEC
see NECROTIZING ENTEROCOLITIS

NECROTIC
The death of a section of tissue.

NECROTIZING ENTEROCOLITIS (NEC)
A disorder of sick premature infants that occurs when a section of either the small or large intestine is damaged or dies. Necrotizing enterocolitis does not always kill all the tissue in a particular area of the intestine.

NEONATAL INDIVIDUALIZED DEVELOPMENTAL CARE AND ASSESSMENT PROGRAM (NIDCAP)
The Neonatal Individualized Developmental Care and Assessment Program or programs like it are increasingly utilized in today's hospitals. It was developed as a result of research in the 1980s by Heidelise Als, PhD (Associate Professor of Psychology [Psychiatry] at Harvard Medical School, and Director of Neurobehavioral Infant and Child Studies, Children's Hospital, Boston). Als' research determined that compromised respiratory status and overall health of preterm and other at-risk infants could be improved by providing care that was guided by direct observation of each infant's behavior in the neonatal intensive care unit.

NEONATAL INTENSIVE CARE UNIT (NICU)

An area of the hospital that provides intensive care for sick newborns.

NEONATAL NURSE PRACTITIONER (NNP)

An RN, certified by the state, who has received additional training as a physician extender to give medical care (as differentiated from nursing care) to neonatal patients under the direction of a neonatologist.

NEPHROCALCINOSIS

Calcium deposits in kidney tissue.

NGT

see NASOGASTRIC TUBE

NICU

see NEONATAL INTENSIVE CARE UNIT

NIDCAP

see NEONATAL INDIVIDUALIZED DEVELOPMENTAL CARE AND ASSESSMENT PROGRAM

NNP

see NEONATAL NURSE PRACTITIONER

OAE

see OTOACOUSTIC EMISSIONS

ORAL DEFENSIVENESS

Resistance to oral feedings.

OTOACOUSTIC EMISSIONS (OAE)

A method of hearing assessment in which sound emissions from the inner ear itself can be measured and used as a means of determining an infant's hearing capabilities.

PARENTERAL NUTRITION

The provision of nutrients through an intravenous (IV) or intra-arterial line, which is more likely to be established for babies with severe respiratory and/or circulatory problems after birth.

PATENT DUCTUS ARTERIOSUS (PDA)

A condition in which the ductus arteriosus, which is a blood vessel in the fetus that connects the pulmonary artery to the aorta, fails to close up after birth.

PCP

see PRIMARY CARE PHYSICIAN

PDA

see PATENT DUCTUS ARTERIOSUS

PEDIATRIC EAR, NOSE, AND THROAT SURGEON (ENT)

A medical doctor who specializes in the surgery of the ears, nose, and throat of infants and children.

PERCUTANEOUS VENOUS CENTRAL CATHETER (PVCC LINE)

A catheter inserted through the skin into the vein of the arm or another peripheral vein, and then threaded all the way up until it reaches the vena cava, which is the large blood vessel in the center of the body that carries blood back to the heart.

PERINATOLOGY

A specialized area of health care concerned with infants throughout antepartum (prior to birth), neonatal, and postnatal care.

PERIODIC BREATHING

Three or more apneic episodes lasting between 3 and 10 seconds within periods of normal breathing of 20 seconds.

PERIPHERALLY INSERTED CENTRAL CATHETER (PICC LINE)

Another term for a PVCC line.

PERIVENTRICULAR-INTRAVENTRICULAR HEMORRHAGE (PV-IVH)

Internal bleeding in the brain. It is a condition that is usually unique to premature babies. Diagnosis is made by ultrasound of the brain; PV-IVH occurs primarily in an area of the brain called the GERMINAL MATRIX. It is also referred to as IVH.

PERIVENTRICULAR LEUKOMALACIA (PVL)

A condition caused by an interruption of the blood flow to the brain tissue and subsequent injury to the brain cells because of the resulting lack of oxygen. It can be associated with any grade of IVH.

PFT

see PULMONARY FUNCTION TESTS

PHOTOTHERAPY

Exposure to light for purposes of treating jaundice in newborns. It can be introduced through the use of a bank of fluorescent lighting or with a fiberoptic blanket.

PICC LINE

see PERIPHERALLY INSERTED CENTRAL CATHETER

PIE

see PULMONARY INTERSTITIAL EMPHYSEMA

PMA

see POSTMENSTRUAL AGE

PNEUMOTHORAX

Air outside the lungs within the chest cavity. It occurs because of a rupture of the alveoli, and is often associated with other lung problems such as RDS. If it is serious, it may be referred to as a collapsed lung, and it can cause respiratory compromise. These severe cases will need to be treated by placing a tube (chest tube) into the chest cavity to remove the air.

POSTMENSTRUAL AGE (PMA)

A method of calculating the gestational age of an infant as determined by counting from the date of the mother's last period.

PREMATURE INFANT

An infant born prior to the completion of the 37th week of gestation.

PRIMARY CARE PHYSICIAN (PCP)

A pediatrician or other suitably trained physician who provides comprehensive, coordinated, family-centered, and continuing care for the children in your family. He is the focus of your children's "medical home." The most effective way to provide for your baby's care after discharge is to promote early involvement of a primary care physician.

PULMONARY EDEMA

Excessive fluid in the lung tissue.

PULMONARY FUNCTION TESTS (PFT)

A series of measurements used to assess the ability of the lungs to function.

PULMONARY HEMORRHAGE

Bleeding into the lungs.

PULMONARY INTERSTITIAL EMPHYSEMA (PIE)

Pockets of air in the lungs outside the airways.

PULSE OXIMETER

A device that is attached to a sensor wrapped around a foot or hand that measures oxygen saturation, an indicator of the level of oxygen in the blood.

PVCC LINE

see PERCUTANEOUS VENOUS CENTRAL CATHETER

PV-IVH

see PERIVENTRICULAR-INTRAVENTRICULAR HEMORRHAGE

PVL
see PERIVENTRICULAR LEUKOMALACIA

RDS
see RESPIRATORY DISTRESS SYNDROME

RECOMBINANT HUMAN ERYTHROPOIETIN
A commercially available product that stimulates the production of red blood cells.

RESPIRATORY DISTRESS SYNDROME (RDS)
Acutely impaired respiratory function in a premature infant caused by insufficient surfactant production. This is the most common single cause of respiratory problems in the premature infant, and is rarely seen in infants of more than 37 weeks gestation.

RESPIRATORY SYNCYTIAL VIRUS (RSV)
A virus spread by the airborne spray of a cough or sneeze, or by hand-to-hand contact with anyone or anything that harbors the virus. It can occur at any time, but is particularly common during the winter months. In a young premature baby, particularly one with BPD, respiratory syncytial virus can cause serious breathing problems, often resulting in rehospitalization.

RESTORE
Trade name for a paraffinlike substance used to keep a nasal cannula in place while protecting an infant's tender skin from being damaged by tape. It comes in paper-thin sheets that are easily cut into the required shape.

RETINA
The light-sensitive nerve tissue that lines the back of the eye.

RETINOPATHY OF PREMATURITY (ROP)
A disorder of the developing retinal blood supply, which occurs in some premature babies. Retinopathy of prematurity may cause mild to severe visual impairment.

ROP

see RETINOPATHY OF PREMATURITY

RSV

see RESPIRATORY SYNCYTIAL VIRUS

SEPSIS

Infection in the bloodstream.

SHORT-BOWEL SYNDROME

A condition that occurs when the bowel's ability to absorb sufficient nutrition is diminished as a result of significant bowel resection (surgical removal). This results in a decrease in the absorptive surface of the bowel, a depletion of vital enzymes, and *hypermotility* (overly rapid movement of nutrition through the bowel).

SURFACTANT

A soapy-feeling substance that coats the surface of the alveoli, changing surface tension and keeping them from collapsing.

TERM

The normal period of gestation, which is approximately 9 calendar months or 37 to 42 weeks gestation.

TOTAL PARENTERAL NUTRITION (TPN)

A method of delivering total nutrition by IV rather than through the gastrointestinal tract. Because of the high glucose concentration that is sometimes necessary for adequate calories, a central catheter is often used.

TPN

see TOTAL PARENTERAL NUTRITION

TPN CHOLESTASIS

see CHOLESTATIC JAUNDICE

TRANSIENT TACHYPNEA OF THE NEWBORN (TTN)

A condition caused by a delay in absorption of lung fluid after birth. It has a characteristic X ray, usually requires only minimal extra-respiratory support, and resolves rapidly within 3 days (usually less than 24 hours) after birth.

TRANSPYLORIC FEEDING

Enteral nutrition provided through a tube inserted into either the nose or mouth, through the stomach, and directly into the jejunum.

TROPHIC FEED

A small amount of enteral feeding. Trophic feeding does not supply sufficient calories for growth, but is effective in stimulating gastrointestinal maturation and function.

TTN

see TRANSIENT TACHYPNEA OF THE NEWBORN

ULTRASOUND

A diagnostic imaging tool that produces a picture of an organ or other tissue by recording the echoes as sound strikes tissues of varying density, translating them into a visual image.

VENTRICLES

The open spaces in the brain tissue that carry fluid and probably serve to de-crease the weight of the brain.

VENTRICULO-PERITONEAL SHUNT

A thin tube with a one-way valve that is placed into a ventricle in the brain and passed under the baby's skin, all the way to the abdominal cavity.

VP SHUNT

see VENTRICULO-PERITONEAL SHUNT

Conversion Table of Pounds and Ounces to Grams

		0	1	2	3	4	5	6	7	OUNCES
	0	--	28	57	85	113	142	170	198	
	1	454	482	510	539	567	595	624	652	
	2	907	936	964	992	1021	1049	1077	1106	
	3	1361	1389	1417	1446	1474	1503	1531	1559	
	4	1814	1843	1871	1899	1928	1956	1984	2013	
	5	2268	2296	2325	2353	2381	2410	2438	2466	
	6	2722	2750	2778	2807	2835	2863	2892	2920	
	7	3175	3203	3232	3260	3289	3317	3345	3374	
	8	3629	3657	3685	3714	3742	3770	3799	3827	
	9	4082	4111	4139	4167	4196	4224	4252	4281	
	10	4536	4564	4593	4621	4649	4678	4706	4734	
	11	4990	5018	5046	5075	5103	5131	5160	5188	
	12	5443	5471	5500	5528	5557	5585	5613	5642	
	13	5897	5925	5953	5982	6010	6038	6067	6095	
	14	6350	6379	6407	6435	6464	6492	6520	6549	
	15	6804	6832	6860	6889	6917	6945	6973	7002	
	16	7257	7286	7313	7342	7371	7399	7427	7456	
	17	7711	7739	7768	7796	7824	7853	7881	7909	
	18	8165	8192	8221	8249	8278	8306	8335	8363	
	19	8618	8646	8675	8703	8731	8760	8788	8816	
	20	9072	9100	9128	9157	9185	9213	9242	9270	
	21	9525	9554	9582	9610	9639	9667	9695	9724	
POUNDS	22	9979	10007	10036	10064	10092	10120	10149	10177	

	8	9	10	11	12	13	14	15	OUNCES
0	227	255	283	312	340	369	397	425	
1	680	709	737	765	794	822	850	879	
2	1134	1162	1191	1219	1247	1276	1304	1332	
3	1588	1616	1644	1673	1701	1729	1758	1786	
4	2041	2070	2098	2126	2155	2183	2211	2240	
5	2495	2523	2551	2580	2608	2637	2665	2693	
6	2948	2977	3005	3033	3062	3090	3118	3147	
7	3402	3430	3459	3487	3515	3544	3572	3600	
8	3856	3884	3912	3941	3969	3997	4026	4054	
9	4309	4337	4366	4394	4423	4451	4479	4508	
10	4763	4791	4819	4848	4876	4904	4933	4961	
11	5216	5245	5273	5301	5330	5358	5386	5415	
12	5670	5698	5727	5755	5783	5812	5840	5868	
13	6123	6152	6180	6209	6237	6265	6294	6322	
14	6577	6605	6634	6662	6690	6719	6747	6776	
15	7030	7059	7087	7115	7144	7172	7201	7228	
16	7484	7512	7541	7569	7597	7626	7654	7682	
17	7938	7966	7994	8023	8051	8079	8108	8136	
18	8391	8420	8448	8476	8504	8533	8561	8590	
19	8845	8873	8902	8930	8958	8987	9015	9043	
20	9298	9327	9355	9383	9412	9440	9469	9497	
21	9752	9780	9809	9837	9865	9894	9922	9950	
POUNDS 22	10206	10234	10262	10291	10319	10347	10376	10404	

Recommended Childhood Immunization Schedule[1]

Vaccine Age ▶ ▼	Birth	1 mo	2 mos	4 mos	6 mos	12 mos	15 mos	18 mos	4-6 yrs
Hepatitis B [2,3]	Hep B-1	Hep B-1							
		Hep B-2	Hep B-2		Hep B-3	Hep B-3	Hep B-3	Hep B-3	
Diphtheria, Tetanus, Pertussis [4]		DTaP or DTP	DTaP or DTP	DTaP or DTP		DTaP or DTP[4]	DTaP or DTP[4]	DTaP or DTP[4]	DTaP or DTP
H. influenzae type b [5]		Hib	Hib	Hib [5]	Hib [5]	Hib [5]			
Polio [6]		Polio [6]	Polio		Polio [6]	Polio [6]	Polio [6]		Polio
Measles, Mumps, Rubella [7]					MMR	MMR			MMR [7]
Varicella [8] (Chicken Pox)					Var	Var	Var		

United States, January-December 1997

The immunization dose and schedule for a premature baby is the same (with one exception) as for a full-term baby and, beginning at two months of age, is based on actual age, not age corrected for prematurity. See chapter II under the heading "Dr. Klein Comments on the Premature Baby's Schedule of Visits, Immunizations, and the Complete Checkup" for a discussion of the hepatitis B immunization.

Shaded bars indicate range of acceptable ages for vaccination.

Approved by the Advisory Committee on Immunization Practices (ACIP), American Academy of Pediatrics (AAP), and American Academy of Family Physicians (AAFP).

Footnotes

[1] This schedule indicates the recommended age for routine administration of currently licensed childhood vaccines. Some combination vaccines are available and may be used whenever administration of all components of the vaccine is indicated. Providers should consult the manufacturers' package inserts for detailed recommendations.

[2] **Infants born to HBsAg-negative mothers** should receive 2.5 µg of Merck vaccine (Recombivax HB) or 10 µg of SmithKline Beecham (SB) vaccine (Engerix-B). The 2nd dose should be administered +/-1 mo after the 1st dose.

Infants born to HBsAg-positive mothers should receive 0.5 mL hepatitis B immune globulin (HBIG) within 12 hrs of birth, and either 5 µg of Merck vaccine (Recombivax HB) or 10 µg of SB vaccine (Engerix-B) at a separate site. The 2nd dose is recommended at 1-2 mos of age and the 3rd dose at 6 mos of age.

Infants born to mothers whose HBsAg status is unknown should receive either 5 µg of Merck vaccine (Recombivax HB) or 10 µg of SB vaccine (Engerix-B) within 12 hrs of birth. The 2nd dose of vaccine is recommended at 1 mo of age and the 3rd dose at 6 mos of age. Blood should be drawn at the time of delivery to determine the mother's HBsAG status; if it is positive, the infant should receive HBIG as soon as possible (no later than 1 wk of age). The dosage and timing of subsequent vaccine doses should be based upon the mother's HBsAG status.

[3] Children and adolescents who have not been vaccinated against hepatitis B in infancy may begin the series during any childhood visit. Those who have not previously received 3 doses of hepatitis B vaccine should initiate or complete the series during the 11- to 12-year-old visit. The 2nd dose should be administered at least 4 mos after the 1st dose and at least 2 mos after the 2nd dose.

[4] DTaP (diphtheria and tetanus toxoids and acellular pertussis vaccine) is the preferred vaccine for all doses in the vaccination series, including completion of the series in children who have received +/-1 dose of whole-cell DTP vaccine. Whole-cell DTP is an acceptable alternative to DTaP. The 4th dose (DTP or DTaP) may be administered as early as 12 months of age, provided 6 months have elapsed since the 3rd dose, and if the child is considered unlikely to return at 15-18 mos of age. Td (tetanus and diphtheria toxoids, absorbed, for adult use) is recommended at 11-12 years of age if at least 5 years have elapsed since the last dose of DTP, DTaP, or DT. Subsequent routine Td boosters are recommended every 10 years.

[5] Three *H. influenzae* type b (Hib) conjugate vaccines are licensed for infant use. If PRP-OMP (PedvaxHIB [Merck]) is administered at 2 and 4 mos of age, a dose at 6 mos is not required. After completing the primary series, any Hib conjugate vaccine may be used as a booster.

[6] Two poliovirus vaccines are currently licensed in the U.S.: inactivated poliovirus vaccine (IPV) and oral poliovirus vaccine (OPV). The following schedules are all acceptable by the ACIP, the AAP, and the AAFT, and parents and providers may choose among them:

     1. IPV at 2 and 4 mos; OPV at 12-18 mos and 4-6 yr
     2. IPV at 2, 4, 12-18 mos, and 4-6 yr
     3. OPV at 2, 4, 6-18 mos, and 4-6 yr

The ACIP routinely recommends schedule 1. IPV is the only poliovirus vaccine recommended for immunocompromised persons and their household contacts.

[7] The 2nd dose of MMR is routinely recommended at 4-6 yrs. of age or at 11-12 yrs. of age, but may be administered during any visit, provided at least 1 month has elapsed since receipt of the 1st dose and that both doses are administered at or after 12 months of age.

[8] Susceptible children may receive Varicella vaccine (Var) at any visit after the first birthday, and those who lack a reliable history of chicken pox should be immunized during the 11-12 year-old visit. Children +/-13 years of age should receive 2 doses, at least 1 mos apart.

Adapted from The American Academy of Pediatrics. Active and Passive Immunization. In: Peter G. Ed. 1997 *Red Book; Report of the Committee of Infectious Diseases.* 24th, Ed. Elk Grove Village, IL: American Academy of Pediatrics; 1997; 18-19

Growth Charts

Boys: Birth to 18 Months Physical Growth NCHS Percentile*
Premature Boy Born at 27 Weeks Gestation

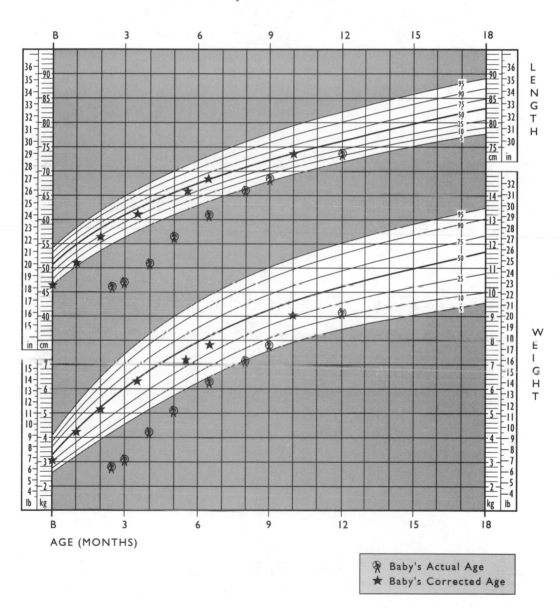

AGE (MONTHS)

| | Baby's Actual Age |
| ★ | Baby's Corrected Age |

Boys: Birth to 18 Months Physical Growth NCHS Percentile*
Premature Boy Born at 34 Weeks Gestation

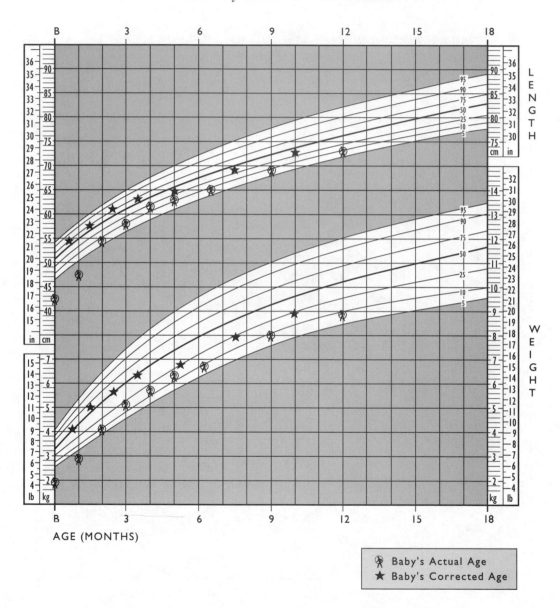

AGE (MONTHS)

🧒 Baby's Actual Age
★ Baby's Corrected Age

* Adapted from Hammil, PVV Drizd, TA Johnson CL, Reed RB Roche AF, Moore WM: Physical growth: National Center for Health Statistics percentiles. AM J CLIN NUTR 32:607-629, 1979. Data from the National Center for Health Statistics (NCHS), Hyattsville, Maryland. ©1992 Ross Laboratories

Resource Guide

ADVOCACY AND SUPPORT

ACCH (The Association for the Care of Children's Health)
(609) 224–1742
fax: (609) 423–3420
e-mail: amkent@smarthub.com
A multidisciplinary committee dedicated to promoting family-centered care, and providing education, information about resources, research, and advocacy.

The Federation for Children with Special Needs
(617) 482–2915
A coalition of parents offering educational information, as well as information regarding medical, legal, and financial resources for families with children with special needs.

IVH Parents
(305) 232–0381
For parents and professionals working with babies and children who have had an intraventricular hemorrhage. They share information, provide support, and conduct ongoing research.

National Perinatal Association
3500 East Fletcher Avenue, Suite 209
Tampa, FL 33613
(813) 971–1008
fax: (813) 971–9306
e-mail: npaonline@aol.com

SNAP (Special Needs Advocate for Children)
Nadine O. Vogel, MBA, President, Executive Director, Founder
(310) 201–9614
(888) 310–9889
fax: (310) 201–9889
http://www.snapinfo.org
e-mail: info@snapinfo.org

Founded to provide information, education, advocacy, and referrals to families with special needs children of all ages and disabilities.

BREAST-FEEDING

Cozy Cuddles Nursing Pillow
(416) 299–5507

Nursing comfort pillows with convenient washable covers.

Lact-Aid International Incorporated
(423) 744–9090

Supplemental feeding system provides oral sucking therapy for infants, as well as nutritional supplementation.

La Leche League International
(847) 519–9585

Many useful items for nursing such as: several styles of nursing pillows, baby cups for tiny infants who have trouble sucking, breast shells for women with inverted nipples, nursing pads, posture-correct nursing stool, heat pads, lanolin cream for sore nipples, milk freezer bags.

Maternity and Nursing Additions
(800) 571–5837

Medela
(800) 435–8316
Breast pumps and nursing aids; directs customers to most convenient
rental station and/or breast-feeding consultant.

CAR SEAT HEAD ROLLS

Sew Baby
(800) 249–1907
This company sells patterns for car seat head rolls.

CHILD-PROOFING AND SAFETY

KidCo
(800) 553–5529

Office of Information and Public Affairs
U.S. Consumer Product Safety Commission
Washington, DC 20207
Publication #202, *The Safe Nursery–A Buyer's Guide*

One Step Ahead
(800)950–5120

Perfectly Safe
(800) 837–KIDS

Rev-a-Shelf
(800) 762–9030

Right Start catalog
(800) 548–8531

The Safety Zone
(800) 999–3030

CLOTHING AND OTHER ITEMS FOR PREMATURE BABIES

American Sewing Guild
(816) 444–3500
Contact the Guild for referrals to chapters who do sewing for premies.

Children's Medical Ventures, Inc.
(888) 766–8443
Diapers and other clothing and support items.

Commonwealth Premature Pampers
(800) 543–4932
Diapers for babies up to five pounds.

Cottage Heirlooms
323 East Adams Avenue
Alhambra, CA 91801
(626) 281–9211
Heirloom-quality infant christening gowns, imported lace, Swiss batiste, Irish linen, and silk.

The Preemie Store
(800) 676–8469
fax: (714) 434–7510
Clothing, books, headrests, womb sounds, items for developmental support, NICU Diaries.

Preemie Yums
(503) 370–9279
Preemie Yums has a comprehensive list of patterns for premies. Fabrics at reasonable prices, precut fabric, and ready-to-wear premie outfits are also available.

COMPLICATED PREGNANCY

Sidelines National Support Network
(714) 497–2265
http://www.sidelines.org
Peer counseling, printed information, and support for families having complicated pregnancies.

GASTROINTESTINAL PROBLEMS

UOA (United Ostomy Association)
(800) 826–0826
Consists of 550 chapters across North America. It is a volunteer-based health organization providing support for those who have or will have ostomy procedures.

HEARING PROBLEMS

American Society for Deaf Children
(916) 641–6084
fax: (916) 641–6085
Parent Hotline: (800) 942–ASDC
e-mail: ASDC1@aol.com
A tax-exempt organization furthering the services of the International Association of Parents of the Deaf.

MAGAZINES, NEWSLETTERS, AND BOOKS

TWINS® magazine (published six times each year)
(800) 328–3211
5350 South Roslyn Street
Suite 400
Englewood, CO 80111
Twins World Magazine
(219) 627–5414

CLIMB
c/o Jean Kollantai
P.O. Box 1064
Palmer, AK 99645

The National Parenting Center Newsletter (published monthly)
  TNPC
(800) 753–6667

Our Newsletter (published quarterly)
Center for Loss in Multiple Birth, Inc.
(907) 746–6123

The Browne Twins Series
(800) TWIN–BKS
Written by Patricia Frechtman, illustrated by Ric Harbin.
The Twins' Beginning, The Twins Come Home, The Twins' First Walk, The Twins' First Visit to the Doctor, The Twins Are on the Go, The Twins' First Birthday

Drawings from the Newborn
Poems and drawings of infants in crisis by Heather Spears; medical afterword by Jorgen Paulin, MD.

Kangaroo Care: The Best You Can Do to Help Your Preterm Infant
Written by Susan M. Luddington-Hoe and Susan K. Golant.

MULTIPLE BIRTH

CLIMB (Center for Loss in Multiple Birth, Inc.)
c/o Jean Kollantai
P.O. Box 1064
Palmer, AK 99645
(907) 746–6123
A nonprofit organization offering support and resources to parents

who have experienced the death of one, both, or all of their children during a twin or higher-order multiple pregnancy, at birth, or during infancy.

Mothers of Supertwins (MOST)
P.O. Box 951
Brentwood, NY 11717
(516) 434–MOST
A nonprofit organization serving the needs of families expecting multiples or those already the parents of triplets, quadruplets, or quintuplets.

The National Organization of Mothers of Twins Clubs, Inc.
    (NOMOTC)
P.O. Box 23185
Albuquerque, NM 87192–1188
(505) 275–0955
http://www.nomotc.org
A nonprofit nationwide network of parents of multiples clubs sharing information, concerns, and advice.

Twin Services
P.O. Box 10066
Berkeley, CA 94709
(510) 524–0863
fax: (510) 524–0894
Se habla español.
Offers free counseling and referral services.

VISION PROBLEMS

American Foundation for the Blind
11 Penn Plaza
New York, NY 10001
(800) 232–5463
(212) 502–7600

The American Printing House for the Blind
P.O. Box 6085
Louisville, KY 40206
(800) 223–1839
(502) 895–2405
fax: (502) 899–2274
http://www.aph.org

Blind Children's Fund
c/o Sherry Raynor
4740 Okemos Road
Okemos, MI 48864–1637
(517) 347–1357
fax: (517) 347–1459
http://www.blindchildrensfund.org
e-mail: blindchildren@aol.com

Blind Children's Fund Resource Center
2971 53rd Street SE
Auburn, WA 98072
(253) 735–6350

Future Reflections: The National Federation of the Blind Magazine for
     Parents of Blind Children
National Organization of Parents of Blind Children
1800 Johnson Street
Baltimore, MD 21230
(410) 659–9314

Grasp and Hand Skills
Baby Discovering His Hands
The Perinatal Team Office
c/o Sue Wolff
The Children's Medical Center
One Children's Plaza

Dayton, OH 45404–1815
(937) 226–8468
Two pamphlets for the parents of visually impaired infants.

Library of Congress Division for the Blind and Physically
   Handicapped
1291 Taylor Street NW
Washington, DC 20213

National Organization of Parents of Blind Children
c/o Barbara Cheadle, President
1800 Johnson Street
Baltimore, MD 21230
(410) 659–9314
fax: (410) 685–5653
ftp.nfb.org
e-mail: nfb@access.digex.net

The VIP Newsletter
(517) 347–1357
Published by the Blind Children's Fund.

Endnotes

CHAPTER FOUR
....

1. *Quarterly Bulletin of the National Perinatal Association* 4, no. 1 (spring 1997).

2. *Los Angeles Times*, 5 February 1997.

CHAPTER FIVE
....

1. *Pediatrics* 1996; 98: 779–783.

2. *J. Pediatrics* 117 (1990): 112.

CHAPTER SIX
....

1. Marcia S. Stevens, RN, DNSc, "Parents Coping with Infants Requiring Home Cardiorespiratory Monitoring," *Journal of Pediatric Nursing* 9, no. 1 (February 1994).

CHAPTER SEVEN
....

1. Avroy A. Fanaroff, MB, FRCP (Edinburgh), DCH, and Richard J. Martin, MB, FRACP, *Neonatal-Perinatal Medicine: Diseases of the Fetus and Infants,* 6th ed. (Saint Louis: Mosby, 1997).

CHAPTER NINE
....

1. *Pediatrics.* 1997; 100: 273.

2. *Pediatrics.* 1998; 101: 1093.

CHAPTER TEN

1. *Pediatrics* 97 (1996): 758–760.

CHAPTER FOURTEEN

1. *Pediatrics* 93, no. 3 (1994).

2. William R. Sexson, MD, and Janet Thigpen, RN, MN, CNNP, *Clinics in Perinatology* 23, no. 3 (September 1996).

3. Ibid.

Index